SIX TREATISES
ATTRIBUTED
TO MAIMONIDES

SIX TREATISES ATTRIBUTED TO MAIMONIDES

Translated and annotated
from the Hebrew editions

by

FRED ROSNER, M.D.

with bibliographies by
Jacob I. Dienstag

JASON ARONSON INC.
Northvale, New Jersey
London

The author gratefully acknowledges permission from the *Bulletin of the History of Medicine* to reprint his article "The Physician's Prayer," which first appeared in 1967.

Copyright © 1991 by Fred Rosner

10 9 8 7 6 5 4 3 2 1

All rights reserved. Printed in the United States of America. No part of this book may be used or reproduced in any manner whatsoever without written permission from Jason Aronson Inc. except in the case of brief quotations in reviews for inclusion in a magazine, newspaper, or broadcast.

Library of Congress Cataloging-in-Publication Data

Six treatises attributed to Maimonides / translated and annotated from the
  Hebrew editions by Fred Rosner; with bibliographies by Jacob I. Dienstag.
    p. cm.
  Includes bibliographical references.
  ISBN 0-87668-804-0
  1. Judaism—Works to 1900. 2. Maimonides—Bibliography.
  I. Maimonides. II. Rosner, Fred. III. Title: Six treatises
  attributed to Maimonides
  BM550.S54 1990
  296.1'7—dc20   89-18590

Manufactured in the United States of America. Jason Aronson Inc. offers books and cassettes. For information and catalog write to Jason Aronson Inc., 230 Livingston Street, Northvale, New Jersey 07647.

Dedicated to my beloved grandchildren

והחיט המשלש לא במהרה ינתק — קהלת ד:יב

And a threefold cord is not quickly broken—
Ecclesiastes 4:12

CONTENTS

Foreword by Rabbi Moshe Greenes — ix
Preface — xvii

Part I
PIRKÉ HAHATZLACHAH
THE TREATISE ON ETERNAL BLISS

Introduction — 3
The Treatise on Eternal Bliss — 17
Bibliography — 57

Part II
SEFER REFU'OT
THE BOOK OF REMEDIES

Introduction — 67
The Book of Remedies — 77
Bibliography — 99

Part III
TEFILAT HAROFÉ
THE PHYSICIAN'S PRAYER

Introduction — 103
The Physician's Prayer — 123
Bibliography — 127

Part IV

SHA'ARE HAMUSAR
THE GATES OF MORAL INSTRUCTION

Introduction	149
The Gates of Moral Instruction	157
Bibliography	173

Part V

MEGILLAT SETARIM
THE SCROLL OF THE UNREVEALED

Introduction	195
The Scroll of the Unrevealed	201
Bibliography	217

Part VI

LETTER TO THE JEWS OF FEZ
ABOUT THE MESSIAH IN ISFAHAN

Introduction	225
Letter to the Jews of Fez about the Messiah in Isfahan	233
Bibliography	251
Index	253

FOREWORD

The prolific Dr. Fred Rosner is at it again. He has given the English-reading public yet another volume of Maimonidean classics. Although this latest in the series may be properly categorized as pseudo-Maimonidean, its worth to the scholar and lay reader should not be underestimated.

Firstly, the translator's introduction and notations are a work of scholarship in their own right. In these, Dr. Rosner assembles in one volume, albeit succinctly, the research of scholars and students of the past who labored diligently to establish or disprove the authenticity of these works and then, with typical humility, offers his own findings.

An added value in the publication of these manuscripts is that it may serve to awaken contemporary scholarship to the beauty and sheer delight inherent in literary research. This branch of Judaic studies experienced a golden age during the nineteenth century, producing masterpiece after masterpiece. However, the entire field has, with some exceptions, been neglected by contemporary scholars.[1] Exposing serious stu-

---

[1]The past twenty to thirty years have seen the stirrings of a reawakening in

dents to such literary research will, I am certain, develop their taste for such undertakings and enrich Torah learning as a whole.

Research papers establishing the authorship of medieval manuscripts read very much like detective stories told by a master storyteller. We start with a totally confounding mystery without apparent clues. The author's star detective then sniffs out a seemingly minor clue here, another one there, until he finally unravels the mystery. These novels are popularly referred to as "thrillers."

Personally, I find engaging in literary research projects, as well as reading the work of others, a thoroughly suspenseful and entertaining activity. It is an almost euphoric experience when the author closes his work with a definitive statement such as, "It is thus clear beyond doubt that the author of the so-called *Thirteen Middos of Reb Yisrael Salanter* is not Reb Yisrael, but none other than the American patriot and statesman, Benjamin Franklin."[2]

Dr. Rosner honored me by inviting me to read his recent manuscripts before publication. Because of an already overburdened schedule, it was my original intention to review them "once over lightly," but I soon found myself so fascinated that I was thoroughly engrossed in the study on a line by line, clue by clue, basis. Dr. Rosner combines the skills of scholar and detective in reaching conclusions that are both articulate and convincing.

There is, however, one significant premise on which I must disagree with the authorities Dr. Rosner cites. They seem to accept as a self-evident truth that Maimonides did not study Kabbalah, nor was he even familiar with that branch of Torah learning. This view is based mainly on the fact that nowhere in his works do we find any reference to that Torah discipline.

---

research, especially in Israel, but it pales alongside the nineteenth-century golden age of Judaic literary research.

[2]This closing sentence is found in one of the studies in my collection, *Forgeries and Plagiarisms in Sacred Jewish Literature*, a work being prepared for publication.

A closer study of the subject, however, reveals quite the opposite to be true. This brief foreword is hardly the appropriate forum for a comprehensive presentation of the proofs that Maimonides was indeed steeped in Kabbalah.[3] I will merely cite some salient evidence to that effect, and will also show that the seeming absence of references to Kabbalah in his writings is very much in keeping with accepted practice of that period and is also consonant with his personal literary style.

Firstly, is it not unrealistic to assume that so vast an area of Torah learning was unknown to Maimonides while his contemporaries and near-contemporaries delved into its depths and related to it as a sacred branch of Torah? Included in this group are such immortals as Rabbi Abraham ibn Ezra and Rabbi Moses Nachmanides (Ramban), both of whose commentaries on the Bible are rich with kabbalistic interpretations of enigmatic passages, and Rabbi Abraham ben David (Raibad), the interpreter of *The Book of Creation (Sefer Yetzirah)*.

Furthermore, many *Rishonim* (early Torah scholars) who lived not long after Maimonides and who studied his writings intensively examined each fine point in great detail to be sure its meaning was not overlooked, and labored to resolve any seeming inconsistency or contradiction between Maimonides' position and talmudic law. They state unequivocally that Maimonides was a master of Kabbalah. To list a few briefly: *Sefer HaChinuch* 545; *Sefer HaZikaron*,[4] and Ramban in his *Peirush* of Torah (see *Koran P'nei Moshe, Devarim* 22:6,7).

In addition, the nineteenth-century scholar Rabbi Gershon Henoch of Radzin (known as *Baal HaTcheilet*), published a thoroughly convincing study which demonstrates that the *Taamei HaMitszvot* (Rationales of the Torah Commandments) of the *Guide of the Perplexed* are actually kabbalistic teachings

---

[3] I have done a more detailed study in my treatise *The Rambam as a Master of Kabbalah*.

[4] A few examples of such *Rishonim* include the author of *Sefer HaChinuch* (545); Rabbi Yom Tov of Seville, known as *Ritvah*, in his treatise *Sefer HaZikaron* in which he defends Maimonides' *Guide of the Perplexed* against the refutations of Nachmanides; and Nachmanides' own commentary on the Torah (see *Koran P'nei Moshe, Devarim* 22:6,7).

couched in rationalistic terms.[5] All this, of course, raises the obvious question: "How is it, then, that nowhere in Maimonides' work do we find any unambiguous references to Kabbalah?" To that I offer two equally obvious explanations:

A) Torah study in all its branches was always considered a universal obligation and the propagation of Torah knowledge the highest worth in Judaism. To quote Maimonides, "Each man in Israel is required to study Torah; both pauper or man of wealth, whether sound of body or in poor health and pain, whether he be youthful or of advanced age and with impaired faculties. Even a destitute person who subsists on alms or a door-to-door beggar, even a man burdened with a wife and children [he is struggling to support] is obligated to set aside time for the study of Torah during the day and during the night, as it is written, 'And you shall engage in it [Torah study] day and night.'"[6] Yet, there is one area of Torah that is "off limits" to the average student, and that is the study of Kabbalah.

In the introduction to his commentary on Torah, Nachmanides explicitly cautions his readers against learning Kabbalah from books or independent study. He, therefore warns his readers not even to delve into his token allusions to Kabbalah in his own commentary because it can only be learned orally "from the mouth of a master [kabbalist] to the ear of an understanding recipient" and any attempt to study Kabbalah on an intellectual level is "nonsense and foolhardy," fraught with danger and destined to end in disaster. Nachmanides closes his introduction with a final admonition: "That which is closed to you do not pursue, do not seek [or ask for] that which is above you. Study that which is permitted to you. You have no business with the hidden [branches of the Torah]." The study of Kabbalah is variously referred to as *Sissrei Torah*, meaning

---

[5]This study originally appeared as a foreword and introduction to his father's book, *Bais Yaakov*, and was later republished as a separate volume titled simply *Sefer HaHakdama V'HaPesicha* (The Foreword and Introduction).
[6]*Hilchot Talmud Torah* 1:8. See also 9–12 there.

the hidden, or not to be revealed, facets of the Torah; *Sod*,[7] meaning the secrets of the Torah; and *Chen*, an acronym for *CHochma Nistar*, meaning the hidden or secret wisdom.

Some of the veils of secrecy surrounding Kabbalah were partially lifted by Rabbi Isaac Luria, known as Ari, in the sixteenth century, and even more so by eighteenth century's Rabbi Israel Baal Shem Tov and his disciples.[8]

Many later scholars studied Kabbalah diligently but did so in isolation, keeping it a secret even from their families. The biographers of Rabbi Ezekiel Landau, known as Noda B'Yehudah,[9] write that he had a small room in the attic of his house to which no one but he had a key. He would lock himself in during the early morning hours, when all members of the household were sound asleep, and there he would study Kabbalah. This fact was discovered only after his death, when the family entered the room and found volumes of kabbalistic dissertations and notes that he had written over the years. He also left instructions that these were not to be published or even shown, but buried in the cemetery, explaining that they had been written only for him. The family further revealed that they at times heard sounds from the attic that indicated he had visitors, but no one ever noticed anyone arriving or leaving, or knew who the visitors were, whether students or masters or perhaps even Elijah or other heavenly emissaries who had come to instruct him. Similar reports were heard from such luminaries as Rabbi Meshulam Igra and Rabbi Moshe Schreiber, known as *Chasam Sofer*.

Maimonides was apparently an adherent of the position that Kabbalah was, in fact, a "hidden" and "secret" branch of Torah, and its study must not be conveyed by any other means than "from the mouth of the master to the ear of an understanding

---

[7]The Torah consists of four facets, P.R.D.S. (in acronym *PaRDeS*), the *S* standing for *Sod*, or the secret aspect of Torah.

[8]The causes for this change in attitude toward the teaching of Kabbalah in publications available to the public and in open assemblies makes a most interesting study unto itself.

[9]Eighteenth century rabbi of Prague and the recognized leading rabbinic authority of Eastern European Jewry.

recipient." It is no wonder, then, that Maimonides avoided any reference to Kabbalah in his writings.

B) Another explanation for the absence of references to Kabbalah in Maimonides' known works is a matter of style, if I may call it such. Many great rabbis were exceedingly disciplined in their studies, and even more so in their writings, and always confined their teachings to the subject at hand. They studiously avoided any midrashic (homiletical) references when dealing with halachah (Jewish law). Similarly, there is an almost total absence of hasidic thought in the halachic dissertations of the great masters and teachers of Hasidism.

Had the *Guide of the Perplexed* not been published in Maimonides' lifetime, but appeared sometime in the last hundred years as a "discovered" manuscript with a title page attributing its authorship to Maimonides, it would almost universally have been ruled fraudulent, completely out of character with the Maimonides we know in the *Mishneh Torah* and *Commentary on the Mishnah*. This, too, is a demonstration of Maimonidean compartmentalization of disciplines, confining the *Mishneh Torah* to the codification of talmudic law exclusively, without allowing any other aspect of his many-faceted intellectual personality to become engaged.

Torah scholarship is replete with such literary compartmentalization and I shall cite one more example to reinforce the premise. Rabbi Yechezkel Sarne, one of the truly outstanding sages and Torah academy heads (Slobodka, Hebron) of this century, considered Rabbi Moshe Chaim Luzzatto among the all-time giants of Torah learning. Rabbi Sarne writes[10] that Luzzatto's work *Mesilat Yesharim* (Paths of the Righteous) "achieved that which those who preceded him and those who have come after him did not." He further compares the author of *Mesilat Yesharim* to no less an immortal than Maimonides and his *Mishneh Torah*. One of the qualities that Rabbi Sarne takes particular note of in the writing of Luzzatto is the ability to confine his writing to the discipline being dealt with without

---

[10] In the foreword to his marginal *Eeyunim* to Rabbi Moshe Chaim Luzzatto's work *Derech Etz HaChaim* (The Path of the Tree of Life).

crossing its boundaries to other, though closely related, disciplines. When writing on ethics and the advancement of spiritual qualities in *Mesilat Yesharim,* Luzzatto gives his reader no inkling that the author is one of the foremost kabbalists of his era.

Rabbi Sarne writes, "One stands in wonderment [awe] that our master, who was among the heads and fathers of the Torah of Kabbalah, leaves no trace or hint [of Kabbalah] in the entire *Mesilat Yesharim.* From this we see how brightly lit all areas of the Torah were to him . . . each of its various components were independent . . . each wellspring being nurtured from its own unique sources of living waters that do not dwindle or run dry."

One cannot thus interpret the absence of Kabbalah in Maimonides' other works as evidence that he was not a kabbalist.

One final observation I should make regarding the question of Maimonides' authorship in Rosner's two books, especially *The Existence and Unity of God,* is that while the subject matter itself is not incompatible with Maimonidean views, I cannot help but join the doubters for one simple reason: *It is too chatty.*

To Maimonides, words were precious gems to be dispensed as needed, not indiscriminately. He does not use five words where four would suffice. He does not sprinkle his writings with liberal doses of adjectives and adverbs for effect or emphasis, nor does he add analogies to make it "interesting." Maimonides says what he has to say briefly, without repetition or reexplanations. Some of the manuscripts in question are replete with overexplanations and other redundancies to the point where my intuitive reaction is, "This is not the Maimonides I know."

Rabbi Moshe Greenes

PREFACE

Undoubtedly, the most important personality in medieval Judaism is Moses Maimonides. This rabbinical, philosophical, and medical giant had an incredible literary ability and encyclopedic knowledge. He had mastered nearly everything in the fields of theology, mathematics, philosophy, medicine, astronomy, and ethics of his own time. He was the "prince of physicians" and served princes and sultans. He was the spiritual leader of the Jewish community and was recognized by Jews worldwide who corresponded with him on halachic, ethical, philosophical, and other topics.

At 33 years of age, Maimonides completed his first major work, the *Commentary on the Mishnah*, which represents a halachic and talmudic discussion of all sixty-three tractates of the Talmud. Ten years later, his magnum opus, the *Mishneh Torah*, was finished. This work was a monumental compilation, organization, and systematization of all biblical and talmudic law in fourteen books and one thousand chapters. This gigantic codification and digest of biblical and rabbinic rules, practices, and customs became an instant success. It remains unprecedented and unrivaled. It was written in beautiful Mishnaic Hebrew instead of the vernacular Arabic, in which Maimonides wrote all his other books. In the year 1190, he completed his great philosophical masterpiece, the *Guide of the Perplexed*.

Each of this trilogy of masterful works would have indelibly recorded Maimonides' name for posterity. However, he was an extremely prolific writer and composed a variety of additional works including a *Book on Logic* (*Ma'amar Hahigayon*), a *Book of Commandments* (*Sefer Hamitzvot*), an *Epistle to Yemen* (*Iggeret Teman*), a *Treatise on Resurrection* (*Ma'amar Techiyat Hametim*), ten medical treatises including the *Medical Aphorisms*, *Regimen on Health*, *Book of Poisons*, treatises on *Asthma*, *Hemorrhoids*, and *Sexual Intercourse*, commentaries on several tractates of the Talmud, and many hundreds of rabbinic responsa. Many of these works, including nine of the ten medical treatises, have been translated, edited, annotated, and published in English by me.

It is not surprising that many writers in medieval and modern times would not only try to emulate Maimonides, but even attach his name to their own writings. Such is the case for several famous works including the well-known and widely quoted "Prayer of Maimonides" for physicians which was actually written by Marcus Herz in Germany in 1783. Other treatises have also been falsely attributed to Maimonides for a variety of reasons. These works have never been available to the English-speaking world and, although spurious, are important for those interested in medieval Judaism in general and Moses Maimonides in particular. It is also important to emphasize and demonstrate, once and for all, that works commonly spoken of as Maimonidean, such as the *Treatise on Eternal Bliss* (*Pirké HaHatzlachah*), the *Book of Remedies* (*Sefer Refu'ot*), his *The Gates of Moral Instruction* (*Sha'are Hamusar*), the *Scroll of the Unrevealed* (*Megillat Setarim*), and the *Letter to the Jews of Fez about the Messiah in Isfahan* are all medieval fabrications and not written by Maimonides.

The author of the *Treatise on Eternal Bliss* intentionally tried to create the impression that the treatise emanated from the pen of Maimonides, perhaps to dissuade people who were influenced by Aristotle and others. In spite of the fact that these works were not written by Maimonides, they are important enough to be made known to the English language reader.

After all is said and done, the reputation of the great Moses Maimonides remains unblemished. His great writings are increasingly appreciated as they become available in English. To the Jewish people, he symbolized the highest spiritual and intellectual achievement a man could attain on this earth. As is so aptly stated: "From Moses ben Amram to Moses ben Maimon, there never arose a man like Moses."

Acknowledgment

I am indebted to Professor Jacob Dienstag for the bibliographies; to Rabbi Moshe Greenes for his foreword to this book and for his helpful suggestions; to Mr. Louis Gross, Rabbi Dr. David Novak, Rabbi Yonah Munk, and Mr. William Wolf for reviewing the manuscript; to Mrs. Annette Carbone, Mrs. Sophie Falk, and Mrs. Miriam Regenworm for secretarial assistance; and to the staff of Jason Aronson Inc. for guiding the book through to publication.

I again affirm my love and devotion to my wife Saranne and to my cherished children Mitchel and Lydia, Miriam and Motty, Aviva and Michael, and Shalom. I thank them for their infinite patience during the long hours of painstaking work. I ask their forgiveness for having spent so much time on attributed Maimonidean translations rather than devoting it to them.

Part I

PIRKÉ HAHATZLACHAH

THE TREATISE ON ETERNAL BLISS

INTRODUCTION

The *Treatise on Eternal Bliss* attributed to Moses Maimonides was published in a critical Arabic and Hebrew edition in 1939 by Davidowitz[1] and includes textual and philological corrections and explanatory notes by Baneth. The *Treatise*, originally written in Arabic and translated by an unknown scholar into Hebrew, is extant in two manuscripts in both languages. The Arabic manuscript, preserved in a Code in the National Library in Paris[2] as Hebrew Codex 719, begins in the middle of p. 29a and ends in the middle of p. 34b. The end is missing and there is no doubt, says Davidowitz, that it was missing as well in the manuscript from which it was copied.

The Hebrew manuscript, lost for hundreds of years, was discovered by Baer[3] who states that the translator was the famous scholar Rabbi Zerachyah Halevi (the Levite). The portion of the manuscript which is the *Treatise on Eternal Bliss* fills three and a half pages (pp. 176b–179b). Steinschnei-

---

[1]H.S. Davidowitz, *Perakim BeHatzlachah HaMeyuchasim LeRambam*. Jerusalem: Mekitze Nirdamim, 1939, XXXI and 39 pp.

[2]*Catalogues des Manuscripts hébreux et samaritains de la Bibliothèque Impériale.* Paris, 1866, p. 116, no. 719.

[3]F. Baer, *Die Juden im Christlichen Spanien*, 1979, Vol. 1. p. XVII, footnote.

der[4-5] states that the translator is unknown. Davidowitz decries the fact that Baer did not specify which of the several scholars named Zerachyah Halevi he believes to be the Hebrew translator. Davidowitz lists the various scholars known by this name and offers reasons why each is not likely to have been the translator of the *Treatise on Eternal Bliss*. He concludes that he was most likely Rabbi Zerachyah ben Yitzchok ben Shealtiel Chen of Barcelona, who lived in Rome in the second half of the thirteenth century and wrote and translated many works from Arabic into Hebrew including Maimonides' *Medical Aphorisms*.[6] The main problem with this conclusion is that Rabbi Zerachyah ben Shealtiel Chen was not known as a Levite, contradicting Baer's assertion above.

The *Treatise on Eternal Bliss*, known in Hebrew as *Pirké HaHatzlachah* or *Perakim BeHatzlachah* (literally: *Chapters on Eternal Bliss*) was first cited in the middle of the fourteenth century by Joseph ben Eleazar, the famous commentator of Ibn Ezra, as "a short essay" composed by Maimonides (*Ma'amar katzar shechibar*).[7] Davidowitz asserts that this unusual citation indicates that even then there was doubt about the true name of the treatise or else they just did not know. According to some writers, Joseph ben Eleazar is referring to the *Treatise on the Unity of God* and not to the work discussed at present. The *Treatise on Eternal Bliss* is also quoted towards the end of the fourteenth century by Don Beneviste ben Labi under the title *Letter of Salvation*.[8] In addition to these two early citations

---

[4]M. Steinschneider, *Catalogus Librorum Hebraeorum in Bibliotheca Bodleiana*. Berlin: A. D. Friedlander, 1852–1860, pp. 1719 and 1917.

[5]M. Steinschneider, *Die Arabische Literatur der Juden*. Frankfurt: a. M. Kauffmann, 1902, p. 209.

[6]F. Rosner and S. Muntner, *The Medical Aphorisms of Moses Maimonides*. New York: Bloch for Yeshiva Univ. Press, Vol. 1 1970, 264 pp. and Vol. 2, 1971, 244 pp. (reprinted 1973).

[7]Joseph ben Eleazar Tov Elem (Bonafil). *Ohel Joseph* (Commentary on Ibn Ezra on the Torah), in the book *Margolit Tovah*. Amsterdam, 1721, p. 13:1 #233.

[8]Don Beneviste ben Labi. Cited in the study of M. Steinschneider in *Hamazkir*, Vol. 6, 1863, p. 14.

INTRODUCTION

mentioned by Steinschneider,[9] Vajda[10] mentions a third in the commentary on talmudic tractate *Abot* by Rabbi Joseph Yabetz who died in 1507. In his commentary on *Abot* 2:16, Yabetz writes: "In a separate chapter known as the *Chapter* [singular] *on Eternal Bliss*, Maimonides wrote . . ."

The *Treatise on Eternal Bliss* or the *Chapters on Salvation* was recommended as a Maimonidean writing worthy of study by Joseph Salomo del Megido in his letter to the Karaite, Serach ben Nathan in 1623.[11] The *Treatise* was printed for the first time in 1567 as an appendix to a dictionary of terms composed by Menachem ben Abraham of Perpignan,[12] a work that was meant to serve as an aid in reading Maimonides' *Guide of the Perplexed*. The treatise was then embodied in a collection of Maimonides' responsa edited by Mordechai Tama in 1765[13] between responsa 155 and 156 and thus separates the Maimonides' responsa of the collection from those that are not his. The *Treatise on Eternal Bliss* was reprinted in 1795, again in 1840, twice in 1859, again in 1905 and 1927, and at least ten more times since.[14]

In 1897, Bacher[15] published an in-depth analysis in English of the *Treatise* with his explanations of the allegory of the sanctuary, especially of the candlestick, the ceremonial commandments and prayer, ecstasy, repentance, the allegorical interpretation of Psalm 45, the symbol of the delights of eternal

---

[9]M. Steinschneider, *Die Hebraeischen Uebersetzungen des Mittelalters und die Juden als Dolmetscher*. Berlin, 1893, p. 437, para. 253.

[10]G. Vajda, Une citation non signalée du *Chapitre sur la Béatitude* attribué à Moïse Maïmonide. *Revue des Etudes Juives*. Vol. 130, no. 2–4, 1971, pp. 305–306.

[11]M. Geiger, *Melo Chofnayim*. Hebrew part p. 18, German part pp. 24 and 73.

[12]Menachem ben Abraham of Perpignan, *Sefer Hagedarim*. Saloniki, 1567, pp. 47–50.

[13]Mordechai Tama, *Responsa Pe'er Hador . . . Teshuvot She'elot LehaRambam*. Amsterdam, 1765, pp. 33a to 35b.

[14]See bibliography by Jacob Dienstag in this book.

[15]W. Bacher, The Treatise on Eternal Bliss Attributed to Moses Maimuni (*Pirké HaHatzlachah*). *Jewish Quarterly Review*, Vol. 9, old series, pp. 270–289, 1896–1897.

salvation (*chupah*), the biblical evidences for the continuation of the soul after death, and miscellaneous remarks on eternal salvation. Bacher was convinced of the authenticity of the *Treatise on Eternal Bliss* as a Maimonidean work, although he admits that the generally adopted view of most writers is that Maimonides was not the author. In support of his opinion, Bacher cites Steinschneider[16] who not only lists the *Treatise* among Maimonides' other writings, but says that "there is nothing therein to prove that it is a forgery. The mystical shadow which overspreads this rather theological and frequently rhetorical exposition is not in direct contradiction with the spirit of Maimonides."[17] In his later work,[18] Steinschneider wrote somewhat differently but arrived at the same conclusion:

> The sometimes mystical shadow and rhetorical tone of this treatise suggest a later age [of Maimonides]. According to Rapoport, this treatise is a codicil to the *Guide* written for Maimonides' cherished disciple Joseph Ibn Aknin. The unfounded suspicion of Graetz that the treatise is spurious is rejected by Bacher.

Bacher asserts that the mere testimony of the treatise itself does certainly not suffice to vindicate it as an authentic Maimonidean work if the contents would compel us, for valid reasons, to number it among the spurious writings that were made under Maimonides' name. However, continues Bacher, the judgment of Steinschneider "is of sufficient force to shake the belief in the spuriousness of our treatise." Bacher's analysis of the *Treatise* attempts to prove the Maimonidean character of the greater part of its contents by comparing it with authentic utterances of Maimonides. Bacher divides the *Treatise* into separate chapters according to the subjects dwelt on. He confines himself to the essential points and does not deal with all particulars of the text

---

[16] M. Steinschneider, *Catalogus Librorum Hebraeorum in Bibliotheca Bodleiana*, op. cit.; *Die Arabische Literatur der Juden*, op. cit.; *Die Hebraeischen Uebersetzungen des Mittelalters*, op. cit.

[17] M. Steinschneider, *Die Hebraeischen Uebersetzungen des Mittelalters*, op. cit.

[18] M. Steinschneider, *Die Arabische Literatur der Juden*, op. cit.

INTRODUCTION 7

because "a minute understanding and eventual corrections can only be expected from a consideration of the Arabic original." At the end of his analysis, Bacher concludes[19] that

> the treatise on Eternal salvation, bearing Maimonides' name, harmonizes, both in its leading thought and in a number of details, with ideas and utterances that are undoubtedly Maimonides'. Essential portions of the treatise, e.g., the allegorical interpretation of Psalm 45, are, it is true, not otherwise attested; yet do they not contain anything which would contradict Maimonides' authorship . . . The contents of the second chapter [ceremonial commandments, prayer, ecstasy] deviate somewhat strongly from Maimonides' mode of thought; and as to several details of the other sections, I could point to divergences from Maimonides' opinions expressed elsewhere. But taking it all in all, it appears unjustifiable to pronounce on our treatise the harsh judgment of Graetz, as to exclude it without further cause, from the list of Maimonides' works . . . this treatise, which, in view of the greater part of its contents, is by no means unworthy of Maimonides.

The "harsh judgment" to which Bacher refers is the following statement by Graetz[20] about the *Treatise on Eternal Bliss*: "It contains so many trivialities, and such a shallow moral doctrine, interspersed with a symbolic interpretation of the Temple, and of the Aggada, that it is impossible for such inane matter to have emanated from a Sage."

Bacher and Steinschneider stand alone in their support of the authenticity of the *Treatise on Eternal Bliss* as a Maimonidean work. In 1869, Schmiedl[21] wrote that the mania of using allegory in medieval writings resulted in the attribution of some allegorical works to Maimonides, including the apocryphal *Treatise on Eternal Bliss*. Similarly, continues Schmiedl, to increase the prestige of Kabbalah, it would not have been surprising for writers to attribute kabbalistic works to Maimonides.

---

[19] W. Bacher, loc. cit. pp. 288–289.
[20] H. Graetz, *Geschichte der Juden*, 3 Auflage, Vol. 6, Leipzig, 1894, p. 389.
[21] A. Schmiedl, *Studien über jüdische, insonders jüdisch-arabische Religionsphilosophie*. Vienna: Herzfeld and Bauer, 1869, p. 233.

In 1939, Davidowitz[22] published his critical edition of the *Treatise on Eternal Bliss* in Arabic and in Hebrew. Baneth markedly improved Davidowitz's work by adding diacritical points, corrections, amplifications, notes, and comments, all in brackets to indicate their authorship. Baneth points out that the *Treatise* is totally contrary to the spirit of Maimonides' *Guide of the Perplexed* and praises Davidowitz for proving that the *Treatise on Eternal Bliss* was not written by Maimonides, even in his old age as suggested by some writers.[23] Baneth notes that Arabic and Hebrew manuscripts usually have the author's name at the beginning and not at the end. The beginning of the *Treatise on Eternal Bliss*, however, is missing so that it is uncertain whether the name of the treatise is *Chapter(s) on Eternal Bliss* or *The Chapter(s) Concerning Eternal Bliss*. Many editions cite the so-called reference in the *Treatise* to Maimonides' *Guide*, but the original Arabic manuscript has the word *almakala*, which means *treatise*, and was mistranslated as *Guide*. Hence, the supposition by Steinschneider, Bacher and others that the *Treatise* serves as a codicil or conclusion for Maimonides' *Guide* is incorrect.

Baneth further states that the fact that certain philosophical concepts of Maimonides' *Guide* are incorporated into the *Treatise* is of no help in determining its authorship since many Jewish philosophers after Maimonides also incorporated ideas from the *Guide* in their works. The *Guide* was the most fundamental philosophical work of the Middle Ages. On the contrary, when Maimonides quotes from his *Guide* in his other works, he usually writes, "as we have explained." Yet nowhere in the *Treatise on Eternal Bliss* is such a phrase to be found. Therefore, concludes Baneth, the *Treatise* was not written by Maimonides. Nevertheless, it is an important work that should be studied on the basis of its merits.

The strongest evidence of the spuriousness of the *Treatise on Eternal Bliss* is provided by Davidowitz[24] in his critical edition of this work. He points out that the Hebrew translation was widely

---

[22] H. S. Davidowitz, op. cit.
[23] S. Zaks, *Tosafot Lishney Hama'amarim Hanal* in *Hayonah*, 1850 (5611), p. 68.
[24] H. S. Davidowitz, op cit.

accepted by most Jews as representing a legacy from the "Great Eagle" Moses Maimonides and for hundreds of years was considered to be a codicil for the *Guide of the Perplexed,* so that over the years the name of the translator was forgotten. One should not be astonished at the esteem in which this work was held in those days because this little booklet is small in quantity but large in quality. Within the work, continues Davidowitz, the reader finds the allegory of the sanctuary and especially the analogy of the candlestick in the sanctuary, encouragement to people that there is eternal life, depiction of the fascinating power of the ceremonial commandments, and prayer. He who fulfills commandments with fervor and enthusiasm can reach the level of a prophet with prophetic visions. The reader is enchanted with a discussion of the power of repentance, rejoices in the allegorical interpretation of Psalm 45, and delights in the amazing explanation of the term *chupah* as a symbol of the pleasures of the world to come. Finally, in words of the Middle Ages, the ultimate kernel, which is eternal bliss or salvation, is described. The *Treatise* speaks only of eternity for the soul. There is no mention of physical or bodily permanence. The *Treatise* concludes with a promise to the reader that if he delves into it constantly and studies it repeatedly, he will be assured of his ultimate goal of spiritual perfection and eternal bliss.

However, states Davidowitz, the style and character and contents of the book lead one to the conclusion that Maimonides did not write the *Treatise on Eternal Bliss.* The very complicated and involved style has no comparison in the *Guide of the Perplexed.* It is true that the *Treatise* may have had wide influence in those days, but "do not judge a barrel by its outward appearance but by its contents."[25] It is also true that the *Treatise* is imbued with basic and fundamental principles enunciated by Maimonides in his *Guide* and in his introduction to the tenth chapter of talmudic tractate *Sanhedrin.*[26] Neverthe-

---

[25] Talmud, Tractate *Abot* 4:20.
[26] F. Rosner, *Maimonides' Commentary on the Mishnah. Tractate Sanhedrin.* New York: Sepher-Hermon, 1981, pp. 134–158.

less, Davidowitz rejects the arguments offered by Bacher (*vide supra*) to authenticate the *Treatise* as a Maimonidean work. Based on content and style, the overwhelming evidence indicates that the *Treatise* is spurious and was falsely attributed to Maimonides.

Davidowitz cites six major areas in the *Treatise on Eternal Bliss* where the contents are at variance with or totally contradictory to Maimonides' statements in the *Guide of the Perplexed*. First, the author of the *Treatise* tells the reader that it was written as a conclusion to the *Guide*, but Maimonides accords this honor to chapter 51 of part 3 of his *Guide* where he states, "This chapter is a kind of conclusion . . ." Second, the *Treatise* attributes a direct relationship between prayer and prophethood: if a person prays with fervor and enthusiasm, he rises from the world of physical sensations to the world of the intellectuals and even to the level of prophethood. But in his *Guide*, Maimonides does not attribute such a grandiose function to prayer. In chapter 51 of part 3, he depicts prayer as a type of training for a person to separate himself from his daily worldly matters and to concentrate on understanding God. Third, the author of the *Treatise* exhorts each of us to strive to reach the spiritual level of Moses, but Maimonides does not consider this level achievable except by the Messiah.[27] Fourth, in the *Treatise*, the senses are compared to the candelabra of the sanctuary, but in his *Guide*, Maimonides does not depict the candelabra as a symbol but as one of the means by which one strengthens the fear of God in the hearts of the people. Fifth, the author of the *Treatise* derives the word *chupah* from *chof*, meaning shelter or haven, and enlarges this meaning to include the sun with its power *like a bridegroom going forth from his wedding chamber*. Just as the harbor for ships serves as a shelter for sailors from ocean storms, so, too, a bridegroom is relieved from the danger of dying childless when he goes forth from his bridal chamber. So, too, when the sun sets and is below the sphere of the earth, it is comparable to the nuptial chamber which is a sheltered and protected place. What casuistry! The sun is not like a groom!

---

[27]M. Maimonides, *Mishneh Torah, Hilchot Teshuvah* 9:2.

What kind of comparison is there between a bridal chamber and a shelter? What perversion of phraseology by the author of the *Treatise*! Sixth, the author also erred in comparing the powers of speech and rational thinking with the sun and the moon at the very beginning of the *Treatise*. This analogy is an expression of neo-Platonic writings but not at all in keeping with the spirit and philosophy of Maimonides.

Davidowitz then offers numerous stylistic reasons why he concludes that the *Treatise on Eternal Bliss* is a spurious work that did not come from the pen of Maimonides. First, the Arabic style of Maimonides often contains the words "as we have explained" or "as we have already mentioned" or "as already stated" and their like. These phrases refer to matters that he has already discussed and/or explained in that same work or in another of his writings. Maimonides does not repeat himself word for word. However, in the *Treatise on Eternal Bliss*, two sections are cited from the *Guide*[28] without reference to the fact that they have been previously mentioned. Furthermore, the *Treatise* contains a number of whole sections from the *Sefer Hashoroshim*[29] of Rabbi Yonah ibn Ganach without any reference to the author. Yet, in his *Guide*, Maimonides only cites ibn Ganach once[30] and in laudatory terms: "It is a good explanation." Another stylistic proof of the spuriousness of the *Treatise on Eternal Bliss*, according to Davidowitz, is the use of technical terms, common nouns, homonyms and synonyms in the *Guide*, which are different from those in the *Treatise*.

Davidowitz then cites several examples of words and phrases found in the *Treatise* such as "stand on your feet" and "your organs of speech," that are never mentioned by Maimonides in his *Guide* or in any of his other authentic writings. The *Treatise* uses the term *ruach* to mean respiration, whereas it usually signifies wind or spirit. In all of Maimonides' writings, the analogy of the sanctuary as representing the human body does not occur.

---

[28] Part 1, chapters 16 and 70.
[29] *Sefer Hashoroshim*, literally *Book of Hebrew Roots*.
[30] Part 1, chapter 43.

All the above facts, asserts Davidowitz, lead one perforce to the conclusion that the *Treatise on Eternal Bliss* was not authored by Maimonides and should not be considered among his authentic writings. One should also not think that an unintentional error of the printer or publisher attributing this work to Maimonides led people for generations to falsely believe it to be authentic. Rather, the character, contents, and style of the *Treatise* clearly indicate that the author intentionally tried to create the impression that the *Treatise* emanated from Maimonides. The author who added Maimonides' name to the *Treatise* is not guilty of ordinary literary plagiarism, where he substitutes *his* name for that of the true author. It is possible that this falsification was perpetrated with the best of intentions to aggrandize the name of God and to strengthen Jewish beliefs and practices. In those days, many people had come under the influence of Aristotle and his followers. The author of the *Treatise on Eternal Bliss*, perhaps an ardent admirer of Maimonides, tried to justify the contents of Maimonides' *Guide of the Perplexed* and defend it against jealous critics by calling the *Treatise* "the conclusion of the *Guide*."

Davidowitz's 1939 critical edition of the *Treatise on Eternal Bliss*, presented as his doctoral thesis at Dropsie College, was reviewed by Vajda.[31] Vajda agrees that the *Treatise* is spurious, although he does not consider the philological evidence presented by Davidowitz to be very strong. He cites the neo-Platonic mysticism in the *Treatise*, of which certain traces of Bachya and of *Ma'ani an-nafs* of ibn Tofayl are only external signs, highly uncharacteristic of the writings of Maimonides. Most writers who cite the *Treatise on Eternal Bliss* agree with Graetz, Davidowitz, Baneth, and Vajda that it is a forgery and was not written by Maimonides. Even Zaks, who thought first[32] that Maimonides wrote it in his old age, later changed his

---

[31] G. Vajda, [Review of:] De Beatitudine Capita Duo R. Mosi Ben Maimon Adscripta, ed. H. S. Davidowitz. Textum recognovit notas explicativas additit. Jerusalem, D. H. Baneth, 1939, pp. XXXI and 39. *Revue des Etudes Juives*, Vol. 107, 1947, pp. 212–213.

[32] S. Zaks, op. cit.

INTRODUCTION 13

mind[33] and clearly called it a spurious work. Dinor[34] asserts that "the authorship of the *Treatise* is not without doubt and the matter needs additional clarification." Shalom[35] expresses himself as follows: "I strongly believe that this *Treatise* is a forgery and was written by a skilled scribe who attempted to emulate Platonism more than Maimonides himself. Vidor[36] points out that, in his opinion, the author of the *Treatise on Eternal Bliss* was associated with the contemporaries of Abraham, son of Moses Maimonides. More recent writers such as Kreditor[37] and Stitskin[38] also consider the *Treatise* to be spurious.

In summarizing the contents of the *Treatise*, Bacher subdivides it into seven sections, the first of which he entitles "Allegory of the Sanctuary, especially of the Candlestick. Perfecting the Spirit." The heart is said to resemble the ark in which the tablets of the law were kept, as the law is fostered in the heart, and is inscribed in the tablets of the heart. The "pure candlestick" is the soul, the "lamp of the Eternal" in man. Its "seven lamps" are the five senses together with the two powers of the soul, thought and imagination, all of which must be devoted to the perfecting of the soul and the service of God. Then one's house is lit up by divine light. The soul that learns to know God becomes itself the "holy spirit." This perfected soul unites, after its severance from the body, with its source. But a soul polluted by sins cannot return to God. He who makes his soul subservient to the senses is referred to as "the servant that becomes the king."

Bacher names the second section of the *Treatise on Eternal Bliss* "Ceremonial commandments and prayer. Ecstasy." One should

---

[33] S. Zaks, *Shir Hashirim Asher LiShlomo ben Gavriel*. Paris 5628 (1867), p. 29.

[34] B. Z. Dinor, *HaRambam*. Tel Aviv: Dvir, 5695 (1934), note 15.

[35] G. Shalom, *Mechoker Limekubal (Igeret Hamekubalim al HaRambam)* in *Tarbitz*, Year 6, Book 3, Nissan 5695 (1934), p. 535.

[36] N. Vidor, Islamic Influences on Jewish Worship (*Hashpa'ot Islamiyot al Hapulchan Hayehudi*). Oxford: East and West Library, 1947, pp. 45–46.

[37] L. S. Kreditor, *Der Rambam*. London: *Yiddishe Stimme*, 5716 (1955), pp. 69–71.

[38] L. D. Stitskin, *Letters of Maimonides*. New York: Yeshiva Univ. Press, 1977, pp. 33, 178–181 (notes 15–17).

devote oneself to the service of God with both external and internal senses. For example, in blowing the *shofar* on Rosh Hashanah, all one's body parts should be involved: the hands outstretched to grasp the *shofar*, the fingers clenched to hold it, the ears listening, the eyes closed, and other members trembling and shaking. Then follows a lengthy exposition about the ecstatic condition, removed from the sensual world, into which fervent prayer can place the soul. Bacher points out that particular emphasis is given

> to the clairvoyance of the person in ecstasy, whose imagination knows no difference between past and future, who has knowledge of future events in the world, such as war, famine, pestilence, death, and life . . . The soul, when in such a condition, is transferred into the world of intelligences [spirits], and man belongs to the category of those beings who are described by the words: living, accomplished, intelligent.

Bacher entitles the third section of the *Treatise on Eternal Bliss* "Repentance. Isaiah 6." Once a man becomes conscious of his deficiencies and understands that he is thereby hindered from attaining eternal salvation, he is seized by the desire to repent and he loudly and humbly confesses his guilt. He who repents and reaches spiritual perfection can then also make others perfect "like a stream that never runs dry." The fourth section of the *Treatise* is a lengthy allegorical interpretation of Psalm 45 in which the perfection of a person who fully adopts all the fundamentals described earlier in the *Treatise* is portrayed. The second chapter of the "*Chapters on Eternal Bliss*," is also the beginning of section five in Bacher's subdivision of the *Treatise*. In this section, entitled "*Chupah*, a symbol of the delights of eternal salvation," the author begins with the proposition that eternal salvation, vouchsafed to man, is commensurate with the perfection attained and the preparations made therefor. There are thus "degrees of salvation." The word *chupah*, usually translated as *nuptial chamber*, is said to refer to eternal salvation and is compared with the highest delight of sensual man. Then follows the etymological explanation of the word

INTRODUCTION 15

that, like *chof* meaning *harbor,* is derived from the verb *chafof* meaning to protect or shelter. The sun is also designated by the word *chupah.* Just as the harbor affords security to the ship, and just as the sun, on its rising, gives a sense of security after the darkness of the night, so, too, the nuptial chamber after the wedding gives a sense of security against the danger of dying childless. Thus, the preparation of the soul for the life after death is compared to the preparation of the bride, and eternal bliss is compared to a wedding chamber.

Bacher calls the sixth section of the *Treatise* "Biblical evidences for the continuation of the soul after death." Numerous references from the Bible and Prophets are cited in support of the existence of spiritual life after death. The final section, entitled "Miscellaneous remarks on eternal salvation," represents a series of rather loosely connected observations and interpretations providing further evidence that this salvation is vouchsafed for every righteous person in proportion to his merit.

My English translation was made from Davidowitz's critical Hebrew edition. I have retained the seven-section subdivision as suggested by Bacher. In spite of the fact that the *Treatise on Eternal Bliss* was not written by Maimonides, it is an important essay worthy of being made available to the English reader. Hence this translation.

THE TREATISE ON ETERNAL BLISS

Perhaps[1] if you purify your heart and separate from the clouds, what was clear to the ancient Sages,[2] who were intellectuals,[3] will become clear to you. Know and understand that I am directing you to it. For every person [destined] to come into the world[4] who desires perfection, can approach [the level of perfection of] Moses our teacher.[5] But if he desires imperfection,[6] he will be like Jeroboam, son of Nebat.[7]

---

[1] Most printed versions of *The Treatise on Eternal Bliss* begin with the words "Esteemed disciple," probably an addition of the first printer as a foreword to the fragmentary beginning of the manuscript.

[2] Pious ones who reached the level of holiness and proximity to God.

[3] Alternate translation: those "in the know" or cognoscenti.

[4] Davidowitz suggests that the author is alluding to the talmudic assertion: "All Israelites have a share in the world to come" (*Sanhedrin* 10:1).

[5] Davidowitz points out that Maimonides reserves this level of perfection for the Messiah. See *Mishneh Torah, Hilchot Teshuvah* 9:2, where it states: "Because the King who will arise from the seed of David will possess more wisdom than Solomon and will be a great prophet, approaching Moses, our teacher . . ."

[6] Literally: deficiency or loss.

[7] First king of post-Solomonic Israel. He reigned for twenty-two years (1 Kings 14:20), approximately from 928 to 907 B.C.E. He led a rebellion against King Solomon (1 Kings 11:26–28), split the kingdom of Israel, and made two

Perhaps there is something that can move you [toward perfection]. These are the cherubim that are allegorically compared to you when Scripture states: "And the cherubim shall spread out their wings on high."[8] When the word of the Lord, blessed be He, emanated from between the cherubim[9] and when the Lord, blessed be He, spoke, souls that died came back to life, like respiration that is the life of the heart and its health and which heals it from abnormal[10] movements that harm it. And the term "breath"[11] is a word with a double meaning, sometimes referring to respiration[12] and sometimes referring to prophecy. Just as the life of the heart is dependent on this air that cools its fires and flames and, if it[13] ceases for even a brief moment, causes the death [of the heart], so too, in your life, if the holy spirit is lost[14] from the heart it dies immediately and that is its death. "Shielding the ark-cover with their wings"[15] is a phrase with a double meaning, which is allegorically used to denote the wings of the lung and there are truly two.[16]

1. Allegory of the Sanctuary, especially of the Candelabrum Perfecting the Spirit

Know that the dwelling place[17] of your heart is comparable to the dwelling place of the ark in which the Tablets of the

---

golden calves (1 Kings 12:25–33). He is considered as one of the most evil kings of Israel.

[8]Exodus 25:20.
[9]See Exodus 25:22.
[10]Literally: ill or sick.
[11]Hebrew: *ruach* or spirit which here means air or breath to conform with Maimonides' *Guide of the Perplexed* 1:40. Bacher points out that spiritually, the breath of God is also expressed by the word *ruach*.
[12]Air, that is.
[13]The air.
[14]Literally: nullified or voided.
[15]Exodus 25:20.
[16]Both wings of the lungs cover the heart, just as both wings of the cherubim covered the ark.
[17]Hebrew: *mishkan*, literally habitation, tabernacle, or sanctuary.

Law[18] were kept.[19] [Just as the Tablets of the Law were kept in the ark],[20] so too the law should be kept in your heart, inscribed on the tablet of your heart.[21] Surely, you see that Scripture states: "The people in whose heart is My Torah."[22] Indeed, the cherubim move you and elevate your essence higher and higher. And if you occupy yourself with your usual activities that are outside the Holy of Holies, you destroy your true house and darken your sun and withdraw your moon.[23] But if you devote yourself to the service of that which is within you at the level of the Holy of Holies and especially to the service of the pure candelabra[24] when you clean the lamps,[25] do so in a manner where you devote your senses and your thoughts[26] towards Him, may He be praised. These [lamps] are the five senses, and the sun and the moon,[27] and [the powers of] thought[28] and imagination, [all of which should be turned]

---

[18] Literally: Tablets of the Testimony.

[19] Literally: concealed or hidden. See Exodus 25:21.

[20] Davidowitz states that the phrase in brackets is missing from the original Arabic manuscript but should be added here.

[21] Allusion to Proverbs 7:3 where it states: "Write them upon the tablet of thy heart."

[22] Isaiah 51:7.

[23] Allusion to Isaiah 60:20 where it states: *Thy sun shall no more go down, neither shall thy moon withdraw itself.* Bacher points out that a similar passage appears in Maimonides' *Guide* 3:51 where it states, "He who recognizes God and gives himself entirely up to this subject of his thoughts, is placed, as it were, in the clear light of the sun; but he who allows himself to be diverted by his occupations is, as it were, in the darkness of a cloudy day."

[24] Exodus 31:8 and 39:37 and Leviticus 24:4. Bacher posits that the "pure candlestick" is the soul, the "lamp of the Eternal" in man, as stated in Scripture: "The spirit of man is the lamp of the Lord" (Proverbs 20:27).

[25] Allusion to Exodus 30:7 where it states: "when he dresseth the lamps."

[26] Literally: intentions.

[27] Bacher explains that the seven lamps of the pure candelabra are exemplified by the five senses together with the two powers of the soul, thought (literally: speech) and imagination, which should all be turned towards the candlestick (Numbers 8:2). The functions of the two powers of thought and imagination are described in greater detail in Maimonides' doctrine of prophecy in his *Guide* 1:47 and 2:36.

[28] Literally: speech.

towards the body[29] of the candelabrum[30] which refers to the westernmost lamp,[31] because the Divine Presence is in the West.[32] See also the position of the sun in the middle of the planets; this is so because its brightness reaches you in such a way that your house remains lit with divine light and angelic honor: "She perceiveth that her merchandise is good, her lamp will not be extinguished in the night."[33]

And you, my brother, observe your lamp, and its ascent, and the perfection of its shape, because it is His handiwork: "The spirit of man is the lamp of God."[34] Sometimes it is called the light of God, other times it is called the breath of God,[35] and yet other times the image or likeness[36] or good spirit[37] or willing spirit[38] or glory[39] or soul of God.[40] And when the soul has

---

[29] Literally: face.

[30] Numbers 8:2.

[31] See Maimonides' *Mishneh Torah, Hilchot Bet Habechirah* 3:8 where he states that the six lamps all faced the middle lamp which was on the shaft of the candelabrum. The middle lamp faced the Holy of Holies and was called the western lamp.

[32] In his *Guide* 3:45, Maimonides explains that pagans worshiped the sun toward the East; therefore Abraham chose the west of Mount Moriah for his prayers because he thought that the most holy place was in the West. This is why the talmudic Sages say that the Divine Presence is in the West (*Baba Bathra* 25a).

[33] Proverbs 31:18. In his *Guide* 3:8, Maimonides gives an allegorical interpretation of Proverbs 31:10–31.

[34] Proverbs 20:27.

[35] Allusion to Job 33:4.

[36] Allusion to Genesis 1:26.

[37] Allusion to Psalm 143:10 and Nehemiah 9:20.

[38] Allusion to Psalm 51:14.

[39] See Maimonides' *Guide* 1:64.

[40] Bacher points out that there are eight biblical expressions denoting the soul, insofar as it shows itself worthy of life after death: *nefesh* (soul) as defined by Maimonides in his *Guide* 1:41; *tzelem* (image) and *demut* (likeness) as defined in the *Guide* 1:1; *ruach* (spirit) as defined in the *Guide* 1:40 but here divided into *ruach tovah* (good spirit) and *ruach nedivah* (willing spirit) on the ground of Psalm 143:10 and Psalm 51:14 (see also Maimonides' *Mishneh Torah, Hilchot Yesodei HaTorah* 4:9); *ner elokim* (light of the Lord) corresponding to *ner hashem* (light of God) as in Proverbs 20:27; and *nishmat elokim* (breath of God) as in Job 33:4. Bacher concludes that the meaning of "soul"

learned to know God, it becomes the holy spirit.[41] Indeed, it is written: And "take not Thy holy spirit from me,"[42] and it is also written "the spirit of the Lord spoke in me."[43] And when it separates [from the body, the soul] unites with its original source,[44] as it is written: "And the spirit returneth unto God who gave it."[45]

The opposite of this occurs if [the soul] does not become learned but becomes defiled by sins;[46] then it is called the spirit of defilement.[47] Indeed, it is written: "Defile not yourselves in any of these things"[48] for thereby [the soul] becomes defiled.[49] And it is written: "And I will cause the spirit of defilement to pass out of the land."[50] As a result, it is written: "A spirit that passes away and does not come again"[51] in regard to the afflicted body with its pollution and its deficiencies and the fact that during its youth it offered sacrifices and poured libations

---

was not included by Maimonides among the meanings of *kavod* (glory) in the *Guide* 1:64. Davidowitz points out that Rabbi David Kimchi, known as *Radak*, in his book *Hasherashim*, uses the expression *kavod* for "soul." Other authors also use the term *kavod* as one of ten names for the soul.

[41] Allusion to Psalm 51:13.
[42] Psalm 51:13.
[43] 2 Samuel 23:2.
[44] Bacher explains that the intelligent soul that has learned to know God is the angel, the organ of divine revelation. The soul, having become perfect in this way, unites, after its severance from the body, with its source. A similar thought is expressed in the *Treatise on the Unity of God (Ma'amar HaYichud)*. See *The Existence and Unity of God: Three Treatises Attributed to Moses Maimonides*. Northvale, NJ: Jason Aronson, 1990.
[45] Ecclesiastes 12:7. See also Maimonides' *Guide* 1:40 and his *Mishneh Torah, Hilchot Yesodei HaTorah* 4:9.
[46] Allusion to Leviticus 18:24.
[47] Allusion to Zechariah 13:2.
[48] Leviticus 18:24.
[49] Contrast the spirit of defilement (*ruach tumah*) with the spirit of holiness (*ruach hakodesh*).
[50] Zechariah 13:2.
[51] Psalm 78:39. Bacher points out that in his *Guide* 1:40, Maimonides cites this passage from Psalms by the side of Genesis 7:15 as an example of the meaning "vital spirit" (breath of life) for the word *ruach*, that is, the principle of animal life, bound up with the body and perishing with it. See Maimonides' *Treatise on Resurrection* (F. Rosner, trans.) New York: Ktav, 1982.

to strange gods. How can it then come into the King's chamber?[52] The King is pure and holy and His ministers are holy and pure.[53] And it is also written: and "ye shall not defile yourselves therein, for I am the Lord your God"[54] that is to say, I am pure and therefore you should be pure. And it is written; "Ye shall be holy, for I [the Lord your God] am holy."[55]

And [the soul] can be compared to the pure candelabrum that is before the Lord,[56] the whole of it made of one piece of beaten gold;[57] and its seven lamps are never extinguished but burn continuously and the flame rises in perpetuity.[58] And if you wish, you might compare the candelabrum to the five senses[59] which are the five physical powers[60] all of which should act to serve the Lord, as it is written: "And the souls which I have made."[61] Understand that when it is written: "for the spirit[62] that enwrappeth itself is from me,"[63] it refers to the thinking soul, the image of God and its likeness which is

---

[52] Allusion to 1 Kings 1:15.

[53] See *Niddah* 30b where it says: "The Holy One, blessed be He, is pure, His ministers are pure and the soul which He gave you is pure. If you preserve it in purity, well and good, but if not, I will take it from you."

[54] Leviticus 18:30.

[55] Leviticus 19:2. Bacher points out that the opinion in Maimonides' *Guide* 3:47 and 3:33 about defilement and holiness denoting the noncompliance and compliance with the divine commandments is fully in accord with this interpretation of these consecutive verses.

[56] Allusion to Leviticus 24:4.

[57] Allusion to Exodus 25:36.

[58] Allusion to Leviticus 24:2.

[59] Davidowitz cites Kaufman quoting Rabbi Levi Ben Gerson, known as *Ralbag*, who compares the senses to the candlestick in an allegorical manner. By contrast, continues Davidowitz, Maimonides, in his *Guide* 3:45, states that the "candelabra was put in front of the curtain as a sign of honor and distinction for the Temple. For a chamber in which a continual light burns, hidden behind a curtain, makes a great impression on man, and the law lays great stress on our holding the Sanctuary in great estimation and regard, and that at the sight of it we should be filled with humility, mercy, and loving kindness."

[60] Literally: powers of the soul, *kochot hanefesh*.

[61] Isaiah 57:16.

[62] Hebrew: *ruach*.

[63] Isaiah 57:16.

enwrapped[64] by the notions[65] of the physical body. The phrase "And the souls[66] which I have made"[67] refers to the service of the thinking soul.[68] Do not rest[69] until you make the soul subservient to the senses and thus reverse your normal tendencies.[70] And you, my brother, serve idols [although] in purity[71] in that you imitate idolaters in eating, drinking, dressing, and cohabitating and consider these things to be permissible.[72] But, in fact, you are enslaving your senses and

---

[64] Literally: surrounded.

[65] Literally: habits or conduct.

[66] Hebrew: *neshamot*.

[67] Isaiah 57:16.

[68] Bacher points out that the figure of the candelabra with its seven lamps representing the five senses and the mental powers (thought and imagination), which must be devoted to the perfecting of the soul and the service of God, is an idea also expressed by the words of Isaiah 57:16. Bacher also states that the term *ruach* here refers to the soul destined for immortality, the image of God, and that *neshamot* here refers to the senses and powers of the soul assigned to the service of that soul. Bacher further asserts that the ingenious interpretation of the verse of Isaiah agrees to some extent with Maimonides' exposition of the talmudic passage in *Chagigah* 12b in his *Guide* 1:70. Contrary to Saadiah and Ibn Ezra, Maimonides does not attribute to the term *neshamah* the meaning "of the highest phase of the soul (spirit)," but "the soul of life," bound up with the body, and perishing together with it. See Maimonides' *Mishneh Torah, Hilchot Yesodei Hatorah* 4:9, and *Hilchot Teshuvah* 8:3.

Davidowitz points out that Maimonides interprets the word *neshamot* to refer to general physical powers which ancient philosophers called *neshamot*, such as the growing force (*nefesh hatzomachat*) and the vital force (*nefesh hachiyunit*).

[69] Literally: do not reverse its desire in you.

[70] Literally: reverse its desire in you, for normally the evil inclination or physical senses prevail over the spiritual or divine soul within man. One must strive to reverse this situation and make the physical senses subservient to the soul.

[71] Davidowitz asserts that "in purity" here means "with the pure soul."

[72] See *Abodah Zarah* 8a where it states that "Israelites who reside outside Israel serve idols, though in pure innocence. If, for example, an idolater gives a banquet for his son and invites all the Jews in his town there, even though they eat of their own and drink of their own and their own attendant waits on them, Scripture regards them as if they had eaten of the sacrifices of dead idols."

using your pure and princely soul[73] for degenerate activities as I discussed in my introduction [to this treatise]. King Solomon alluded to this thought [when he wrote]: "For three things the earth quakes,[74] for a servant when he becomes king[75] and a churl when he is filled with food."[76] And King David said: "There shall be no strange God within thee, neither shalt thou bend down to any foreign God,"[77] which our ancient Sages explained as follows: Who is the strange God that resides within the body of a human being? Say that it is the evil inclination.[78]

2. Ceremonial Commandments and Prayer Ecstasy

My brother, devote yourself[79] to the service of God with your external and internal[80] senses.[81] Thus, when you prepare yourself to properly blow and listen to the sound of the Shofar[82] on Rosh Hashanah,[83] consider that its sound should involve all your organs:[84] your hands should be outstretched to take the Shofar; your fingers should be clenched to hold it; your throat, your tongue and your organs of speech should serve to make the sound [of the Shofar] pleasant; your ears should be attentive; your feet should stand straight; your eyes should be closed; and the remainder of your members should tremble and shake. The same applies to one who makes a

---

[73] Literally: dear soul which is a princess.

[74] Proverbs 30:21.

[75] Solomon considers a person who makes his soul subservient to his senses like a servant who becomes the king.

[76] Proverbs 30:22.

[77] Psalm 81:10.

[78] Shabbat 105b. Maimonides discusses the evil inclination (*yetzer hara*) more fully in his *Guide* 3:22.

[79] Literally: come.

[80] Literally: revealed and hidden.

[81] External senses refer to the senses of touch, vision, hearing, taste, and smell. Internal senses refer to intellect, memory, imagination, and so on.

[82] Ram's horn.

[83] Jewish New Year.

[84] Literally: Its movement should be complete in your organs.

Sukkah[85] or [takes] the *Lulav*[86] or fulfills[87] other [commandments] of the Torah.[88] And he who prays should turn to the Lord, may He be blessed, standing on his feet, with joy in his heart and on his lips,[89] his hands outstretched, his organs of speech articulating words, and his other members trembling and shaking.[90] And he should not cease from uttering pleasant sounds, subdue himself, supplicate [to God], bow down, prostrate himself and cry, because he [is standing] before a great and mighty King.[91]

And he will achieve [a feeling of] ecstasy and wonderment to the point that he finds his soul in the world of the intellectuals. His glorious soul becomes subdued and he extracts it from the [physical] sensations as if it is devoid of them. And he observes with his power of imagination, and sees and hears that about which there is no doubt, for there is no difference between future and past events in regard to these matters because they [the past and the future] are the same in matters that are clear to them and he regards future events the same as he regards past events and when he describes them they are true. And when they are verified and accepted by scholars of the truth, and their correctness is approved, certainly he can foretell[92] that which will happen in the world such as war, famine, pestilence, death, and life. And he knows how to protect

---

[85] Tabernacle.

[86] One of the four species of plants used on the holiday of Tabernacles.

[87] Davidowitz points out that the original Arabic manuscript here adds: and he who affixes a *mezuzah* (parchment scroll containing Deuteronomy 6:4–9 and 11:13–21 to the doorpost, usually in a case made of wood, metal or plastic) or dons *tefillin* (phylacteries) or reads from the Torah or prays . . .

[88] Bacher points out that Maimonides cites in his *Guide* 3:52 objects of the various religious practices; all of them are meant to promote the fear of God, and to be the means to the perfection of the individual.

[89] The original Arabic manuscript has: with internal joy and (joy) in his speech.

[90] The original Arabic manuscript here adds: as it is written "And the posts of the door were moved" (better: the foundation of the thresholds shook) "at the voice of them that called" (Isaiah 6:4).

[91] Perhaps an allusion to Deuteronomy 10:17.

[92] Literally: reveal, that is, have prophetic foreknowledge.

himself from hidden dangers and is able to correct his own imperfections.[93] He can also distinguish friend from adversary and beloved from enemy, and nothing in the world is hidden from him. Worldly events are as clear to him as the events in his own house that relate to his servants and his children. And [when in this state of ecstasy], he is in the category of those being characterized as living, accomplished [94] and intelligent.[95]

3. Repentance. Isaiah 6

The opposite applies to a man's deficiencies. Once he realizes his deficiencies and the deficiencies of his position,[96] so that when he is awake he considers himself to be unworthy,[97] insignificant,[98] and degraded, and it becomes clear to him that he is greatly hindered and prevented from attaining eternal salvation,[99] he is seized by [the sensation of] repentance[100] and cries out with a loud and bitter cry,[101] and he is filled with

---

[93] Literally: fill in that which he is lacking.

[94] Literally: complete or perfect or whole.

[95] Literally: achieved (an understanding of God). Bacher comments on this lengthy exposition about the ecstatic condition, removed from the sensual world, into which fervent prayer can place the soul. Some of the traits recall the description by Maimonides in his *Guide* 2:41 of those conditions into which the prophets are placed during their visions when awake. Particular emphasis is given to the clairvoyance of the person in ecstasy, whose imagination knows no difference between past and future, who has knowledge of future events in the world, such as war, famine, pestilence, death, and life. He distinguishes friend from enemy, and nothing in the world is hidden from him. The soul, when in such a condition, is transferred into the world of intelligences, that is, spirits, and man to the category of those beings who are described by the words: living, accomplished, intelligent.

[96] Bacher points out that this statement is closely connected with the earlier description of the ecstatic condition of him who has arrived at perfection.

[97] Literally: small.

[98] Literally: base.

[99] Hebrew: *hatzlachah*. Literally: success.

[100] Bacher notes that Maimonides discusses the significance of repentance for spiritual perfection in his *Guide* 3:36, end.

[101] Allusion to Esther 4:1.

remorse and humility as stated by Isaiah: "Woe unto me for I am silenced; because I am a man of unclean lips."[102] He felt guilty[103] because he was negligent in the exhortation of the people and because he feared them and this was his sin. But when the prophet [Isaiah] achieved perfection and was purified of his sins,[104] he became worthy of his mission. This fact is confirmed [in Scripture]: "Then flew unto me one of the Seraphim."[105] And when he was filled with remorse and repented from his sin, having already been punished [and forgiven] as stated in Scripture: "And thine iniquity is taken away, and thy sin expiated,"[106]—as soon as he heard [God ask]: "Whom shall I send?"[107] he answered: "Here am I, send me."[108] And he suffered by being torn and oppressed[109] by the people as it is written: "I gave my back to the smiters, and my cheeks to them that plucked off the hair,"[110] but was not torn or oppressed by the Lord, blessed be He. He became equal to the angels who acquire the knowledge of God from one to another and who cause it to flow from one to another.[111] And it shall never cease flowing from the highest, which is the first intellect, to the lowest, which is the actual intellect that is called *Ishim*,[112]

---

[102]Isaiah 6:5.

[103]Literally: He said: Isaiah thought he was unworthy of his prophetic mission because of his negligence in exhorting the people because he feared them."

[104]That is, when Isaiah repented.

[105]Isaiah 6:6. *Seraphim* are angels.

[106]Isaiah 6:7.

[107]Isaiah 6:8.

[108]Isaiah 6:8.

[109]The original Arabic manuscript has: his glory was profaned.

[110]Isaiah 50:6.

[111]Bacher points out the allusion to the words of Isaiah 6:3, which *infra* are applied to the praise of God by the angels, quite in accord with Maimonides' interpretation of Psalm 19:2 (see his *Guide* 2:5 and the *Ma'amar HaYichud*, chapter 1). The words of the text are taken here in the sense of the idea of emanation, which is in accord with Maimonides' views in his *Mishneh Torah, Hilchot Yesodei HaTorah* 2:7 and 4:6, the *Ma'amar HaYichud*, chapter 1, and his *Guide* 2:6.

[112]Maimonides describes ten ranks or levels of angels, the highest of which are the *Chayot HaKodesh*, which are just below the Throne of Glory, and the

and it is that [intellect] that flows to the prophets and gives each form its ultimate perfection according to the level of preparation of the *Ishim*.

Therefore, a man who has reached perfection must also make others perfect and must cause to flow [from himself] to them that which had flowed to him from God, blessed be He, as stated by Solomon: "Let thy springs be dispersed abroad, and courses of water in the streets."[113] And God spoke through Isaiah: "and thou shalt be like an irrigated garden, and like a spring of water whose waters do not fail."[114] Our Sages also spoke about a [spiritually perfect] man who is subject to the constant[115] influence of the Divine Emanation and to which he cleaves without any separation. They said: from heaven are revealed to him the secrets of Torah and he becomes like an everflowing fountain and like a river that never runs dry.[116]

4. Allegorical Interpretation of Psalm 45

And when a person reaches this level [of perfection] towards which strives the man who has fully adopted[117] the aforemen-

---

lowest of which are *Ishim* (literally: men or individuals), who speak to the prophets and appear to them in prophetic visions. *Ishim* approximate the intelligence of human beings. See previous note for sources.

[113] Proverbs 5:16. Bacher points out that this interpretation of Proverbs 5:16 is based on the agreement of the word of the text *yofutzu* with *futz*, the Arabic expression for emanation (Hebrew *shefa*). Maimonides himself, in his *Guide* 2:12, explains this Arabic expression by saying that emanation is like the source from which water flows, and then gushes over all. In the same passage, he finds the idea of emanation in the biblical expressions for God; (*Me*) *the fountain of living waters* (Jeremiah 2:13), and (*for with Thee*) *is the fountain of life* (Psalm 36:10). However, cautions Bacher, in the *Guide* 3:54, the verse in Proverbs 5:17 is interpreted by Maimonides to mean that the highest perfection attainable by man, namely intellectual perfection, "is only for him and for no other besides him."

[114] Isaiah 58:11.

[115] Literally: permanent.

[116] *Abot* 6:1. The secrets or mysteries of Torah, according to Bacher, here mean the profound knowledge of the contents of the Bible.

[117] Literally: perfected.

tioned fundamentals and has done that to which I directed him by conquering all obstacles and by following the path of righteousness,[118] his perfection is portrayed [in Scripture as follows]: "My heart overfloweth[119] with a goodly matter; I say: my work is dedicated to a king; my tongue is the pen of a ready writer."[120] Indeed, when it says *rachash*, it refers to the man who reflects in his mind the prophecy that he is given, without trembling and without sound but with understanding of the subject. And I will not criticize[121] such a man when he follows the prophecy and meditates it in his mind without trembling and without sound[122] because he is portrayed as one who moves his lips when praying, as the Sages said: his lips are springing forth[123] his prayers.[124] The explanation of the word *rachash* is the springing forth of water,[125] that is to say bringing it forth by digging; and the springing forth is that which originates from the mountains as if it is perspiration issuing from a stone. And this word [*rachash*] and this subject can be explained by comparing the movement of the lips in prayer to the bringing forth of water by digging.

And the searcher for wisdom attaining the prophetic under-

---

[118]Bacher and Davidowitz both point out that the transition from the preceding section is formed by a passage that is corrupted in many instances, but the sense is that the degree of perfection, already mentioned in preceding remarks, is attainable by man only in the way allegorically indicated in Psalm 45.

[119]Hebrew: *rachash*. Bacher says *rachash* really means to cause water to spring forth by means of digging; the word also means the trickling of the water from the mountain; a sort of perspiration issuing from stone. According to Bacher, these interpretations are based on Abulwalid's explanation of the Hebrew verb *rachash* which is compared with the Arabic *rashach*.

[120]Psalm 45:2.

[121]Literally: distance.

[122]The Hebrew word *rachash*, explains Bacher, also means the motion of the lips in prayer without sounds or words (see *Chagigah* 3a), and is therefore a suitable expression for the inspiration that affects man only in thought, and not in words and sounds.

[123]Hebrew: *rachash*.

[124]*Megillah* 22b.

[125]The motion of the lips when praying is compared to the springing forth of water.

standing [of the knowledge that flows from God] is designated by Scripture as if he is digging: "If thou seek her as silver, and search for her as hidden treasures, then shalt thou understand the fear of the Lord, and find the knowledge of the Holy Ones."[126] And when he attains the fear of the Lord, blessed be He, which is the ultimate goal of the Torah, he will arrive at the knowledge[127] that flows to him from the Holy Ones that are the angels, in that Scripture states: "Then I heard a Holy One speaking."[128]

One can complete this essay on the [interpretation of the] scriptural phrase: "My heart overfloweth"[129] with an extraordinary rhetorical account of a case in which knowledge[130] came forth without speech or language or sound, other than the movement of lips. And the Lord, may He be blessed, placed[131] [this knowledge] on the person's tongue, and without thought and meditation about the subject matter that came forth. [The Talmud relates that] there were dumb men in the neighborhood of Rabbi,[132] sons of the daughter of Rabbi Yochanan ben Gudgada, and according to others, sons of the sister of Rabbi Yochanan, who, whenever Rabbi entered the house of study, went in and sat down before him and moved their lips. And

---

[126]Proverbs 2:4–5. The meditation of the inquirer for wisdom and the seeker of perfection is designated as "digging." Bacher notes that Maimonides here inserts a novel interpretation of Proverbs 2:5 which states: "Then shalt thou understand the fear of the Lord; and find the knowledge of God" by substituting "Holy Ones" (Hebrew: *kedashim*) for "God" (Hebrew: *elokim*). The changed form of the verse is probably related to Proverbs 30:3 and is explained thus: He who has attained the fear of God, which is the ultimate object of the Torah, will arrive at the knowledge that flows to him from the "Holy Ones," that is, the angels (see Daniel 8:13). That the fear of God is the ultimate object of the Torah is expounded by Maimonides in his *Guide* 3:24.

[127]Literally: fear. The text is somewhat corrupted here but the sense is clear.

[128]Daniel 8:13.

[129]Psalm 45:2. The Hebrew phrase *rachash libbi*, which here means "my heart overflows," is ordinarily translated as inner thoughts or emotions or prayer of the heart or heartfelt wishes.

[130]Literally: prophecy.

[131]Literally: sent.

[132]Popular name for Rabbi Judah the Prince, compiler of the Mishnah.

Rabbi prayed for them and they were cured, and it was found that they were well versed in Halachah,[133] Sifra,[134] Sifre,[135] Tosefta,[136] and the entire Talmud.[137] Behold [the Talmud] compares the issuing forth of speech and the movement of the lips in speech to digging and pouring forth.

And bend your ear, my brother, to understand that which follows about this subject matter because I placed it at the end of the treatise and it will completely encompass all its contents. At that point your glorified soul will be incessantly [filled] with divine possessions and artificial wares as stated by the wise King Solomon: "The heart of her husband safely trusts in her, and he has no lack of spoil."[138] And David said: "I rejoice at Thy word, as one that finds great spoil."[139] He thus compares[140] that which he knows about what is concealed to that which he does not have in terms of spoils.[141]

And I now return to my earlier treatise to complete the [discussion of the scriptural] phrase: "My tongue is the pen of a ready writer."[142] The latter refers to an expert scribe and is derived from the Arabic[143] vernacular and, therefore, means [a scribe] who writes unhesitatingly[144] because he writes that which is clear[145] to him and registered [in his mind]. And it is written: "Gird thy sword upon thy thigh, O mighty one,"[146]

---

[133]Final legal adjudication.
[134]Homiletical exposition on Leviticus.
[135]Homiletical exposition on Numbers.
[136]Supplemental or additional Talmud.
[137]The text here differs slightly from that in the Talmud, *Chagigah* 3a.
[138]Proverbs 31:11.
[139]Psalm 119:162.
[140]Literally: combines.
[141]Davidowitz suggests that the author compares what he learned from the concealed things and from those things that are not known to him, to spoils.
[142]Psalm 45:2.
[143]The Hebrew word *mahir* (usually translated as rapid, quick, swift), is derived from the Arabic *maahir*, which is here translated as expert or skilled.
[144]Literally: improves his writing.
[145]Literally: guarded or watched.
[146]Hebrew: *gibbor*.

"thy glory and thy majesty."[147] [This verse] refers to a person who rules over his senses so that they do not divert him[148] [from spiritual perfection]. And our Sages said: "who is a mighty one, he that subdues his [evil] inclination."[149] And it is written: "And in thy majesty prosper, ride on,"[150] which is like: "Who rideth upon the heaven"[151] and this is an extraordinary comparison. Just as God[152] rules over the heaven, the rider [rules over the animal he rides] and this is an extraordinary comparison. For the rider is the one who makes the animal move and causes it to go wherever he desires, and it is his instrument and he can use it in any manner he pleases. And he is removed from it and not attached thereto but separate from it. Similarly, God[153] is the one who moves the sphere through whose movement all things move and He is separate from it and is not a power in it.[154] Human beings[155] are figuratively comparable to their Creator as it is written: "prosper, ride on in behalf of truth,"[156] which refers to the small world.[157] You can also derive the same idea[158] from the scriptural phrases: "And

---

[147] Psalm 45:4.
[148] Literally: distress or trouble him.
[149] Abot 4:1.
[150] Psalm 45:5.
[151] Deuteronomy 33:26.
[152] Literally: the Lord, may He be blessed.
[153] Ibid.
[154] Bacher points out that the explanation here of Deuteronomy 33:26 agrees completely with Maimonides' *Guide* 1:70. God "rides" or rules over the world as a man rides or rules over his animal. The rider is more important than the animal upon which he rides and which he leads, and he is separate from it, apart from it, and not connected with it. In like manner, the uppermost sphere, whose rotation sets everything moveable into motion, is moved by God, who is separate from the sphere and not a power in it.
[155] Literally: speaking or thinking souls.
[156] Psalm 45:5.
[157] As God directs the universe consisting of the spheres, the thinking soul directs the little world, the body, by means of its likeness to God. The idea of man as a microcosmos is discussed by Maimonides in his *Guide* 1:72 and the *Ma'amar HaYichud*.
[158] Literally: you can see.

he was riding upon his ass,"[159] and she was riding on her ass."[160]

And it is written: "Thine arrows are sharp,"[161]—arrows with which to kill the enemies of the king. This [analogy] refers to the killing of the lust of the evil inclination which is the enemy of the good inclination.[162] And it is written: "myrrh, and aloes, and cassia are all thy garments."[163] These [plants] are an allusion to the bodily senses, which are victorious over the soul. And it is written: "Out of ivory palaces stringed instruments have made thee glad,"[164] which is also an allusion to this palace,[165] and the analogy is as follows: when you become cleansed like strong white ivory. Then it is written: "Kings' daughters are among thy favorites";[166] this is an allusion to the powers of the thinking soul. And it is written: "At thy right hand stands the Queen in gold of Ophir,"[167] which is an allusion to the animal soul that is endowed with the attribute of humility with which to serve the thinking soul. The desire [of the animal soul] is to adorn [the thinking soul] with good actions such as self restraint and determination to acquire excellent moral and intellectual virtues.[168]

Then it is written: "Hearken, O daughter, and consider and incline thine ear; forget also thine own people, and thy father's house";[169] this [statement] refers to the animal soul and means to say that you should divest yourself of your animal nature and subject yourself to humility and obedience to the intellect. And it is written: "So shall the king desire thy beauty; for he is thy Lord, and do homage unto him."[170] And subject your humility

---

[159]Numbers 22:22.
[160]1 Samuel 25:20. Davidowitz points out that the exact scriptural citation should be: "And it was so, as she rode on her ass . . ."
[161]Psalm 45:5.
[162]The intellect, that is.
[163]Psalm 45:9.
[164]Psalm 45:9.
[165]In Arabic *heychal*, meaning palace, is a nickname for "the body."
[166]Psalm 45:10.
[167]Psalm 45:10.
[168]See Maimonides' *Guide* 3:54, at the beginning.
[169]Psalm 45:11.
[170]Psalm 45:12.

to the primary cause of your existence which is the Lord, may He be praised: "Is He not thy father that hath gotten thee?"[171] Then it is written: "And, O daughter of the Rock[172] with a gift . . ."[173] This [daughter of the Rock] is the thinking soul that has its origin [174] from the primary cause and from the primary beginning, which is responsible for all other things. Thus God[175] is called Rock when it states: "The Rock, His work is perfect[176] and of the Rock that begot thee thou wast unmindful."[177] And it is also written: "and thou shalt stand near the Rock,"[178] which refers to the Lord, may He be praised. And it is written: "the richest of the people shall entreat thy favor with a gift."[179] This statement is an allusion to the powers of the soul and the senses and the body[180] and other [organs] just like the scriptural passage: "All my bones shall say: [Lord, who is like unto Thee]."[181]

And it is written: "All glorious is the king's daughter within the palace,"[182] which means that the intelligent soul becomes perfect only when she withdraws and isolates herself [from the external world].[183] Then it states: "She shall be led unto the king on richly woven work."[184] That phrase is similar to: "and thy raiment was of fine linen and silk and richly woven work,"[185] and these are the [moral and spiritual] excellences.

---

[171]Deuteronomy 32:6.

[172]Hebrew: *tzur*, also translated Tyre, but here in the allegorical sense "daughter of the Rock" referring to the thinking soul that has its origin in the "Rock," the primary cause, that is God (Bacher).

[173]Psalm 45:13.
[174]Literally: is hewn from.
[175]Literally: truth; epithet for God.
[176]Deuteronomy 32:4.
[177]Deuteronomy 32:18.
[178]Exodus 33:21.
[179]Psalm 45:13.
[180]Hebrew: *heychal*. See note 165.
[181]Psalm 35:10.
[182]Psalm 45:14.
[183]See Maimonides' *Guide* 3:51.
[184]Psalm 45:15.
[185]Ezekiel 16:13.

And the phrase "She shall be led unto the king" refers to the Lord, may He be praised[186] [to whom the soul is led] when the soul becomes purified and rules over the senses and turns them to its service. The same applies to the other bodily forces that are under its dominion. Indeed, Scripture speaks thereof: "The virgins, her companions in her train;"[187] and this occurs when moral character is perfected before Him, may He be praised, and the pure spirit[188] is revealed before Him[189] so that the beauty of the powers of the soul and their excellence and exaltation are visible [before God] and they adorn themselves and rejoice in the happiness of [obeying] His commandments.[190] And [the perfect soul is helped] by listening to[191] beautiful music and musical instruments and then becomes like a bride with her accompanying musical instruments and beautiful and pleasant songs heard from her virgin companions who are adorned and perfumed and whose beauty compares favorably with their [palatial] dressing room. That which Scripture says: "the virgins, her companions in her train,"[192] is an allusion to the powers of the soul and the senses that listen to the intellectual soul. The phrase: "being brought unto thee"[193] means to say that they will serve thee. The soul thereby becomes purified and its light[194] will shine in the glitter of its appearance[195] and

---

[186] The acquired moral virtues or "excellences" are the means by which the soul is led to God, the King.

[187] Psalm 45:15.

[188] Davidowitz cites Kaufman who quotes Rabbi Judah ben Barzilai, author of *Commentary on the Book of Creation*, who states that the soul of a person is the "pure spirit."

[189] Literally: between his hands.

[190] Perhaps "they shall be led with gladness and rejoicing" (Psalm 45:16), is here being paraphrased or explained.

[191] Literally: being attached to.

[192] Psalm 45:15.

[193] Psalm 45:15.

[194] Literally: its candle.

[195] Literally: glitter of its face. Davidowitz points out that the comparison of the soul or the heart to a vision or appearance or spectacle was common in Arabic moral literature. So too in the work known as *Chovot HaLevavot* in the section entitled *Cheshbon HaNefesh*.

it is turned to the form of the sun and it is transformed from divine spirit in potentiality and becomes divine spirit in actuality.[196] And this is the holy spirit that belongs to the saints and they are the world of intelligences.[197]

Then Scripture states: "Instead of thy fathers shall be thy sons,"[198] [namely when the sons] learn the virtues [and excellences of their fathers]. "Whom thou shalt make princes in all the land"[199] means that they cannot achieve this perfection unless they rule over the land,[200] as it is written: "And the fear of you and the dread of you shall be upon every beast of the earth."[201]

I have explained this psalm in much greater detail than that which God granted us from His Divine table.[202] The [perfect man] can succeed thereby and not waste these explanations[203] among the masses of the people[204] and be like a person of whom Scripture says: "Like a small stone in a heap of stones, so is he that giveth honor to a fool,"[205] It is not good for someone to throw a precious jewel on a heap of stones for he causes it to be lost in a place not its own. And [the perfect man] should be like a person of whom Scripture says: "for her gain shall be for them that dwell before the Lord, to eat their fill, and for stately clothing."[206]

---

[196]See Maimonides' *Guide* 1:70.

[197]See note 95.

[198]Psalm 45:17.

[199]Psalm 45:17.

[200]Ruling over the land, according to Bacher, means ruling over the material world and the senses.

[201]Genesis 9:2.

[202]Alternate translation: heavenly treasures. Bacher points out that in his allegorical interpretation of the prologue to Job (*Guide* 3:22), Maimonides says that the ideas had come to him, as it were, through revelation.

[203]Literally: treatises or essays.

[204]Literally: many men.

[205]Proverbs 26:8. Bacher notes that the explanation of this scriptural phrase is based on Saadiah.

[206]Isaiah 23:18. Both Bacher and Davidowitz point out that the application of this scriptural phrase is based on its interpretation in *Pesachim* 119a. In his *Guide* 3:1, Maimonides makes use of the same verse from Isaiah 23:18 and its talmudical interpretation.

5. Chupah [Isaiah 4:5], a Symbol of the Delights of Eternal Salvation. Chapter 2

I have already informed you earlier that, according to the views of the philosophers,[207] the eternal salvation[208] vouchsafed [to man] is commensurate with the perfections attained and the preparations therefor[209] as expressed by our ancient Sages in the Talmud in *Baba Bathra* in the chapter entitled "He who sells a ship":[210] Rabbi Yochanan said that in the future, the Holy One, blessed be He, will make seven canopies[211] for every righteous man, as it is written: "And the Lord will create over the whole habitation of Mount Zion, and over her assemblies, a cloud of smoke by day, and the shining of a flaming fire by night, for over all the glory shall be a canopy."[212] This means that the Lord compares eternal bliss to the delight that the sensual power [of man] experiences, which only delights in material things. And He also [allegorically] compares [eternal bliss] to the enjoyment[213] of the soul and the delight[214] of the eyes when they see it, namely the wedding chamber.[215] Thus, Scripture states: "And which is like a bridegroom coming out of

---

[207] Bacher and Davidowitz both note that since this information about the opinions of the philosophers on eternal beatitude is not to be found in the present text, it must have been lost in a missing chapter. Maimonides discusses the opinions of the philosophers on the immortality of the soul in his *Treatise on Resurrection* (see F. Rosner translation, New York: Ktav, 1982). See also Maimonides' *Guide* 1:74.

[208] Literally: the ultimate success or beatitude.

[209] The "degrees" of salvation are most clearly expressed at the end of this chapter.

[210] *Baba Bathra* 75a.

[211] Hebrew: *chupah* meaning canopy or bridal chamber.

[212] Isaiah 4:5.

[213] Literally: profit.

[214] Literally: repose, rest, tranquility.

[215] Bacher explains that the word *chupah*, meaning canopy or bridal chamber, is interpreted allegorically to denote eternal salvation. The latter, being denoted by the word that means wedding chamber, is compared with that which is, for the sensual man, the highest delight, and the look of which affords enjoyment to the soul and the eyes.

his wedding chamber,"[216] and "Let the bridegroom go forth from his chamber, and the bride from her wedding pavilion."[217]

The root of the word *chupah* is *chaphof*,[218] which refers to something that is used as a shelter and which hides and protects. Thus, Scripture states: "And he shall be for a haven of ships,"[219] meaning a refuge for ships, that is to say, a harbor, and it is so called by the masses of people[220] because it is a place where ships find tranquility from the winds and where they find shelter from destruction and sinking. When ships are afraid of large numbers of clouds and of changing winds, they do not feel safe until they reach the harbor and lower their sails and cast out the iron implement called the anchor.[221] Thereby the ship is relieved of its fright and its sailors have good tidings in that they are safe from occurrences at sea.

The word *chupah* is used[222] as a comparison to the rising of the sun and its shining after [the previous day's] sunset.[223] And the verse: "Let the bridegroom go forth from his wedding chamber,"[224] is a very wonderful analogy in that when the bridegroom leaves his wedding chamber his soul rejoices and is tranquil from the relief that he feels from bad thoughts concerning his fertility and ability to propagate his race, and his fear is alleviated. And Scripture states: "Weep ye not for the dead, neither bemoan him; but weep sore for him that goeth away, for he shall return no more, nor see his native

---

[216]Psalm 19:6.

[217]Joel 2:16.

[218]According to Bacher, this etymological explanation is based on Abulwalid's *Dictionary*, article *chaphof*.

[219]Genesis 49:13.

[220]Davidowitz points out that this phrase in Hebrew is without explanation.

[221]Davidowitz notes that Maimonides also speaks of ships' anchors in his *Commentary on the Mishnah, Baba Bathra* 5:1.

[222]Literally: borrowed.

[223]As the harbor affords security to the ship, so the sun, on its rising, gives a sense of security after the darkness of the night, which causes fear. Later, the sun is also designated by the word *chupah*.

[224]Psalm 19:6.

country."[225] This verse is explained [in the Talmud] to refer to one who goes away [from this world] without children;[226] and the Sages said that three people are accounted as dead [one of whom is a person who is childless].[227] And a person does not lose his fear of death until he has consummated his marriage,[228] which represents the desire [to create] a child, and until he has completely fulfilled this [goal] in the covered and hidden and protected place.[229] The same [analogy] can be applied to the sun when it sets and is below the sphere of the earth; and it is comparable to the *chupah*,[230] which is a sheltered and protected place. And people do not lose their fear of the darkness of the night and its coldness and the interruption of work and activities[231] until the sun rises and shines.

And the place where the union of the bridegroom and the bride takes place is called the *chupah* as we mentioned earlier. Every man of means concerns himself with its beautification and adornment. Some people erect poles [around the nuptial bed] and surround it with embroidered fabrics and picturesque designs;[232] and they make its ceiling from myrtle branches and on its floor they create a background of flowers of various colors. And some people tie shining pearls and precious stones thereto and different types of adornments and decorations.

And this subject of *chupah* is well known among the masses of the people, as are the beautiful adornments[233] as a result of which the people[234] rejoice and find tranquility with their

---

[225] Jeremiah 22:10.

[226] *Moed Katan* 27b and *Baba Bathra* 116a. Thus, the bridal chamber, after the wedding has been consummated therein, gives a sense of security against the danger and fear of dying childless.

[227] *Nedarim* 64b. The talmudic statement lists four who are accounted as dead: a poor man, a leper, a blind person, and one who is childless.

[228] Literally: until he has engaged in the biblically commanded sexual intercourse.

[229] The nuptial chamber.

[230] The nuptial chamber.

[231] Literally: movement.

[232] Davidowitz states that the original Arabic text has "flags."

[233] Literally: pictures.

[234] Literally: souls.

beloved and desired ones; and they lose their fear and their fright and their terror so that the enemy, which resides within them,[235] does not prevail. This is what God said: "As a bridegroom putteth on a priestly diadem, and as a bride adorneth herself with her jewels."[236] And about this individual[237] Scripture commands that: "he shall be free at home one year."[238]

The reason why the place of the bridegroom and bride is called *chupah* is because there one finds the friends of the bridegroom whom he has identified [and asked] to be close to him in his shelter and with whom he previously exchanged presents, offerings, and gifts. These [friends] are called groomsmen and are found with the bridegroom in the *chupah* during the seven days of feasting after the wedding.[239] Each of the groomsmen has his own *chupah*, which is apportioned according to his means.[240] One can make an analogy between this [*chupah*] and the *chupah* of the second world in that the souls that reach it rejoice and delight, and are secure against perdition and destruction. Each person's salvation and eternal bliss[241] is vouchsafed in measure to his preparation.[242] This [thought is expressed in Scripture] which states: "for over all the glory shall be a canopy,"[243] And the Sages use *garden*[244] as a synonym for *chupah* when they explain the essay of the wise [King Solomon] in relation to the soul rejoicing when it reaches

---

[235]The evil inclination.
[236]Isaiah 61:10.
[237]The bridegroom.
[238]Deuteronomy 24:5.
[239]Literally: after the (biblically) prescribed cohabitation of the wedding night.
[240]The groomsmen are assigned their own rooms or shelters in accordance with the presents sent by them to the bridegroom.
[241]Literally: his cup and his portion.
[242]Davidowitz points out that Maimonides discusses the obligation of groomsmen to bring presents to the groom in his *Mishneh Torah, Hilchot Zechiyah Umatanah*, chapter 7.
[243]Hebrew: *chupah*. Isaiah 4:5.
[244]Aramaic: *ganunita*.

[the world to come]. "I am come into my garden,[245] my sister, my bride":[246] . . . [247] Then the intelligent soul, after it separates itself from this earthly shelter, is like a bride who is given[248] to her bridegroom and who approaches him with her ornamented garments and pleasant melodies [of rejoicing]. And she has already separated herself from the clouds [of sensuality] that covered her[249] and the screens have been removed and the turbid spirit has become purified and she acquires radiance and effulgence.

Concerning beatitude,[250] which refers to eternal bliss that is vouchsafed for the soul after it separates [from the physical and sensual body], Scripture states: "And the Lord will create over the whole habitation of Mount Zion and over her assemblies."[251] The term *create* is used to denote the creation of the world from nothingness as stated: "In the beginning God created the heaven and the earth."[252] And the wise [King Solomon] said: "Because man goeth to his eternal home,"[253] which the Sages interpret: to teach us that every [righteous] person is given a habitation that befits his honor.[254] So too they said: "The Holy One, blessed be He, will at a future time cause every righteous person to inherit a world for himself."[255] And the aforementioned eternal bliss, which is vouchsafed for her,[256] is like an ever renewing beatitude and eternities that renew themselves.[257]

---

[245] Hebrew: *gani*.
[246] Song of Songs 5:1.
[247] Bacher and Davidowitz both point out that one or more sentences are missing here.
[248] Joyful.
[249] The clouds of sensuality interfere with the true knowledge of God.
[250] Hebrew: *gemul*, literally, recompense, reward.
[251] Isaiah 4:5.
[252] Genesis 1:1.
[253] Ecclesiastes 12:5.
[254] *Shabbat* 152a.
[255] *Uktzin* 3:12. The talmudic assertion is somewhat different in that it ends with the phrase "to inherit three hundred and ten worlds."
[256] The soul.
[257] Hence the appropriateness of the word "create." For additional discus-

And the scriptural verse: "over the whole habitation of Mount Zion and over her assemblies"[258] refers to those who are prepared for and designated to find beatitudes, as it is written: "every one that shall be found written in the book."[259] And it is also written: "And a book of remembrance was written before Him, for those who feared the Lord and who thought upon His name."[260] This situation is analogous to that of the people designated by the bridegroom to stand near the *chupah* and they are the groomsmen. The phrase *her assemblies* refers to the place where [the righteous] assemble at specific times,[261] and these are the times of holy convocations as it is written: "New moon and Sabbath, the holding of convocations."[262]

[In the Talmud] the Sages ask:[263] why is fire required in a *chupah*? Rabbi Yochanan[264] said: this teaches us that each person will be burned by reason of [his envy of the superior] *chupah* of his friend. Alas, for such shame! Alas, for such reproach! Another question that is asked [in that talmudic passage] relates to the statement of the Sages that one of the seven *chupahs* [that are prepared for every righteous man] is a *chupah* of fire. How is it possible for a person to live in a shelter and survive there if it is burning with fire? The fire would consume all that is near it. The Sages answer by quoting Rabbi Yochanan who says that every person will be burned by reason of [his envy of the superior] *chupah* of his friend. This means that he will be burned from the fire and the conflagration as [figuratively] expressed in the phrase "affliction of fire." A later

---

sion of the word "create" by Maimonides, see his *Guide* 2:30 at the end; 3:10 at the beginning, and 3:13. The conclusion is that the preparation of the soul for life after death is compared with the preparation of the bride for her wedding.

[258] Isaiah 4:5.
[259] Daniel 12:1.
[260] Malachi 3:16.
[261] Festivals or religious assemblies.
[262] Isaiah 1:13. This scriptural quotation, according to Davidowitz, is missing in some of the manuscripts and early editions.
[263] *Baba Bathra* 75a.
[264] The Talmud has Rabbi Chanina rather than Rabbi Yochanan.

commentator[265] explained that [a person will be burned because of the envy of his friend] who is a more righteous person than he because his friend is dwelling in a tabernacle of fire and he cannot reach nor approach his friend's tabernacle. Indeed, his friend sits in a tabernacle of fire that provides light for him day and night and is not harmed. And if in this world a fire does not rule over all righteous people, how much more so in the world to come where they come to reap their reward. The Sages therefore responded [appropriately] when they said: Alas for such shame! Alas for such reproach![266] because there[267] people will be separated into categories[268] and the benefits are [distributed] according to the level of preparation of each person and the amount of perfection he was able to achieve [in this world].

Thus, eternal bliss is compared to a wedding chamber [269] in that souls that are prepared delight in it; and it is vouchsafed for every individual according to the level of his means. A bride does not prepare herself for her bridegroom until the time is ready for her transfer from her father's house to her husband's dwelling, and she has learned well the activities and responsibilities that she needs to fulfill on behalf of her husband as it is written: "A woman of valor, who can find?"[270]

6. Biblical Evidence for the Continuation of the Soul after Death

The transfer of the soul to its world [of eternal bliss] can be compared to a bride preparing to [transfer herself to] her

---

[265]Davidowitz states that according to Professor Louis Ginzberg in his essay "Compte rendu des Mélanges Israel Levy," *Revue des Études Juives*, 1914 Vol. 67, pp. 150–151, this commentator is Ibn Migash, the teacher of Maimon, father of Moses Maimonides.
[266]*Baba Bathra* 75a.
[267]In the world to come.
[268]Literally: levels or steps.
[269]*Chupah* meaning bridal canopy or wedding chamber.
[270]Proverbs 31:10.

husband as she stands in the dwelling of the Master of [all] Worlds,[271] the world of the intellectuals and the spirits of the righteous ones.[272] This analogy is expressed in Scripture[273] as follows: "And Enoch walked with God, and he was not; for God took him."[274] Onkelos the proselyte[275] translates the latter phrase: "for God caused him to die."[276] The meaning is not clear as to whether God caused him to die to protect him and to spare him [from the ills of this world] in order to reward him for his excellent activities, or just the opposite. The opposite is obviously untrue, namely that God would do something bad to a person who extends himself to serve Him. Therefore, the only remaining [explanation] is that He was kind[277] to Enoch by transferring him[278] from this turbid and painful world into the world of spiritual beings. The latter [explanation] is alluded to in Scripture when it states: "that it may be well with thee,"[279] which means in a world where all goes well,[280] "and that thou mayest prolong thy days,"[281] which refers to a world that is all enduring.[282] And Scripture also states: "Oh how abundant is

---

[271] One of God's titles.

[272] Davidowitz claims that the phrase "the world of the intellectuals and the spirits of the righteous ones" represents an additional phrase that explains the aforementioned "its world" and does not refer to "Master of (all) Worlds" since the world of the intellectuals and the spirits of the righteous ones is a single world. Hence, continues Davidowitz, it would seem preferable to omit the entire phrase.

[273] Literally: is expressed by God.

[274] Genesis 5:24.

[275] Second century translator of the Bible into Aramaic under the guidance of Rabbi Eliezer and Rabbi Joshua (*Megillah* 3a).

[276] Bacher argues forcefully against a variant reading of the Targum: "for He did not let him die."

[277] Literally: did good.

[278] Literally: giving him rest.

[279] Deuteronomy 22:7.

[280] *Kiddushin* 39b and *Chullin* 142a.

[281] Deuteronomy 22:7.

[282] The text here differs slightly from that in Kiddushin 39b. See also Maimonides' *Guide* 1:42 at the end, his *Mishneh Torah*, *Hilchot Teshuvah* 8:1, and his *Mishnah Commentary on Tractate Sanhedrin*, introduction to *Chelek* (see

Thy goodness which Thou hast laid up for them that fear Thee."[283] This is the [eternal] bliss that has no comparison in this world and its value is inestimable.[284] And it is also written: "Neither hath the eye seen a God, only Thou."[285]

And if you, discerning reader, assert that the explanation of [the scriptural verse] *for God took him*[286] is that "He did not let him die" but transferred him from place to place and he is still living on earth to this day[287]—this assertion cannot be correct[288] in that it is refuted by the fact that his life span cannot be longer than that stated in Scripture: "And all the days of Enoch were three hundred and sixty-five years."[289] It is, therefore, a certainty that his days [on this earth] ended and God took him to the perfect pleasantness[290] like a person who recompenses the one who loves him; when he observes his friend exerting himself on his behalf, he takes him to his special place and leaves him there in pleasantness forever. This is what King Solomon alludes to when he states: "The King hath brought me into his chambers. We will be glad and rejoice in thee."[291] This is also the meaning of the scriptural phrase: [*The*

F. Rosner. *Maimonides' Commentary on the Mishnah, Tractate Sanhedrin.* New York: Sepher-Hermon Press, 1981, p. 145).

[283] Psalm 31:20.

[284] In his *Mishneh Torah, Hilchot Teshuvah* 8:1, Maimonides states that the reward of the righteous is that they will attain this bliss and abide in this state of happiness. Later in the same chapter (8:7), he states that naught can be compared nor likened to the bliss in the world to come.

[285] Isaiah 64:3. Eternal bliss is incomprehensible to the human mind. In *Berachot* 34b, the Talmud suggests a different meaning, viz. "no eye but Thine, O god, has seen what He will do for those who wait for Him."

[286] Genesis 5:24.

[287] Literally: sphere of the earth.

[288] Literally: is nullified.

[289] Genesis 5:23. Bacher points out that the biblical passage (Genesis 5:23–24) is adduced in proof of the continuity of the soul after death by Judah Halevi and Abraham ibn David.

[290] That is, the world to come, the world of souls.

[291] Song of Songs 1:4. This statement is an allusion to the world to come. In his *Guide* 3:51, Maimonides gives an allegorical interpretation of the phrase "let him kiss me with the kisses of his mouth" (Song of Songs 1:2). This kind of death, which in truth is deliverance from death, has been ascribed by the

righteous perish] . . . "That the righteous is taken away from the evil to come,"[292] which refers to the fact that God [causes him to die and thus] preserves him from observing and seeing the sufferings that befall[293] the people of his generation. This is also the meaning of the scriptural phrase: "My beloved is gone down to his garden, to the beds of spices, to pasture in the gardens, and to gather lilies."[294] These refer to the souls of the righteous about which Scripture clearly states: "He entereth into peace, they rest in their beds."[295]

Among the assertions[296] concerning everlasting bliss in relation to the patriarch Abraham is the scriptural phrase: "But thou shalt go to thy fathers in peace."[297] This verse is testimony of the fact that after death he went to the dwelling place of his honorable forefathers such as Noah, Enoch, and Methuselah,[298] and not like Terach and his like.[299] Since he [Abraham] was not buried near any of his forefathers or relatives, the [aforementioned scriptural] phrase cannot mean that he was buried in their grave. In fact, only his children but not his forebears are buried in his grave. In the same honorable manner, concerning the other patriarchs as well as Moses and Aaron, Scripture states: *and was gathered to his people*,[300] which means that each of them was placed with those who were like him in that they had purified their souls and, after being

---

Sages to none but Moses, Aaron, and Miriam. The other prophets and pious men are beneath that degree.

[292] Isaiah 57:1.

[293] Literally: are appropriate.

[294] Song of Songs 6:2. According to Song of Songs *Rabbah* 6:2, *to gather lilies* means to gather the souls of the righteous.

[295] Isaiah 57:2.

[296] Literally, testimonies.

[297] Genesis 15:15.

[298] In his *Guide* 2:39, Maimonides speaks of Methuselah in a positive and complimentary manner.

[299] Davidowitz points out that Terach, Nachor, and their like, although ancestors of Abraham, were idol worshipers.

[300] Genesis 25:8; 35:29, and 49:33 and Deuteronomy 32:50.

severed from the body, those souls ascended to the world of everlasting continuity.[301]

And this [eternal] bliss is also clearly [pointed out to us by God] through His prophets in that one finds it mentioned in the words of the prophets. [For example], it is stated by Malachi, the last of the prophets: "For, behold, the day cometh, it burneth as a furnace[302] . . . But unto you that fear My name shall the sun of righteousness arise with healing in its wings."[303] And He said to Joshua, son of Yehotzadak:[304] "If thou wilt walk in My ways, and if thou wilt keep My charge, and wilt also judge My house, and wilt also keep My courts, then I will give thee free access among these that stand by."[305] These [scriptural verses] mean to say that [eternal bliss] will be your reward if you walk in the paths of the Torah, as is alluded to in the biblical phrase: "that they may keep the way of the Lord";[306] and it also states: "and you shalt walk in its ways."[307] [God promises that]: your reward will be your continuity and your eternity, like the eternity of the angels that always stand before Me.[308]

---

[301]Bacher states that Abraham ibn David explains this scriptural verse in the same way.

[302]Malachi 3:19.

[303]Malachi 3:20.

[304]Joshua was the son of Yehotzadak, the last High Priest, who was carried captive to Babylon (1 Chronicles 5:41), and grandson of Seraiah who was put to death by Nebuchadnezzar at Riblah after the capture of Jerusalem (2 Kings 25:18 ff).

[305]Zechariah 3:7.

[306]Genesis 18:19.

[307]Deuteronomy 28:9. The actual verse is: "and you shall walk in His ways."

[308]Bacher points out that the interpretation that the sentence "If you walk in My ways, I shall give you free access among those who stand," refers to God's promise to give righteous man continuity and eternity like angels, is also subscribed to by Bachya ben Pekuda in his *Duties of the Heart* (Section 9:1) and by Joseph ibn Tzaddik in *Microcosmus* (ed. Jellinek, p. 73 sq). Davidowitz also cites Bachya's *Duties of the Heart* where the author asserts that if man is pure and his deeds are good in this world, his soul will leave his body after death and assume the form and character of angels who are incorporeal.

7. Miscellaneous Remarks on Eternal Salvation[309]

And I will not cite[310] all the biblical allusions to the eternal salvation. Rather, the intent of this chapter is to inform you that this salvation is vouchsafed for every righteous person in proportion to his worth.[311] There is no difference between our belief [in eternal salvation] and that of philosophers[312] and Torah believers,[313] and this is why I prefaced my remarks as I did.

The talmudic Sages state[314] that the elders of that generation said: the countenance of Moses was like that of the sun, the countenance of Joshua was like that of the moon,[315] woe for such shame; woe for such reproach. Thus, "the skin of the face of Moses shone"[316] as a result of the purification of his soul which increased his spiritual perfection[317] as it is written: "and they were afraid to come near him"[318] because he thereby became an angel and he who sees an angel is afraid of death. And you, my brother, know that the moon is one part of 6,800 parts of the sun as is explained by natural scientists. Observe the level of achievement of Joshua in relation to Moses. Indeed, he was the most worthy and most appropriate person [to succeed Moses] from among the various levels of [spiritual perfection of] the righteous.[319] How extremely wonderful is

---

[309]Bacher characterizes the last part of this treatise as "a series of rather loosely connected observations and interpretations."

[310]Literally: prolong the discussion of.

[311]See Maimonides' *Mishneh Torah, Hilchot Teshuvah* 9:1 where he states that a person's merit is in proportion to his deeds and his Torah learning.

[312]Philosophers also admit to eternal salvation for pious and worthy people.

[313]This expression is also used by Maimonides in his *Guide* 3:20.

[314]*Baba Bathra* 75a.

[315]Joshua's glory was less than that of Moses.

[316]Exodus 34:30.

[317]Literally: ascent.

[318]Exodus 34:30.

[319]Davidowitz points out that if there was such an enormous difference between the exalted position of Moses and that of Joshua, how much more so are there differences between the various levels of spiritual perfection of righteous people.

the scriptural phrase [about Moses]: "and I will emanate from the spirit which is upon thee."[320] Moses attained the level of the acting intelligence in that [Torah] knowledge emanated from his exalted soul upon the elders and also upon the multitude of Israelites. It is written: "and the Lord hath not given you a heart to know and eyes to see [*until this day*]."[321]

And about Joshua it is written: "And thou shalt put of thine splendor upon him,"[322] which the Sages interpret: *of thine splendor* but not all thine splendor.[323] The moon acquires light from the sun. And this is what we mentioned about the Sages of that generation comparing Joshua to Moses.[324] For the light that shines from the sun[325] is natural and the moon acquires light therefrom as it [326] stands opposite it[327] and when it inclines away from the sun, its light is diminished. The further it[328] becomes distanced from the sun, the less its light, until it[329] becomes its natural dark self.

Indeed, in this distinguished analogy, the Sages teach us that Joshua paid heed to the messenger [of God][330] and followed in his footsteps and did not fail to remain opposite him to serve him and to glitter from his light.[331] Scripture states: "And Joshua the son of Nun was full of the spirit of wisdom; for Moses had laid his hands upon him."[332] Indeed, the other prophets and even the early Sages were compared to the form of the sun in that they were seen as reflections in which one

---

[320] Numbers 11:17.

[321] Deuteronomy 29:3.

[322] Numbers 27:20.

[323] *Baba Bathra* 75a.

[324] Joshua derived spiritual teaching from Moses as the moon derives light from the sun.

[325] The rays of the sun.

[326] The moon.

[327] The sun.

[328] The moon.

[329] The moon.

[330] Moses, that is.

[331] Just as the sun's light is reflected onto the moon, so, too, Moses' light was reflected onto Joshua.

[332] Deuteronomy 34:9.

form is reflected from another that is opposite the sun. And the brightness of the reflection varies according to the level of [spiritual perfection] and the preparation of each individual person. The perfection of each person is indeed [measured] according to the amount of heed that he pays to the Torah of Moses, our teacher; and one should not turn away from being opposite its light. The further one becomes distanced from the Torah, the more one's light weakens and one's lamp becomes extinguished.

In this way the Torah is compared to light, as are its followers. Thus, it is written: "For the commandment is a lamp and the Torah is light."[333] And it is also written: "Woe unto them that call evil good, and good evil."[334] The reverse is true about one who separates himself from the Torah, about whom it is written: "But the wicked shall be put to silence in darkness."[335] And it is further written: "They know not, neither do they understand; for their eyes are bedaubed, that they cannot see, and their hearts that they cannot understand."[336] And about the return of the Jews to the Torah during the time of Mordechai, Scripture states: "The Jews had light and gladness."[337]

Through the words of Malachi, Scripture teaches that salvation is attained and achieved through the fulfillment of the commandments of the Torah.[338] It is written: "Remember ye the Torah of Moses My servant,"[339] and the continuation of this [thought] is in the next scriptural verse: "Behold, I will send

---

[333] Proverbs 6:23. Whoever seeks perfection must turn to the Torah and the teaching of Moses.

[334] Isaiah 5:20.

[335] 1 Samuel 2:9. Bacher and Davidowitz point out that in his *Guide* 3:51 and 3:18, Maimonides applies this passage in a similar manner when he asserts that those who have no knowledge of God are like those who are in constant darkness and have never seen light.

[336] Isaiah 44:18.

[337] Esther 8:16.

[338] Literally: the deeds of the Torah.

[339] Malachi 3:22.

you Elijah the prophet,"[340] which means that God will return Elijah to this world after he was separated from it.[341] This [verse] is absolute proof that the resurrection of the dead is connected with the [coming of the] Messiah as it is written: "And thou shalt rest, and stand up to thy lot, at the end of the days."[342]

He who believes that Elijah did not die and that the greatness[343] of Elijah rests in the fact [that he did not die], must perforce also believe in the destruction of a fundamental principle [of Judaism]. This principle states that Moses, our teacher, the father[344] of all prophets, died, even though he was the master of all prophets. How can it then be said that Elijah remained physically alive? Indeed, remaining in corporeal form relegated to a desert or to a mountain rather than being part of the world of intellectual [souls] is in fact a deficiency. This [entire line of reasoning] is a distortion[345] of our faith.[346]

---

[340] Malachi 3:23.

[341] Died.

[342] Daniel 12:13. Here Maimonides does not clearly enunciate the relationship between the resurrection of the dead and the messianic age. See, however, his *Treatise on Resurrection*, F. Rosner, translator and editor. New York: Ktav, 1982; his *Mishneh Torah, Hilchot Teshuvah*, chapter 8; and his *Commentary on the Mishnah, Tractate Sanhedrin*. F. Rosner, translator and editor. New York: Sepher-Hermon, 1981, pp. 147–158.).

[343] Literally: perfection.

[344] Literally: teacher.

[345] Literally: badness.

[346] That Elijah died is proved because otherwise a fundamental article of our faith, namely the unequaled greatness of Moses, would be destroyed. See Maimonides' *Mishnah Commentary to Tractate Sanhedrin* that includes the widely read tenth chapter, *Perek Chelek*. In his lengthy commentary to this chapter, he discusses the basic tenets of the Jewish faith, such as the existence, unity, eternity and incorporeality of God, prophethood in general and the prophecy of Moses in particular, reward and punishment, the messianic age, and the resurrection of the dead. The first Mishnah in *Perek Chelek* begins with the words "Every Israelite has a share in the World to Come." To answer the questions as to who is an Israelite and what is the World to Come, Maimonides goes into a lengthy explanation of the concepts of immortality. He scorns those who perceive eternal bliss in the materialistic sense as a Garden of Eden in which milk and honey flow abundantly. His main thesis is that man should

It is important for you to know that the words "taking away" stated in relation to Elijah proves that he died and that he was separated from his physical body just as Moses was separated [from his physical body]. At the time when Elijah was being separated from Elisha, Scripture states: "today the Lord will take away thy master."[347] Similarly, Scripture speaks about Enoch: "for God took him,"[348] meaning He caused him to die. And it is also written: "But God will redeem my soul from the power of the netherworld; for He shall receive me. Selah,"[349]— which refers to the loss of the soul when the body is lost. Pray to the Lord that one's soul should remain without perdition when the body disintegrates. Furthermore, in its description of the death of the wife of Ezekiel, Scripture, states: "Behold, I

---

obtain wisdom for wisdom's sake, obey God for obedience's sake, and serve Him without anticipating any reward whatsoever. Then follow the formulation and analysis of the *Thirteen Articles or Principles of Jewish Faith*. The first five of these deal with the belief in God: that He is One, that He is the Creator, that He is Incorporeal and Eternal, that He alone is worthy of man's praise and worship. Principles six through nine are concerned with prophecy and revelation. Principles ten and eleven are the beliefs in reward and punishment for observance or transgression of God's commandments. The final two principles deal with the belief in Redemption and Resurrection of the Dead. According to Maimonides, if one rejects any of these doctrines, he has excluded himself from the community of Israelites; he is a heretic and unbeliever who has no share in the World to Come. This systematic formulation of a specific number of basic principles of belief generated a long, sometimes acrimonious debate concerning dogma in Judaism and provided the impetus for the creation of an extensive literature on the subject. (See M. Kellner, *The Role of Dogma in Medieval Jewish Thought*, Oxford, 1986.) Some of his critics asserted that it was temerity on Maimonides' part to select only thirteen of the many tenets of Judaism. Others objected that some of the articles are not specific to Judaism or are not indispensable foundations of the Jewish faith. The most prominent of Maimonides' critics in this regard were the philosophers Chasdai Crescas and Joseph Albo. The critics notwithstanding, Maimonides' *Thirteen Principles* have gained wide acceptance by the Jewish people, and they have even become incorporated in the daily liturgy as the *Yigdal* prayer.

[347] 2 Kings 2:3.
[348] Genesis 5:24.
[349] Psalm 49:16.

take away from thee the desire of thine eyes with a plague."[350]

Know now this [principle well] and your faith will not be faulty. The expression used by the Sages that "Elijah did not die" means that he left this earthly world when he was perfect and it only appeared as if he died, but he actually went to the world of the angels where there is no death. So, too, by your life,[351] the Sages speak of a minority of other righteous people such as Yishai, the father of David, and Kilab, the son of David.

Matter[352] forms a partition between man and his Master.[353] This [separation from God] is the ultimate worldly pain[354] for the one who has tasted of the delights of the senses but who yearns for communion with God in the world. On the other hand, those who are [spiritually] blind, who only understand the delights of the senses and who have no other pleasure but sensual delights in this world, know no pain or punishment except the want of their sensual enjoyments. Since this is the trend of thought of the great multitude of the people or even all the people, the Torah promises rewards[355] for the fulfillment of commandments and the opposite for transgressions as it states: "And it shall come to pass, if ye shall hearken diligently [unto My commandments]."[356] And it is also written:[357] "If ye walk in My statutes, and keep My commandments, and do them; then I will give you rains in their season, and the land shall yield her produce."[358] Since the prevention of misfortunes[359] and the abundance of rewards are the needed conditions, they are promised to those who seek spiritual

---

[350]Ezekiel 24:16.

[351]An expression for an oath.

[352]That is, sensuality.

[353]See Maimonides' *Guide* 3:9 where he states that the corporeal element in man is a large screen and partition that prevent him from perceiving abstract ideals.

[354]Literally: punishment.

[355]Literally: the coming of good things.

[356]Deuteronomy 11:13.

[357]Davidowitz points out that the Arabic manuscript ends here. The remainder of the text is found only in the Hebrew manuscript.

[358]Leviticus 26: 3–4.

[359]Such as hunger or illness.

perfection and the attainment of truth[360] and who are worthy thereof[361] as Scripture asserts: "Let the humble eat and be satisfied; let them praise the Lord that seek after Him; may your heart be quickened forever."[362] And it is also written: "And delight themselves in the abundance of peace."[363] And prostitution and perversion belong to the spiritually blind as it is written: "But Jeshurun waxed fat, and kicked."[364] And it is also written: "When they were fed they became full; they were filled and their heart was exalted; therefore they have forgotten Me."[365] Who can these verses refer to but to the multitude who have no delights but the pleasure of their senses![366]

The prophets also spoke of the eternal salvation in that they used the analogy cited by the Sages: in the future, the Holy One, blessed be He, will make seven canopies for every righteous person in the Garden of Eden,[367] as we have previously discussed. Thus, the entrance to the Garden of Eden and its orchards[368] is described in Scripture as it is.[369] And the entrance to Gehenna and its fire is described by Scripture as follows: "For an abyss is prepared of old."[370] This trend of thought is also accepted by those who follow in the path of the Torah from among[371] the nations.[372] All this is an allegory to

---

[360]See Maimonides' *Mishneh Torah, Hilchot Teshuvah* 9:1.

[361]Bacher explains that the promises of terrestrial rewards and terrestrial punishment also refer to those who find their highest enjoyment in the perfecting of the spirit.

[362]Psalm 22:27.

[363]Psalm 37:11.

[364]Deuteronomy 32:15. The next verse states: "They roused Him to jealousy with strange gods; with abominations did they provoke Him."

[365]Hosea 13:6.

[366]Davidowitz points out the difficulty in the transition from this sentence to the next paragraph and suggests that the text may be defective or missing some words.

[367]*Baba Bathra* 75a.

[368]Literally: its paradises.

[369]Perhaps this statement refers to Isaiah 4:5 where the word *canopy* (Hebrew: *chupah*) is used.

[370]Isaiah 30:33.

[371]Literally: as stated by.

denote the delight of the soul and its level[373] in her proximity to her Creator and her pain caused by her distance from His habitation. Thus it is written: "As for me, I shall behold Thy face in righteousness."[374]

When physical bodies separate [from the soul at the time of death], the bodies putrefy and disintegrate and eventually we observe that they become dissolved and that plants that can serve as animal food grow [from the gravesite]. This observation confirms the truth that reward and punishment are not corporeal but are only vouchsafed for the soul. Scripture states: "Who art thou, that thou art afraid of man that shall die; and of the son of man that shall be made as grass?"[375] Earlier, this verse is explained: "All flesh is grass,"[376] and: "The grass withereth, the flower fadeth; but the word of our God shall stand forever."[377] And it is also written: "The dead praise not the Lord; neither any that go down unto silence."[378] The matter is as follows: all living beings[379] die in this world and their end is to descend in silence.[380] Not so, however, for the children of Israel: "But we will bless the Lord from this time forth and forever. Halleluyah."[381] This is an allusion to the [Jews] who serve Him in this world and do so because of the pure delight of their communion with Him. They retain that delight that they derived from Him and they increase this [servitude] manifold until the end of the world.[382]

---

[372]Davidowitz suggests the following meaning: even the Christian and Moslem religions that posit a God also accept the concept that eternal bliss is purely spiritual.

[373]Davidowitz here points to an erroneous word in the Hebrew text. Perhaps it should be "tranquility."

[374]Psalm 17:15.

[375]Isaiah 51:12. See also Maimonides' *Mishneh Torah*, *Hilchot Teshuvah* 8:3–5 and his *Treatise on Resurrection*.

[376]Isaiah 40:6.

[377]Isaiah 40:8.

[378]Psalm 115:17.

[379]Literally: flesh, perhaps to include animals.

[380]Into their terrestrial grave.

[381]Psalm 115:18.

[382]Davidowitz suggests: the righteous people who serve God with delight in

Scripture also states about this world: "So that my glory may sing praise to Thee and not be silent; O Lord my God, I will give thanks to Thee forever."[383] This verse does not mean that man will praise and laud [God] in this world without interruption to the point that Scripture says: "and not be silent." How is this possible since various hindrances such as illnesses and other occurrences interrupt him from doing so? Rather this verse denotes that if a person's soul delights in serving Him, then when that [perfect soul] is transferred [from the body at the time of death] it increases its delight [in serving Him] and never ceases praising Him, like the spheres and the intelligences.[384] About the spheres, Scripture asserts: "The heavens declare the glory of God";[385] and about the angels, it is written: "And one called unto another and said: [Holy, holy, holy is the Lord of hosts, the whole earth is full of His glory]."[386]

I have discussed this topic in great detail because I saw great benefit therein. I gathered together statements from the prophets and the rabbinic Sages and philosophical viewpoints that support, as much as possible, the concept of eternal salvation. Do not set aside that which I have [herein] brought to your attention. Place this booklet before you[387] and delve into it at all times and study it repeatedly[388] for all the days of your life. By my life, it will bring you to your ultimate goal [of spiritual perfection] and will insure that all your deeds are righteous: "For then thou shalt make thy ways prosperous, and then thou shalt have good success.[389] It shall be healing to thy navel, and potation to thy bones."[390]

---

this world continue to do so and even increase their servitude in the world to come.
[383] Psalm 30:13.
[384] Angels.
[385] Psalm 19:2.
[386] Isaiah 6:3.
[387] Literally: opposite your eyes.
[388] Literally: counted times.
[389] Joshua 1:8.
[390] Proverbs 3:8.

BIBLIOGRAPHY

by Jacob I. Dienstag

רשימה ביבליוגרפית זו של פרקים בהצלחה (או: פרקי הצלחה) היא חלק
מביבליוגרפיה מקיפה של כל חיבורי הרמב״ם ומשנתו. החלק על ביאור מילות
ההגיון הופיע בארשת, ספר ב׳ (תש״ך); על איגרת תימן-שם, ספר ג׳ (תשכ״א); על
ספר המצוות-שם, ספר ה׳ (תשל״ב); על משנה תורה-בספר היובל לכבוד יצחק קיוב
(תשל״ב); על מאמר תחיית המתים קרית ספר, כרך מ״ח (תשל״ג); על איגרת השמד-
שם, כרך נ״ו (תשמ״א); איגרת הרמב״ם לחכמי פרובאס-שם, כרך ס״א (תשמ״ד-
תשמ״ד); שמונה פרקים-בספר היובל לרבי יוסף דוב סולוביצ׳יק (ירושלים: מוסד הרב
קוק, תשמ״ד); מאמר העיבור לרמב״ם-יד להימן, לזכר א״מ הברמן (לוד: מכון
הברמן, תשמ״ד); מורה נבוכים-בספר זכרון לאלכסנדר שייבר (בודאפעסט, 1988);
שירים ומכתמים על מורה נבוכים-בספר היובל לכבוד פרופ׳ אהרן מירסקי (לוד:
מכון הברמן, תשמ״ו); פירושים והערות על מורה נבוכים — בגבורות הרמ״ה לכבוד
ר׳ משה חיים וייל. ירושלים, תשמ״ז; ספרי רפואה של הרמב״ם: הנהגת הבריאות;
ס׳ הסבות; ס׳ קצרת — במכון הרמב״ם בחיפה (בדפוס); פירוש הרמב״ם למסכת
ראש השנה — בספר זכרון להרב אליהו יונג. בדפוס.

התוכן:
א. פרקים בהצלחה, מקור ותרגום, מספר 1-20.
ב. על פרקים בהצלחה בספרות ימי הביניים, מספר 21-22.
ג. מאמרים ומחקרים, מספר 23-51.
ד. ציונים ביבליוגרפיים לכתבי-יד של פרקים בהצלחה, מספר 52-56.

א. פרקי הצלחה-מקור ותרגום

שכ״ז 1567

1] פרקים בהצלחה להרמב״ם. בסוף ספר הגדרים לר׳ מנחם בן אברהם המכונה
בונאפוס. שאלוניקי, שכ״ז 1567, דף [47-50]. (ש. ווינער, קהלת משה, עמ׳ 233, סימן
1897; ב. וואקשטיין, מנחת שלמה, חלק ב׳, מספר 262).

תקכ"ה 1765
2] פרקי הצלחה להרמב"ם ז"ל. בספר פאר הדור ... תשובות שאלות להרמב"ם. אמשטרדם, תקכ"ה [1765], דף לג, א-לה, ב.

תקנ"ה 1795
3] זבד טוב חלק ראשון והם דברי פרקי הצלחה לרבנו משה בן מימון... והובא בספ' פאר הדור... נדפס ע"י...אהרן יוסף הכהן בודק... לבוב: פיליריש שריפטן, הנשר הגדול [תקנ"ה 1795], [2], 16 דף. 160. (ווינער, שם, עמ' 402, מספר 3353; וואקשטיין, שם, חלק א', עמ' 141, מספר 677).

ת"ר 1840
4] זכר טוב חלק ראשון והם דברי פרקי הצלחה להנשר הגדול רבינו משה בן מיימון הספרדי והוא בספר פאר הדור המכונה בשם שו"ת הרמב"ם ז"ל. יוזעפאף: בדפוס דוד סעדי' ישעי', ת"ר [1840]. [10] דף. °16.

תרי"ט 1859
5] פרקי הצלחה להרמב"ם ז"ל. בספר פאר הדור הוא שאלות ותשובות הרמב"ם... Schrenzel, 1859 Lemberg: D.H. דף לב, ב-לו, א.

6] פרקי הצלחה להרמב"ם ז"ל. בקובץ תשובות הרמב"ם ואגרותיו, חלק ב'. לפסיא [תרי"ט 1859], דף לב, א-לד, ד.

תרנ"ז 1897
7] [by] (פרקי הצלחה) The Treatise of Eternal Bliss Attributed to Maimonides W. Bacher, JQR, o.s. 9 (1897), 270-289.

תרגום חלקי אנגלי של המאמר בלוית מבוא שבו בא בכר לידי הכרעה שהוא יצא מפרי עטו של הרמב"ם. בניגוד לגריץ, שחשב את המאמר הזה לזיוף, בכר בא למסקנה זו: "ברור כי לא נצדק בחרצנו על המאמר הזה את המשפט החמור שחרץ עליו גרץ, ואל לנו להוציאו בלי טעמים נוספים מרשימת הספרים המיוחסים לרמב"ם. הצורה המוזרה במידה ידועה, בה נמסר לנו המאמר, מעוררת בנו את הדעה שלפנינו מלאכה בלתי גמורה מאת הרמב"ם, מלאכה שנכנס אליה גם חומר זר מבחוץ. אפשר כי המקור הערבי, אם נתבונן בו ביתר דיוק, יפיץ אור נוסף על נקודות בודדות בתרגום. אולם, על כל פנים, מבחינת תכנו ברובו המכריע, אינו בלתי-מתאים למלאכת הרמב"ם" (שם, עמ' 289. השתמשנו בתרגומו של ההבאה מאת ש"ץ דווידוביץ במבואו ל"פרקים בהצלחה"-ראה מספר 10).

תרס"ה 1905
8] פרקי ההצלחה להרמב"ם ז"ל. בס' "זכר צדיק" למהר"ל מפראג. פיעטרקוב, תרס"ה, עמ' 17-28.

תרפ"ז 1927
9] פרקי הצלחה. באגרות ותשובות לרבינו משה בן מימון הספרדי (הרמב"ם). ורשה: הוצאת "טרקלין", תרפ"ז/1927. י"ח עמ' (פגינציה מיוחדת).

תרצ"ט 1939
10] פרקים בהצלחה המיוחסים לרמב"ם ז"ל; הוציאם לאור במקורם הערבי בפעם הראשונה ובתרגומם העברי מוגהים על פי כתב יד עם מבוא והערות ש. צ. דווידוביץ.

ערכם לדפוס והגיהם והוסיף הערות מבארות ד. צ. בנעט. ירושלים: הוצאת מקיצי נרדמים, תרצ״ט. XXXI, 39 עמ׳. שער לאטיני:
De Beatitudine Capita Duo R. Mosi Ben Maimon Adscripta. Nunc primum Arabice edidit interpretationem Hebraicam ad fiden codicis m.s. correctam introductionem notasque adiecit H. S. Davidowitz. Textum recognovit notas explicativas addidit D. H. Baneth. Jerusalem: Mekize Nirdamim, 1939.
Rev. by G. Vajda, *REJ*, 107 (1946-47), pp. 212-213.

תש״ה 1945

[11] פרקי הצלחה. בתוך: "קובץ מאמרי הרמב״ם", ניו-יורק, "ישורון", תש״ה/1945. י״ח עמ׳ (פגינציה מיוחדת). דפוס צילום מוגדל מאגרות ותשובות להרמב״ם, ורשה, תרפ״ז (בשינוי נוסח השער-עיין לעיל מספר 9).

תשי״ד 1954

[12] פרקי הצלחה. בתוך אגרות ותשובות להנשר הגדול רבינו משה בן מימון הספרדי (הרמב״ם). ירושלים: לוין-אפשטיין, תשי״ד [1954]. י״ח עמ׳ (פגינציה מיוחדת). דפוס סטראוטיפי של הוצאת ורשה, תרפ״ז (עיין לעיל מספר 9).

תשכ״א 1961

[13] פרקי הצלחה. בתוך: אגדות ותשובות להנשר הגדול רבינו משה בן מימון הספרדי (הרמב״ם). ירושלים: לוין-אפשטיין, תשכ״א [1961]. י״ח עמ׳ (פגינציה מיוחדת).

תשכ״ז 1967

[14] פרקי הצלחה להרמב״ם ז״ל. בתוך: אגרות קנאות; אגרות הרמב״ם. נדפס בלפסיא [תרי״ט], נדפס מחדש, ירושלים, תשכ״ז, דף לב, א-לד, ד. דפוס צלום מהוצאת לפסיא הנ״ל.

תשכ״ח 1968

[15] פרקי הצלחה. בתוך: אגרות ותשובות להנשר הגדול רבינו משה בן מימון הספרדי [הרמב״ם]. ירושלים: לוין-אפשטיין, תשכ״ח [1968]. י״ח עמ׳ (פגינציה מיוחדת). דפוס סטראוטיפי של הוצאת ורשה תרפ״ז (עיין לעיל, מספר 9).

תשכ״ט 1969

[16] פרקי הצלחה להרמב״ם ז״ל. בספר פאר הדור ... תשובות שאלות להמאור ... רבינו משה בן מימון ... תל-אביב, תשכ״ט/1969, דף לג, א-לה, ב. דפוס צלום של הוצאת אמשטרדם, תקב״ה (עיין למעלה, מספר 2).

[17] פרקי הצלחה להרמב״ם ז״ל. בקובץ תשובות הרמב״ם ואגרותיו, חלק ב׳, Farnborough: Gregg 1969 דף לב, א-לד, ד. דפוס צלום של הוצאת לפסיא, תרי״ט (עיין למעלה, מספר 6).

תשל״א 1971

[18] במבחר ספרות המוסר מאת ישעיהו תשבי בשיתוף עם יוסף דן. ירושלים-תל-אביב: הוצאת ספרים מ. ניומן, תשל״א, עמ׳ 353-357. ליקוט מהוצאת פרקים בהצלחה בעריכת ש״צ דוידוביץ (עיין למעלה, מספר 10).

תשמ"ד 1984

19] פרקי ההצלחה להרמב"ם ז"ל. בשאלות ותשובות רבינו משה בן מימון "פאר הדור," יוצא לאור במהדורה חדשה ומתוקנת, עם מקורות ציונים והערות, שינויי נוסחאות, ותשובות חדשות ומפתחות מאת דוד יוסף. ירושלים: מכון אור המזרח, מכון ירושלים, תשמ"ד, עמ' שו-שטז.

1991

20] Treatise on Eternal Bliss. In: *Six Treatises Attributed to Maimonides.* Translated by Fred Rosner. With Bibliographies by Jacob I. Dienstag. Northvale, NJ: Jason Aronson, 1991, p. 3.

חסר מקום ושנת דפוס

21] פרקי הצלחה להרמב"ם ז"ל. בקובץ תשובות הרמב"ם ואגרותיו, חלק ב' [ישראל, תשמ"ג או תשמ"ד], דף לב, א-לד, ד. דפוס צלום של הוצאת לפסיא, תרי"ט (עיין למעלה, מספר 6).

ב. על פרקים בהצלחה בספרות ימי הביניים

22] דון בנבנשת בן לביא, סוף המאה הי"ד. הובא במחקרו של מ. שטיינשניידר, המזכיר, 6 (1863), עמ' 14.

23] יוסף ב"ר אליעזר טוב עלם (בונפיל), הספרדי, המאה הי"ד. אהל יוסף (פירוש על אבן עזר לתורה) בספר מרגלות טובה, אמשטרדם, תפ"ב/1721, דף י"ג, א, סימן רלג. "וכמו זה פירש הרמב"ם ז"ל במאמר אחד קצר שחבר" (לפי שטיינשניידר, העברעישע איבערזעצונגען, עמ' 437, הערה 476). אולם ד"ר דוד הרצוג במהדורה הבקרתית של הספר בשם "צפנת פענח" (קראקא, תרע"ב/1911), פ' בראשית (עמ' 69), סובר שהמחבר מתייחס ל"מאמר היחוד" להרמב"ם.

ג. מאמרים ומחקרים

24] בכר, בנימין זאב, 1850-1913.
הרמב"ם פרשן המקרא. תירגם א"ז רבינוביץ. תל-אביב, תרצ"ב, עמ' 24.
שהרמב"ם הוא המחבר של פרקי הצלחה.

25] בנעט, דוד צבי, 1893-1973.
הקדמת העורך. ב"פרקים בהצלחה המיוחסים לרמב"ם"... עם מבוא והערות ש. צ. דוידוביץ. ערכם לדפוס והגיהם והוסיף הערות מבאורות ד. צ. בנעט. ירושלים: "מקיצי נרדמים", תרצ"ט, עמ' VII-XIII.

26] גריץ צבי הירש, 1817-1891.
דברי ימי ישראל. תירגם שאול פינחס רבינוביץ, חלק ד'. ורשה, תרנ"ה/1894; תרס"ח/1908; תרע"א/1911, עמ' 459.
שפרקי הצלחה הוא זיוף ספרותי.

27] דוידוביץ, ש. צ., -1887
מבוא לפרקים בהצלחה. ירושלים: הוצאת מקיצי נרדמים, תרצ"ט, עמ' XIV-XXXI.
שהמאמר לא נכתב ע"י הרמב"ם.

28] דינור, בן ציון, 1884-1972.
הרמב"ם. תל-אביב: דביר, תרצ"ה, עמ' 100, הערה 15. "יש לציין, כי שייכותם של הפרקים להרמב"ם איננה מחוץ לכל ספק; והדבר טעון ברור נוסף."

29] דינסטאג, ישראל יעקב.
בנימין זאב בכר בתור חוקר הרמב"ם. סיני, כרך נ"ה, חוברת א-ב (ניסן-אייר תשכ"ד), ע"ח-ע"ט.
סקירה ביבליוגראפית אדות בעיית אבהותו של מאמר פרקים בהצלחה.

30] דינסטאג, ישראל יעקב
פרקים בהצלחה המיוחסים לרמב"ם. ביבליוגרפיה של הוצאות, תרגומים ומחקרים. Studies in Bibliography and Booklore, vol. 16 (1986), pp. 51-56.

31] העשל, אברהם יהושע 1907-1972.
ההאמין הרמב"ם שזכה לנבואה ?ספר היובל לכבוד לוי גינצבורג. ניו-יורק: האקדמיה האמרקנית למדעי היהדות, תש"ו 1945, עמ' קע-קעא; דפוס צלום ב- Essays in Medieval Jewish and Islamic Philosophy (ed. A. Hyman). New York: Ktav, 1977, pp. 145-146.
"במקום אחר אשתדל ב"ה לחזק דעתם של שטיינשניידר ובכר שפרקי הצלחה פרי רוחו של הרמב"ם הם".

32] וידר, נפתלי, -1905
השפעות אסלאמיות על הפולחן היהודי. אוקספורד: הוצאת ספרית-מזרח ומערב, תש"ז/1947.
עמ' 45-46: "פרקים בהצלחה" לראב"ם ? "רצוננו רק להעיר שנראה שהמחבר [של פרקים בהצלחה] שייך לסוג החסידים מבית מדרשו של הראב"ם [ר' אברהם בן הרמב"ם]".

33] וידר, נפתלי, -1905
צעקת "הוא". סיני, כרך פ"ט, חוברת א-ב (ניסן-אייר תשמ"א), עמ' לח, הערה 5. כנ"ל.

34] זקש, שניאור, 1815-1892.
תוספות לשני המאמרים הנ"ל. היונה, תרי"א, עמ' 68.
מצטט את הפרקים: "בפרקי ההצלחה אשר חבר הרמב"ם בזקנותו"; אולם ראה הערך הבא:

35] זקש, שניאור, 1815-1892.
שיר השירים אשר לשלמה בן גבירול. פאריש תרכ"ח, עמ' כט.
בניגוד לשי"ר הוא מחליט שהפרקים מזויפים.

36] טייטלבוים, מרדכי.
הרב מלאדי ומפלגת חב"ד, חלק א'. ורשה: הוצאת תושיה, תר"ע, עמ' 20.
על הנגון בשעת התפילה בספרות הקבלה ופרקי ההצלחה.

37] צונץ, יום-טוב ליפמן, 1794-1886.
הדרשות בישראל. תורגם ע"י מ. א. ז"ק. ירושלים: מוסד ביאליק, תשי"ד, עמ' 502, הערה 197.

38] קרעדיטאר, לייב שלום, 1875-1966.
דער רמב"ם, לונדון: אידישע שטימע, תשט"ז. עמ' 69-71: "זוערק אויפן רמב"ם'ס נאמין". שהספר "פרקים בהצלחה" אינו מהרמב"ם.

39] שלום, גרשם, 1897־1982.
מחוקר למקובל (אגדת המקובלים על הרמב״ם). תרביץ, שנה ו׳ ספר ג׳ (ניסן תרצ״ה), עמ׳ 535 [=ספר הרמב״ם של התרביץ, ירושלים: חברה להוצאת ספרים על יד האוניברסיטה העברית, תרצ״ה, עמ׳ 91; מיקראה לחקר הרמב״ם. ירושלים: האוניברסיטה העברית, תשמ״ה, עמ׳ 91].

"...אני מאמין שמאמר זה זוייף בכשרון רב בידי סופר מהיר ומליץ נאמן שהרחיק ללכת בדרכי האפלטונים יותר מהרמב״ם עצמו".

40] Bacher, Wilhelm, 1850-1913.
Die Bibelexegese Moses Maimuni's. Budapest, 1896 (reprint: Gregg International Publishers, 1972), pp. 17-18.

41] Baron, Salo W., 1895-1989.
A Social and Religious History of the Jews. 2nd ed., vol. VIII. New York: Columbia University Press, 1958, p. 273, note 1; 308, note 17 (6).

42] Eppenstein, Simon, 1864-1920.
Moses ben Maimon, ein Lebens-und Charakterbild. In: *Moses ben Maimon* (ed. W. Bacher, M. Brann, D. Simonsen, J. Guttmann), Band II. Leipzig: G. Fock, 1914, pp. 100-101.

43] Fenton, Paul, 1951-
Introduction to his edition of *The Treatise of the Pool by* Obadyah b. Abraham b. Moses Maimonides. London: Octagon Press, (c. 1981), pp. 19, 44-46; 71 (notes).

44] Geiger, Abraham, 1810-1874.
[Review of:] S. Munk, *Notice sur Joseph ben Jehuda.* Paris, 1842. *Der Israelit des Neunzehnten Jahrhunderts (Literaturblatt),* 7 (1846), 136.

45] Graetz, Hirsch, 1817-1891.
Geschichte der Juden. 3. Auflage, Band VI, Leipzig, 1894, p. 389.

46] Sirat, Colette, 1934-
La Philosophie Juive au Moyen Age. Paris: Editions du Centre National de la Recherche Scientifique, 1983, pp. 240-41.

47] Steinschneider, Moritz, 1816-1907.
Die Hebraieschen Ubersetzungen des Mittelalters und die Juden als Dolmetscher. Berlin, 1893 (reprint: Graz, 1956), p. 437.

מתנגד לגרייץ ומיחס את המאמר להרמב״ם.

48] Steinschneider, Moritz, 1816-1907.
Gesammelte Schriften, I. Band. Berlin: M. Poppelauer, 1925, p. 40, note 11 (reprinted from *Ersch und Grubers Allgemeine Enc.* Sektion I, Band 54 (1852), 357-9).

כנ״ל.

49] Steinschneider, Moritz, 1816-1907.
Die arabische Literatur der Juden. Frankfurt a.M.:J. Kauffmann, 1902 (reprint: Hildesheim: Olms, 1964), p. 209.

50] Stitskin, Leon D., 1910-1978.
In his ed. of *Letters of Maimonides.* Translated and edited with introduction and notes. New York: Yeshiva University Press, 1977, pp. 33; 178-181 (notes 15-17).

51] Vajda, Georges, 1908-1981.
[Review of:] *Perakim be-Hatslaḥah (De Beatitudine),* ed. H. S. Davidowitz (Jerusalem, 1939), *REJ,* 107 (1946-47), pp. 212-213.

52] Vajda, Georges, 1908-1981.
"Une Citation non Signalee" du *Chapitre sur la Beatitude attribue a Moise Maimonide.* REJ, 130, no. 2-4 (April-Dec. 1971), pp. 305-306.

53] Weiss, Adolf, 1849-1924.
"Mose ben Maimons Leben unde Werke." In his ed. of *Mose ben Maimon: Fuhrer der Unschlussigen.* I. Band. Leipzig: F. Meiner, 1923, p. CLXII-CLXIII.

54] Zunz, Leopold, 1794-1886.
Die Gottesdienstlichen Vortrage der Juden historisch entwickelt. Berlin: A. Asher, 1832, p. 399; 2. Auflage, Frankfurt a.M.: J. Kauffmann, 1892 (facs. ed. Hildesheim: G. Olms, 1966). p. 412.

ד. ציונים ביבליוגרפיים לכתבי־יד של פרקים בהצלחה

[55 אלוני, נחמיה, 1906־1983 וקופפר, אפרים, ־1905
רשימת תצלומי כתבי־היד העבריים במכון לכתבי־היד העבריים חלק ב' ירושלים:
ראובן מס, תשכ"ד מספר 1272 (יא). פאמפלונה ספרית הקתדרלה.

[56 דוידוביץ, שלום צבי, ־1887
מבוא לפרקים בהצלחה. ירושלים, מקיצי נרדמים, תרצ"ט, עמ' XXVI-XXVII.

57] Loewinger, David Samuel, 1904-1980 and Weinryb, Bernard D., 1901-1983.
Catalogue of the Hebrew Manuscripts in the Library of the Juedisch-Theologisches Seminar in Breslau. Wiesbaden: Otto Harrassowitz, 1965, no. 119 (3).

58] *Revue Orientale.*
Catalogue d'une collection de manuscrits a Constantinople, vol. 2 (1842), p. 209, no. 14.

"Mass. sur papier, petit in 4, 36 pages."

59] Zotenberg, Hirsch
Catalogues des manuscripts hebreux et samaritains de la Bibliotheque Imperiale. Paris, 1866, no. 719 (3).

Part II

SEFER REFU'OT

THE BOOK OF REMEDIES

INTRODUCTION

In 1900, Menashe Grossberg published a booklet in England entitled *Sefer Refuoth LeRabbenu Moshe Maimon Zal, Rofeh LeMelech Mitzrayim* ("The Book of Remedies of Moses Maimonides, Physician to the King of Egypt"). The printer was Yitzchok Zev Metzik. The title page indicates that the booklet "is being published for the first time based on a manuscript in the British Museum in London." The author, Menashe Grossberg of Trestina, is the author of other works including *Alfeh Menashe, Dagel Menashe, Mateh Menashe,* Responsa *Shevet Menashe*, and several others. The 1900 edition of *The Book of Remedies* is bound together with another of Grossberg's works entitled *Chevel Menashe*. Grossberg was convinced of the authenticity of the work as a Maimonidean writing as he described in the foreword to the 1900 edition. However, there is serious doubt as to the accuracy of Grossberg's hypothesis. It seems likely that *The Book of Remedies* has been falsely attributed to Maimonides and was probably authored by Raymon Lull in the thirteenth century, as was proven by the elegant research of Benjamin Richler.

In the Hebrew publication *Kiryat Sefer* (Jerusalem: Hebrew University 1983, Vol. 58, p. 624–625), Richler discusses a *Book of Wisdom* or *Book of Raminos* and its relationship to the fifty sections (literally: gates) attributed to Maimonides. Richler begins by describing the *Sefer HaYosher*, also known as the *Sefer HaYashar*, in which there are collected remedies composed between 1280 and 1300 in France (see M. Steinschneider, *Hebraesch Bibliographie*, 1877, XVII, pp. 59ff). Among the pronouncements of many other renowned physicians such as Avicenna, Yochanan of Damascus, and Isaac the Israelite are the statements of the scholar called "Raminos in the *Book of Wisdom*." His statements are cited many times in the chapter dealing with the preservation of health as follows: "Avicenna, Raminos, and all the physicians . . ." (folio 89a in the Oxford manuscript, Bodleian Oppenheimer 180, film 19948). It is evident that the author considered him to be a respected and expert physician. Steinschneider (*Hebraesch Uebersetzungen*, p. 823, note 329) suggests with great hesitation that Raminos is really Raymon Lull, a contemporary of the author of the *Sefer HaYosher*.

Richler also points out that in the Roma-Costanza manuscript 2834 (film 760, Catalogue Sacerdota 201, pp. 1–13), there is a composition that the copyist called *Sefer Dud HaChochmot* ("The Book of Pot of Wisdoms") within which are cited all the aforementioned statements from the *Sefer HaYosher*. There is no doubt, concludes Richler, that *The Book of Raminos* or *Book of Wisdom* is identical to the *Sefer Dud Hachochmot*, which was written by Raminos as will soon be proven.

The *Book of Raminos* is described by Richler as a book of remedies from the thirteenth century or perhaps somewhat earlier that is almost unknown in the Jewish medical literature of the Middle Ages. Internal evidence alludes to its composition outside Germany. Herbal and pharmacological terms are Arabic. In some places, names of additional herbs are given in another language, apparently Spanish, as for example *alrigla*, which in Spanish is *bordoliga verdoliga, portulacea oleracea* in Latin). The Costanza manuscript was written in Italian, but not before the fourteenth century. The lines that were not copied prove that the original from which the copyist was working was apparently quite old and crumbling.

INTRODUCTION 69

The book consists of the search for wisdom of a young person called *Dud HaChochmot* ("Pot of Wisdoms"), that is to say philosophy, and Raminos in Chaldean. Raminos met the pious and scholarly Avitov or Arimon in Chaldea where he was accepted as a student and studied philosophy and medicine. The book begins: "Thus states the translator of this book from Chaldean into the language of strangers. I found in a Chaldean book that this book was one of the great events that occur only once in a long while." The explanation of this book relates to the time when the Israelites settled on their land when they first came out of Egypt. Raminos stayed with Arimon for a while before he "pursued his goal of going to another city to delve further into and to study other wisdoms." He requested that Arimon teach him one of the wisdoms. Since "your body is the wellspring for your soul," and since "the closest topic to me is my body, and it is proper to study the close before the distant," Raminos decided to study the secrets of medicine. According to Arimon, the knowledge of medicine, which in practical terms means the knowledge of the preservation of health, is divided into three parts. "Know that the Creator placed on this world three enemies that rule over man: wild animals, the four fundamental elements, and the inclination." Arimon does not speak at length about the first enemy. His main discussion concerns the four fundamental elements (fire, water, wind, and earth), each of which rules over one of the seasons, and the inclination, primarily the lust for food. He gives general recommendations for the preservation of health, and practical suggestions for one's conduct during each season, and about topics relating to eating and drinking.

After this chapter, the author writes: "Behold, I am adding to all this fifty sections [literally: gates] which I call fifty gifts. Conceal them as much as you can and do not teach them to every person." Richler points out that his friend, Shmuel Ashkenazi, told him that these fifty sections are identical with the composition by this name attributed to Maimonides in the London manuscript (Add. 27089, film 5769), which was published in London in 1900 by Menashe Grossberg in *The Book of Remedies of Moses Maimonides*. It is still not clear whether the fifty sections are part of the original book or whether they were added by one of the copyists. Early evidence points to the fact that at the end of the thirteenth century they were already considered to be part of *The Book of Raminos*. In the *Sefer HaYosher* the entire twenty-second section is cited in the name of Raminos as follows: "Raminos says . . ."

Finally, Richler points out that the book is composed of parables and proverbs. Arimon asks Raminos:

> What is the meaning of the words of the scholar who said that every detriment of human beings is through stones from flint rock, and their reward is on the wings of bees, and wisdom is the egg of a rooster, and there will be time when it will not exist and it will exist but not exist. And Raminos answered: the meaning is that all detriments come from associating with fools, scoffers and wicked people. Ignoramuses are compared to flint rock. Scholars are compared to the wings of bees because if a person associates with scholars, he can achieve great things just as a person reaches the site of the honey from the wings of the bees. The expression that wisdom is like the egg of a rooster means that there will be born a scholar whose name will be Solomon, son of David. He will enliven all wisdoms and there will not be more like him and he will be like the egg of a rooster which is unique and there is no other [i.e., extremely rare; as rare as a hen's tooth]. His statement: it will exist but not exist means that wisdom will be cut off [e.g., cease] after him and not be reawakened until the ends of time by scholars who will seek it out. They will be Greeks and will be called philosophers. They will think in their hearts that they are scholars but they will speak inappropriate words against the Most High [Daniel 7:25]; and they will err and be led astray. Therefore, he states: it will exist but not exist.

Richler concludes his presentation by informing the reader that he and Dr. Samuel Kottek are preparing a more extensive treatise about this composition (*The Book of Remedies*) and hope to publish their treatise soon.

My own view is that the *The Book of Remedies* is spurious. There is no extant Arabic manuscript, and it is known that with the exception of the *Mishneh Torah*, all of Maimonides' writings were composed in Arabic. The text itself is not similar to other writings of Maimonides with which I am familiar, including his ten authentic medical treatises. *The Book of Remedies* is full of errors and the author jumps from topic to topic. Many of the statements contradict what Maimonides wrote in the fourth chapter of his *Hilchot De'ot* and elsewhere. For example, section 43 asserts that all purgatives are harmful but Maimonides recommends them. Finally, *The Book of Remedies* is not mentioned at all by Steinschneider, Kroner, or Muntner, the renowned Maimonidean scholars. For all of these reasons, I believe that *The Book of Remedies* has been falsely attributed to Maimonides.

Editor's Foreword

King Solomon composed a *Book of Remedies*. If a person became ill or if he suffered from any sickness, he would consult that book and follow the recommendations contained therein[1] and would be healed. This *Book of Remedies* was concealed by King Hezekiah and they approved of his action. It seems apparent that "they approved of his action" refers to the Sages since the Talmud in *Berachot* 10b asks: What is the meaning of "I have done that which is good in Thy sight?"[2] Rabbi Levi said: He concealed the *Book of Remedies*. Hezekiah saw that people did not rely on God for their healing because they were not humbled by their sickness, but healed themselves (by consulting the *Book of Remedies*). Immediately he removed it and concealed it so that the people should supplicate for divine mercy as is explained by Rashi and by Maimonides in their Mishnah commentaries in the chapter entitled "Where it is the custom."[3]

---

[1] Literally: and do that which is written therein.
[2] Isaiah 38:3.
[3] The fourth chapter of *Pesachim*, folio 56a.

Righteous people acted similarly during the era of the prophets when they became sick. They consulted only the prophets as is described by Nachmanides in his commentary on the Torah portion entitled "My statutes."[4] It is my opinion that this custom was also prevalent at the time of the Patriarch Isaac. Thus, when Rebekah had pains during pregnancy, she did not consult with physicians, but sought out God as it is written: "And she went to inquire of the Lord."[5] Hezekiah himself did the same when he was ill: "Hezekiah turned his face to the wall and prayed unto the Lord."[6] And he wanted the people of his generation to do likewise. Therefore, he concealed the *Book of Remedies* and the Sages praised him for this act.[7] Maimonides expressed surprise when he wrote: Now listen to the harm done by this treatise and by the delusions contained therein. How could they attribute this folly to Hezekiah? Such folly should not even be attributed to the basest of the average persons and should not be cited as proof to support him for which the Sages praised him.[8]

In reality, this approval, whereby the Sages praised Hezekiah for concealing the *Book of Remedies*, is not agreed upon by later Sages or even by some Sages who lived in his own generation. This observation is evident from the talmudic statement in *Berachot* 60a: when going for bloodletting, a person should say "May it be Thy will, O Lord, my God, that this operation should be a cure for me, and mayest Thou heal me, for Thou art a faithful healing God, and Thy healing is sure, since men have no power to heal, but this is a habit with them." Rashi explains that they should not occupy themselves with remedies but should ask for divine mercy. Abaye said a man should not speak thus, since it was taught in the school of Rabbi Ishmael: It is written, "He shall cause him to be thoroughly healed."[9] From

---

[4]Leviticus 26:3ff.
[5]Genesis 25:22.
[6]Isaiah 38:2.
[7]*Berachot* 10b and *Pesachim* 56a.
[8]Maimonides, *Mishnah* commentary on *Pesachim* 4:8.
[9]Exodus 21:19.

INTRODUCTION

this we learn that permission has been given to the physician to heal.[10] The same principle is found in the Jerusalem Talmud, in chapter five of *Shekalim* where it states that Ben Achiya cared for those with intestinal ailments. The priests walked barefoot on the [stone] floor [of the Temple] and ate meat and drank water and as a result developed intestinal ailments.[11] He knew which wine was beneficial for the intestines and which wine was detrimental[12] for the intestines. How could he knew this unless he studied the *Book of Remedies*? Furthermore, we find in *Yoma* 83a: if one is seized by a ravenous hunger,[13] he may be fed even unclean things [even on the Day of Atonement] until his eyes are enlightened.[14] Similarly, the Sabbath must be desecrated[15] wherever there is possible danger to the life of a patient. This [cardinal principle of Judaism] clearly indicates that one should not rely on a miracle for a patient and only plead for mercy but one must also apply medical remedies.[16] So, too, in his illness,[17] King Asa did not seek out the Lord but turned to the physicians.[18] His transgression was the fact that he did not also turn to God [for healing]. See also my book Responsa *Shevet Menasheh* 32.

Verily, according to this discussion, it is difficult to understand[19] how Hezekiah could have concealed the *Book of Remedies*. Is it logical that King Solomon composed a *Book of Remedies* and Hezekiah found no benefit therein, either for his own generation or for subsequent generations, and concealed it and the Sages praised him and were not concerned as they were

---

[10]End of quotation from *Berachot* 60a.
[11]Diarrhea.
[12]Literally: loosen or melt.
[13]Bulimia.
[14]See 1 Samuel 14:27. Such ravenous hunger renders the eyes dull.
[15]The laws of the Sabbath are suspended or waived.
[16]Literally: indulge in the ways of remedies.
[17]King Asa probably suffered from gout as cited in 1 Kings 15:23. See the chapter entitled "Gout in the Bible and Talmud" in *Medicine in the Bible and Talmud* by F. Rosner, New York: Ktav, 1977, pp. 59–60.
[18] 2 Chronicles 16:12.
[19]Literally: the mind cannot fathom.

concerned in regard to the concealing of the Book of Ecclesiastes and Ezekiel? Originally, I thought to explain this [seemingly unintelligible] act of Hezekiah in concealing the *Book of Remedies* in that it was not really concealed in the literal sense. Rather, it means that the topic of medical remedies was forgotten by the people of his generation because they were not greatly involved in medical practices[20] and their main approach [in illnesses] was only to plead for [divine] mercy. Hezekiah was responsible for this attitude because he led the people of his generation in this approach and it is, thus, as if he concealed [the *Book of Remedies*]. Therefore, it is attributed to Hezekiah that he concealed the *Book of Remedies*.

I found a comparable situation in *Pesachim* 62b: Since the day that the *Book of Genealogies* was concealed, the strength of the Sages has been impaired and the light of their eyes has been dimmed. Rashi there explains the word *concealed* to mean forgotten. Were it not for the explanations of Rashi and Maimonides, I would have explained this matter in a different way; that is to say as Maimonides wrote in the present work in section 31: "You will make serious errors if you study the *Book of Remedies* by yourself without consulting the great Sages and experts." This is the way the people of his generation conducted themselves. If any individual developed any type of illness, he would look into the *Book* [*of Remedies*] and would follow the instructions written therein. Hezekiah observed that many people erred by consulting this *Book* on their own and were not able to fully understand its contents.[21] From this practice many detrimental outcomes occurred because of their deficient knowledge. Therefore, Hezekiah concealed this book from the average person and entrusted it to the great Sages so that they could teach the people the principles of medicine, as written in the *Book*, in the manner described in the above-cited Jerusalem Talmud. For this act [of Hezekiah] the Sages praised him and it was the proper thing. Perhaps this is the true explanation.

---

[20]Literally: the ways of remedies.
[21]Literally: were not sufficiently expert in the ways of the *Book*.

INTRODUCTION 75

The conclusion for us to draw from all the aforementioned is that in our generation—as was true in the generation of Solomon and Hezekiah—a person with an illness must follow the instructions of the physician and must plead for mercy that [their prescriptions] produce successful results.[22] Undoubtedly this was the situation in the era of the Sages of the Talmud as is all explained in the above-cited sources. This, too, is the opinion of Maimonides who was engaged in the practice of medicine and wrote books on this topic, one of which has been published many times and is called the *Medical Aphorisms*,[23] and others.

Recently,[24] in the collection of manuscripts in the British Museum in London, I found, praise the Lord, a small book containing fifty sections of remedies of Moses Maimonides which, according to the testimony of my close friend, the learned scholar Rabbi Shazach,[25] has not yet been published. I, therefore, found it appropriate to publish it. It is certainly a precious book of great value and of great benefit, especially those items that originate with Moses Maimonides. Unfortunately, the manuscript of this book is written on very old paper and because of its age, there are individual letters and words that are blurred and which I cannot read and restore. Nevertheless, I rejoiced therewith "as one who finds great spoils"[26] and I hope that the readers will also rejoice therewith.

Menashe Grossberg

---

[22] Literally: are beneficial.

[23] Hebrew: *Pirké Moshe*. See English version by F. Rosner and S. Muntner entitled *The Medical Aphorisms of Moses Maimonides*, New York: Bloch for Yeshiva University Press, 1973, 2 volumes.

[24] Literally: and now.

[25] Acronym probably referring to Rabbi Shlomo Zalman Chayim Halberstam.

[26] Psalm 119:162.

THE BOOK OF REMEDIES

These[1] are the instructions[2] that Moses Maimonides sent to his son by which to conduct himself all the days of his life to maintain his strength and his health in order to engage in Torah [study and practices].

---

[1] Grossberg points out in a lengthy footnote that in his preface he wrote that King Solomon wrote a *Book of Remedies*. So wrote Moses Nachmanides (known as *Ramban*) in the introduction to his commentary on the Torah. Abraham di Boton (known as *Lechem Mishnah*), in his Mishnah commentary, writes in the name of *Tashbatz* (acronym for Simeon ben Tzemach or Shimshon ben Tzadok), section 447, that when Noah and his sons were in the ark, demons, spirits, and night devils were also present and harmed Noah so that he became ill. An angel came, took one of Noah's sons to the Garden of Eden, and taught him medical remedies that he wrote in a book. Here ends the citation from *Tashbatz*. In his book *Torat Ha'Adam*, Nachmanides comments on the phrase in *Sofrim*, chapter 15, "the best of physicians go to Gehenna," that all remedies are associated with danger: That which heals one person is lethal for another. The phrase "the best of physicians go to Gehenna" is a criticism of the practices of physicians and their negligent and wanton acts. He does not, however, consider medical practice to be prohibited as the Sages spoke about the worthiest of butchers (who are said to be the partners of Amalek. See *Kiddushin* 82a.) If he (the physician) conducts himself appropriately, however, certainly he has considerable merit for himself. So much for the words of Nachmanides.

[2] Literally: sections on arrangements.

A person should not eat to satiety[3] but should stop eating when he still has the desire to eat more.[4] The Sages suggest the measure of two-thirds [of satiety]. In the summer when it is hot, one should reduce somewhat this measure and in the winter increase it.[5] The Sages also said that it is far better to eat a little of a detrimental food than to eat a lot of a beneficial food.

In the morning after the stomach is empty, that is to say when he has gone into the yard,[6] he should exercise moderately with brief exercises to stimulate natural body heat. However, one should not [exercise] at all [immediately] after eating but calmly walk a little over the length of the house; such [walking] helps the food descend. Exercise shortly before eating is totally detrimental.

Sleep is helpful to the digestion [of food]. A person should not eat unless he is hungry[7] so that food will not enter [the stomach] when food is already there. A person should not eat until he is very hungry and his hunger is very strong, for sometimes hunger is beneficial. The same applies to drinking beverages.

Drinking water after eating is detrimental to digestion except for someone who is accustomed thereto.[8] One should not drink

---

[3]Grossberg points to the biblical verse "Thou mayest eat grapes at thy fill at thine own pleasure" (Deuteronomy 23:25). Rashi interprets the phrase "eat thy fill" to mean "but not excessive eating." See also *Erubin* 83b: he who consumes excessive amounts of dough is a glutton.

[4]See Maimonides' *Mishneh Torah, Hilchot De'ot* 4:2 where he states: a person should not eat until his stomach is replete but should diminish his intake by approximately one-fourth of satiation. See my English translation, in *Medicine in the Mishneh Torah of Maimonides*, New York: Ktav, 1984, pp. 69–107. See also Maimonides' *Medical Aphorisms* (F. Rosner and S. Muntner, trans. and edit, New York: Bloch for Yeshiva Univ. Press, 1973, chapter 17:2), where he quotes Hippocrates who said, "the maintenance of health depends upon the avoidance of satiation. . . ." The Talmud (*Gittin* 70a) also lists eight things which in large quantities are harmful but in small quantities are beneficial, namely, traveling, the "way of the world," wealth, work, wine, sleep, hot baths, and bloodletting.

[5]See *Hilchot De'ot* 4:1.

[6]Alternate translation: when the food has gone to the enclosure, that is, intestines.

[7]See *Hilchot De'ot* 4:1.

[8]Grossberg points out that he found a similar statement in a letter that

during a meal or [immediately] thereafter before digestion has even begun, and this refers not only to water.[9]

One should not retain any superfluities at all. As soon as one feels the need to eliminate them, one should respond thereto.[10]

One should not eat nor wash oneself nor drink nor engage in sexual intercourse nor perform any exercise until one has examined oneself [regarding the need to eliminate wastes].[11] So, too, shortly thereafter. And one should also respond [to the need to excrete wastes] when the food is digested.

Beneficial foods include bread made from wheat that is properly prepared,[12] that is to say from grain that is not very fresh nor very old and not from absolutely pure flour. One should mix[13] it well during its kneading and its baking. Meat of goats, sheep,[14] chicken, *parmatz*,[15] pigeons,[16] turtle doves, and

---

Maimonides wrote to the Sultan, which was published in the work *Keren Chemed*. See also *Shabbat* 41a: if one ate without drinking, one's food is blood and this represents the beginning of intestinal illness. This statement refers to one who did not drink at all after eating.

[9]See *Hilchot De'ot* 4:2 where Maimonides says that one should not drink water during meals save a little and mixed with wine. When the food commences to be digested in the intestines, one may drink as much water as one finds necessary. However, even after the food has been digested, he should not imbibe water excessively. See also *Berachot* 42b where Rashi comments that people used to drink but little during a meal. See also *Niddah* 24b: anybody who takes in more drink than food undermines his health.

[10]See *Hilchot De'ot* 4:1 where Maimonides states that one should not postpone urination or defecation for even a single moment. See also *Makkot* 16b: withholding one's bodily functions comes under the heading of *You shall not make yourselves abominable* (Leviticus 11:43). Further, it gives rise to bad diseases and endangers life (Maimonides' *Hilchot Ma'achalot Assurot* 17:31).

[11]See *Hilchot De'ot* 4:2 where Maimonides states that one should not eat until one has examined oneself carefully lest it is necessary to excrete wastes. See also *Shabbat* 82a: he who requires easing himself and still goes on eating is like a furnace stoked on top of its ashes—which is the beginning of a bad odor.

[12]Literally: fixed.

[13]Literally: pluck or pick or call.

[14]Or lambs.

[15]A type of fowl?

[16]In *Hilchot De'ot* 4:10, Maimonides lists small young pigeons among detrimental foods.

the yolks of chicken eggs [are also beneficial foods].

However, their nature is not equal. Poultry meat is easier to digest [than large cattle meat], and next is goats' [meat] and next is that of sheep. A person should eat the lighter food before the heavier food.[17]

Lambs' [meat] up to one year is beneficial, and that from a castrate soaked in oil is the best type of meat. The meat near the bones and the legs of [large] animals is beneficial.

The best among beneficial milks is that from goats and from cows.[18] It is beneficial for someone in whom it does not become sour in the stomach nor produce sourness. Such a person does not develop swelling in his loins. One should mix a little honey and a grain of salt [into the milk]. Cheese[19] is beneficial if it is one day old, white,[20] sweet, and without fat. All types of butter are not detrimental foods for any person.

Honey is good for the elderly.[21] The small fish whose flesh is white and hard and has a good taste and are derived from the sea or from rivers, like the fish that the Sages called *varveel*, are not nutritionally detrimental[22] but one should only consume a little thereof.

Wine is beneficial, for it nourishes food, dilutes it and accelerates its digestion.

The melon[23] known as *leborika* should only be consumed at the beginning of the day when the stomach is devoid of liquid[24] and does not have a bad constitution. Then it is good because

---

[17] A similar statement is found in *Hilchot De'ot* 4:7.

[18] See Maimonides' *Medical Aphorisms* 20:43 where it states: cow's milk is the thickest of all milks and also the fattest. Camel's milk is the most watery and the least fat. . . . Goat's milk is intermediate. . . .

[19] Cheese is discussed in *Hilchot De'ot* 4:9 and Maimonides' *Medical Aphorisms* 20:42 and 45.

[20] White cheese is mentioned in the *Medical Aphorisms* 23:107.

[21] See *Hilchot De'ot* 4:12 where it states: honey and wine are bad for children but salutary for the elderly.

[22] Literally: their food is not bad.

[23] See *Hilchot De'ot* 4:6 where melons and other fruits are classified as purgatives and where pomegranates and other fruits are called constipating agents.

[24] Humor.

it cools the body a little. It is better, however, to abstain from eating it altogether.[25]

Dried and wrinkled fruit and dried *pistok*[26] are beneficial during a meal. It is even better to consume them after the meal because their sweetness aids one's digestion.

Things that are not good for the body include unleavened bread,[27] cooked or fried dough . . . or other oils. So, too, coarse bread[28] and bread made from fine flour and wheat that was cooked [are detrimental to health].

All that which is within the abdomen of an animal[29] is detrimental [to human health if consumed]. The fat of animal flesh is extremely detrimental, as are the heads of animals. And everything that is made from milk or that contains it is extremely harmful, that is to say curdled milk or cooked milk . . .[30] and all that is cooked with milk. All types of cheese are harmful except one-day old cheese,[31] as cited above. Honey is harmful for young men,[32] especially those with a hot constitution.

Most fish are detrimental[33] and especially fat fish or those raised in bad waters.

Garlic, onions, cress, cabbage, and *kalineesh*[34] are detrimental

---

[25] Literally: to keep one's hands therefrom.

[26] Pistachio? See also *Hilchot De'ot* 4:11 for a discussion of dried versus fresh fruit.

[27] See *Hilchot De'ot* 4:9 and *Kiddushin* 62a where unleavened bread is said to be detrimental to health.

[28] See *Shabbat* 117b where coarse bread and bread made of fine flour are discussed.

[29] Grossberg points out the talmudic discussions in *Chullin* 49a about the internal organs of an animal, in *Berachot* 55a about "the rough parts of the flesh of an animal causing hemorrhoids, and in *Shabbat* 81a.

[30] In the *Medical Aphorisms* 20:39, 43, 44, Maimonides cites certain beneficial effects of milk.

[31] Other beneficial effects of cheese are cited in *Medical Aphorisms* 20:45.

[32] See *Hilchot De'ot* 4:12.

[33] The Talmud (*Berachot* 40a) states that one who eats small fish regularly will not suffer with his bowels. Moreover, small fish stimulate propagation and strengthen a man's whole body.

[34] A type of vegetable?

foods.³⁵ However, cucumbers and green melons are only slightly harmful. On the other hand, fresh fruits produced on trees are mostly harmful to people in general. The most harmful of all are the carob³⁶ and *nispili rabuli*. There are some [fruits] that are only slightly harmful and nearly comparable to those that are beneficial. Examples are figs and grapes because they are not very harmful.³⁷

Galen said³⁸ that a person who once had a fever for an entire year abstained from fruits and was cured . . . in addition, beverages made therefrom, namely a good pharmaceutical with which to heal . . . of the fruits is the cause³⁹ of the fever. If a person wishes to eat of them, he should only eat fresh ones before meals, such as nuts and grapes and figs. He should not eat food after them until they have left the stomach so that they should not mix with the food. He should eat astringent [fruits] after the meal such as *peraglim* and *pirsagu*⁴⁰ but he should only consume a little of these to strengthen and close the mouth of the stomach. The worst types of fruit are the *irsagu* and *anufarsaglu,* and a person should not consume of these two types at all. However, dried fruits such as raisins and dried *pistok* can serve as seasoning for the food. So, too, the consumption of a little of different types of sweet things after the meal is beneficial to strengthen the food and the stomach and the former's digestion.⁴¹

---

³⁵These vegetables are also said to be harmful in *Hilchot De'ot* 4:9. See also *Kiddushin* 62a and *Avodah Zarah* 29a. The latter reference says that boiled cabbage has a curative effect.

³⁶In *Hilchot De'ot* 4:11, Maimonides states that carob pods are always injurious to health. He also advises one to abstain from fruits of trees, especially when they are fresh.

³⁷In *Hilchot De'ot* 4:11, Maimonides states that figs, grapes, and almonds are always good, whether fresh or dried. In *Midrash Kohelet* 5:10, it states that the fig is good to eat, nice to look at, and beneficial to the intellect.

³⁸In his medical writings, especially in his *Medical Aphorisms*, Maimonides frequently quotes Galen.

³⁹Literally: substance.

⁴⁰A type of pear?

⁴¹In his *Medical Aphorisms* 20:5ff, Maimonides quotes Galen more extensively in regard to the beneficial and harmful fruits.

This is as much[42] as I saw fit to mention in regard to this regimen [of health] and it is sufficient, according to our opinion.

Says the author Rabbi Moses Maimonides in his book entitled *Regimen of Health*[43] at the end of the book:[44] I am here adding fifty sections[45] that I call fifty branches. Conceal each and every one that you can and do not teach them to everybody.

The first section. The entire goal[46] in regard to your food consumption is that it should be beneficial. Do with your food as you would do with a therapeutic medicine, in that you do not consume it out of lust but because it benefits you.

The second section. Do not eat unless you are hungry,[47] and do not be like one who adds oil to the lamp so that you do not extinguish the lamp, for such a practice may save you from death but will not save you from harm to the stomach.

The third section. If you are hungry, do not delay in eating, for you will harm the stomach and cause detrimental humors[48] to be drawn into your body.

The fourth section. Your food intake should always be less than satiation[49] by the measure of one *gera* or a *zuz*.[50] If the

---

[42] Literally: the amount or measure.

[43] Among Maimonides' medical writings are two treatises on the regimen of health, both of which contain extensive discussions of beneficial and harmful foods including fruits and vegetables. See the English edition of A. Bar-Sela, H.E. Hoff, and E. Faris, *Moses Maimonides' Two Treatises on the Regimen of Health*. Philadelphia: Transactions of the American Philosophical Society, New Series, Vol. 54, part 4, July 1964, 50 pp.

[44] Grossberg considers this Maimonidean reference to his book entitled *Regimen of Health* to refer to a general medical textbook mentioned by Maimonides in his *Hilchot De'ot* 4:21.

[45] Literally: gates, that is, brief paragraphs or aphorisms.

[46] Literally: thought or intention.

[47] Literally: without lust. See *Hilchot De'ot* 4:1 where Maimonides makes an identical statement. See also *Berachot* 62b.

[48] In medieval times, health was thought to be related to a proper balance in quality and in quantity of the four body humors: white bile (phlegm), red bile (blood), black bile (melancholy) and yellow bile (choler).

[49] See footnote 4.

[50] Grossberg points out the commentary of Rashi on Exodus 30:13 which states: *gera* in Hebrew denotes a *me'ah*, a coin of small value, in

stomach lusts for additional food, more than normal,[51] and is involved in grinding it up . . . [well], do not overburden it; rather, learn a lesson from the burden on an animal which, if excessive, causes the animal to crouch under it or to kick hard and throw its rider to the ground.

The fifth section. Always strive to drink pure and clear[52] water, for if water is turbid it gives rise to stones.[53] Tasteless water[54] gives rise to hydrops and swelling of the intestines.

The sixth section. Contrary to what people say, the intestines are not like a millstone but like a weak sac. Do not cast into them save well-ground food and dishes that have been well cooked. And do not eat excessively of hard fruits and unripe fruits that have not sufficiently ripened because if you burden the intestines with lots of inadequately cooked dishes, the intestines will have to complete your deficiency in that you failed to cook the food properly. Also, do not suddenly ingest[55] excessively hot foods and do not . . . drink cold water nor snow except for small amounts, a little at a time.

The seventh section. A person should not abstain from sleep in the proper position[56] because it is necessary for [the maintenance of] health and is associated with procreation.[57]

The eighth section. If a nocturnal emission[58] causes you to be sexually excited, wait before eating until you are full . . . if it has already caused you to become excited, eat and drink a little and then . . . sleep.

Aramaic . . . a full *shekel* is four *zuz* and a *zuz* was originally five *me'ahs*. Consequently, a *shekel* was twenty *me'ahs* or *geras*.

[51] Literally: more than its portion.
[52] Literally: good.
[53] Bladder or kidney stones.
[54] Unsalted? Yet in his *Medical Aphorisms* 20:38, Maimonides cites Galen who says that the most salutary of drinking waters are those that have no perceptible taste or odor.
[55] Literally: rush into them, that is, the intestines.
[56] Grossberg points out that in *Hilchot De'ot* 4:4–5, Maimonides advises a person to sleep on his left side at the beginning of the night and on his right side at the end of the night, whereas Avicenna recommends the reverse.
[57] Meaning unclear?
[58] Literally: occurrence.

The ninth section. If an occurrence happens to you at night,[59] it should suffice for you. You do not need anything else.

The tenth section. Nature requires that semen be emitted if you are a plethoric man[60] and your body contains much semen. Do not live without a wife because all the Sages are in agreement that [without a wife] one loses one's intellect.

The eleventh section. An excess of coitus weakens the body.[61] Guard against it as you would guard yourself against your enemy who seeks your life. Only engage in coitus for therapeutic reasons, to cleanse your body but not for lust.[62]

The twelfth section. Do not be surprised if you see a person who appears to be accustomed to an excess of coitus and an excess of detrimental foods, and do not . . . it appears as if death occurs as a result rather than bad illnesses. There are many reasons for this [observation], as if this person accustomed to [excessive coitus and an excessive intake of detrimental foods] is a king[63] who saves himself by [taking] excellent

---

[59]That is, a nocturnal emission.
[60]Literally: a man of blood.
[61]Literally: destroys one's life.
[62]See *Hilchot De'ot* 4:19 where Maimonides states: Effusion of semen represents the strength of the body and its life, and the light of the eyes. Whenever semen is emitted to excess, the body becomes consumed, its strength terminates, and its life perishes. This is what Solomon in his wisdom stated: *Give not thy strength unto women* (Proverbs 31:3). He who immerses himself in sexual intercourse is assailed by premature aging. His strength wanes, his eyes weaken, and a bad odor emits from his mouth and his armpits. The hair of his head, his eyebrows, and his eyelashes fall out, and the hair of his beard and armpits and the hair of his legs increase excessively. His teeth fall out, and many maladies other than these afflict him. The wise physicians have stated that one in a thousand dies from other illnesses and the remaining 999 from excessive sexual intercourse. Therefore, a man must be cautious in this matter if he wishes to live wholesomely. He should not cohabit unless his body is healthy and very strong and he experiences many involuntary erections, and when he diverts his thoughts to another thing, the erection persists, and when he senses a heaviness from his loins down, as if the testicular cords were being tightened, and his flesh is warm. Such a person requires coitus, and it is therapeutic for him to have sexual intercourse.
[63]Literally: one of the kings.

medicinal remedies and by [consulting expert] physicians. So, too . . . kings maintain their lives by the multitude of the people or because they are born very strong. It is an observed fact[64] that some people can carry a heavy burden because of their great strength whereas others are weak and cannot even carry a very light burden.[65]

The thirteenth section. Do not seek after things that increase coitus lest you die because of their great warming effect,[66] especially in the summer.

The fourteenth section. If you desire to increase coitus to have many children,[67] be careful to eat foods that are beneficial for this purpose;[68] ask physicians about them.

The fifteenth section. Wait until the season of Nissan [for bloodletting] because that [season] is good for this activity.[69]

The sixteenth section. Do not marry an exceedingly beautiful woman. Do not cause . . . that she give birth. But do not take [as a wife] an exceedingly ugly woman lest you stay

---

[64]Literally: for you observe.

[65]Literally: a burden that (weighs) nothing.

[66]Literally: heat.

[67]Literally: to leave live seed after you.

[68]See Maimonides' *Treatise on Cohabitation* (published together with his treatises on *Poisons* and *Hemorrhoids* by the Maimonides Research Institute, Haifa, Israel, 1984, pp. 153–182), where he enumerates a variety of aphrodisiacs.

[69]See *Hilchot De'ot* 4:18, where Maimonides states that "a person should not accustom himself to constant bloodletting. He should not phlebotomize himself except if there is extraordinary need. One should not let blood either in the sunny (summer) months or in the rainy (winter) season; rather, a little in the month of Nissan (approximately April [spring]), and a little in the month of Tishri (approximately October [autumn]). After fifty years of age, he should not phlebotomize himself at all. A person should not be bled and take a bath on the same day, nor be bled and then undertake a journey, nor be bled on the day he returns from a journey. On the day of phlebotomy, he should eat and drink less than he is accustomed to, and he should rest on the day of phlebotomy and not fatigue or exert himself or promenade." These rules are based in part on discussions in the Talmud, *Gittin* 70a and *Shabbat* 129a. For a detailed discussion of bloodletting in talmudic times see my review article in the *Bulletin of the New York Academy of Medicine*, Vol. 62, pp. 935–946, November, 1986.

separate from her a lot and cause yourself pain . . . which arises as a consequence of [accumulated unexpended] semen. Therefore, marry a woman of moderate beauty[70] for she is good for your body.

The seventeenth section. Do not abstain from vomiting once a month[71] or every other month for this act brightens the eyes and is beneficial for the intestines. If emesis is difficult for you, perform it with items that induce emesis, such as hot water or honey with salt, or spinach seeds ground and cooked in a little water, or roots of bitter cucumbers cooked in water because all these facilitate emesis for a person. Do not[72] induce vomiting on days when you have blood let, for this is very harmful.

The eighteenth section. If you need to cleanse your [body] do not postpone your [elimination of wastes] because that gives rise to a reversal of action in that food which normally attracts them to itself will attract from that which is prepared to be excreted[73] and this is detrimental to your body. The withholding of urine gives rise to afflictions in the depths of the abdomen, the urinary bladder, and the withholding of feces[74] and winds[75] which are usual in the abdomen.[76]

The nineteenth section. The imbibition of water with honey after coitus is beneficial because it enslumbers . . . the organs. If honey is not available, drink water alone because it quenches[77] your thirst.

The twentieth section. When you drink water, drink only a

---

[70]Literally: intermediate.

[71]Grossberg refers the reader to his own book entitled *Shevet Menashe*, section 32:3 as well as to Maimonides' *Aphorisms* 13:13. The latter quotes Galen who said that for some people it suffices to empty their bodies once a year at the beginning of spring whereas others require a second purgation in the fall. However, chapter 13 of Maimonides' *Aphorisms* deals with purgatives and enemas, not with emetics.

[72]Literally: beware.

[73]This sentence is unintelligible in the original but has been translated literally.

[74]The original has: *colong*, ? colon.

[75]Flatus?

[76]Meaning unclear.

[77]Literally: breaks.

little [at a time] and swallow it[78] in a fine stream because the abdomen does not lust for it except for its coldness. If the water passes through the throat all at once, it causes severe harm, but if you drink it slowly, you derive benefit therefrom without harm and it suffices for the lesser. The greatest desire of the abdomen for it occurs because of the foods that heat it.

The twenty-first section. Wine is among the substances that help digest[79] foods. Therefore, drink some two hours after your meal. Do not drink it excessively because it causes great loss of intellect,[80] whereas a little digests the food and gladdens the soul.[81]

The twenty-second section. If you can abstain from drinking wine all the days of your life, it is good for you, because the study of science is not good in its presence.

The twenty-third section. When you drink beers of pomegranate kernels or barley beer or honey beer, drink them when they are still sweet because then they purify and give rise to wind.[82] If you drink them when they are fully fermented,[83] they produce all the harm mentioned above. There is a greater benefit from wine;[84] and the best of all is a honey drink.

The twenty-fourth section. Good seasonings are helpful and beneficial in place of wine to digest[85] the food, because seasonings . . . a preparation of peppers is useful in the winter in place of wine to digest [food]. A sponge[86] seasoning is beneficial in the summer and in the winter in its place . . . for those physicians who assert that there is nothing better than wine because . . . they allow every person to drink wine according to his desire and his craving.

The twenty-fifth section. A person should not mislead you

---

[78] Literally: slide it around your mouth.
[79] Literally: grind.
[80] Alcoholic intoxication.
[81] Euphoria.
[82] Flatus or eructation?
[83] Literally: their action is completed.
[84] Literally: there is a great benefit between them, wine (namely).
[85] Literally: grind.
[86] Arabic *asfig*.

THE BOOK OF REMEDIES

by teaching you that the ancient Sages did not instruct us to [totally] forsake wine . . . they stated an important fact[87] when they asserted that wine makes the lusting soul prevail over the intellectual soul to the point that the latter flees and becomes subservient to the former and becomes totally nullified from its [normal] activity. Another more powerful curse than this occurs as a result of drinking . . . I say that it is a greater harm to the world than a viper or a scorpion or fatal poisons.

The twenty-sixth section. For someone who knows nothing about the science of medicine and is not involved in any science and is an ignoramus, but is active in performing physical exercises and eats large meals,[88] there is nothing better for him than the drinking of wine because for him it is a substitute for life. But it is not good for concerned individuals and depressed souls to drink wine.[89]

The twenty-seventh section. Do not excessively eat food that sweetens because it causes obstruction of the tubes of the liver. Similarly, do not prepare a dish of flour and *isfagis*[90] like the various types of fried dishes made from dough; all the more so if you eat them with honey.

The twenty-eighth section. . . . you should desire to eat vegetables to loosen your bowels for defecation, dip the [vegetables] in the first water[91] and eat them cooked in the second water[92] . . . you need to be constipated.[93]

The twenty-ninth section. Write a treatise on foods for yourself, for they are beneficial to your life. Do not rely on your own knowledge until you study that book, but ask medical

---

[87] Literally: something that suffices for this matter.

[88] Literally: his foods are thick.

[89] There are numerous references in Maimonides' *Medical Aphorisms* to the beneficial effects of wine (see especially chapter 20).

[90] Perhaps referring to euphorbia.

[91] Term usually used to denote the handwashing water prior to a meal.

[92] Term sometimes used to denote the handwashing water at the end of a meal, perhaps here referring to the second "soaking" water in which the vegetables are cooked.

[93] Literally: withheld.

experts about it until you learn all its sections. If the physician is not wise, ask another specialist.

The thirtieth section. There is no constitution . . . of intermediate variety as there was in previous eras and not as will be in the future.[94] Therefore, do not rely on what you see [written] in books of . . . Ali[95] and the Sages of your generation.

The thirty-first section. You are making an error if you study the book of medicines by yourself without doing so under the tutelage of[96] expert and distinguished scholars. But if you are a scholar . . . knowledgeable, you can prevail over them. Nevertheless, I still advise you to learn from them using your own intellect.

The thirty-second section. Every sweet and hot [spice] and every hot seasoning[97] and every mixture containing cold vinegar and every cold sourness and every savory food that does not have . . . a cold part and every mixture containing sweetness or cold vinegar, and every beverage of hot oil and all tasteless things such as cold water and every hot sharpness and all foods are included in these general principles.[98] If you wish to know the characteristics of any one of them, taste it with your mouth and you will observe that it tends towards one of these general characteristics and beware of mistakes.

The thirty-third section. Do not rely solely on these characteristics because there are also constitutional differences in various food categories. Therefore, I advise you not to refrain

---

[94] Grossberg points out the commentary of *Tosafot* in the Talmud (*Moed Katan* 11a), which states that people's body constitutions change over generations and remedies described in the Talmud may not be beneficial in later times.

[95] Grossberg suggests that this Ali may refer to Ali the Ishmaelite who wrote a book found in manuscript form in Oxford and London and published in Leipzig.

[96] Literally: without using.

[97] Literally: salt.

[98] All foods have characteristics such as sweetness or sourness or hotness or coldness.

THE BOOK OF REMEDIES

from consulting with[99] the great scholars of your generation and . . . with many whom I have not mentioned.

The thirty-fourth section. Crusts[100] of dried breads that have been well-baked can serve as substitutes for *brangin* in giving rise to black bile. Stay away from them as much as possible,[101] but if you feel yourself slipping . . . with a lot of moisture you can consume a little thereof. Similarly, refrain from eating strong meat as much as possible.

The thirty-fifth section. There is no beneficial or helpful substance in fried foods, not like grains or seeds such as wheat or barley. Beans are not beneficial at all.

The thirty-sixth section. When you still have wheat bread and lamb's meat, you would be a fool to seek something else except in the hot summer season, when you feel hot and thirsty. Then, eat cooling fruits or grapes after the [aforementioned foods] because these [fruits] are sweetening and cooling foods. So too are *dormaskin* washed in cold water.

The thirty-seventh section. Sharp foods[102] such as leek, onions, and garlic, and bitter foods such as beans and . . . and lentils, all these give rise to thick humor and black melancholic humor and the persons [so affected] have bad dreams.

The thirty-eighth section. Light foods are easily and rapidly lost in the abdomen. These include milk and moist cheese and fish. Therefore, if you wish to consume any of these, be careful that the intestines should be devoid[103] of all food. Do not eat any other food together with them.

The thirty-ninth section. Most people[104] in the world usually mix spices in their food and do not do so properly but rely on the women who do the cooking. Therefore, if you have a decreased desire for coitus . . . from dried coriander, but if you are constipated, do not take any of it at all. If you feel soft

---

[99] Literally: asking.
[100] Literally: peels.
[101] Literally: as much as you are able.
[102] Literally: things.
[103] Literally: cleansed.
[104] Literally: every man.

and bitter humor in your intestines, put a lot of pepper in your food. If it is thick[105] meat, add only a little pepper and ginger. If . . . weakness of the intestines, add a little vinegar. Vinegar is good for all thick meat unless you feel sourness in your intestines.

The fortieth section. Do not cook your food in an old pot but in a new one. If it is an old pot, place water and salt and crushed bran therein before you add your food and boil the upper one in the boiling of these[106] because the old pot gives rise to a taste that is a taste of a lethal poison, especially in the summer season.

The forty-first section. Do not eat truffles or mushrooms. Beware not to eat any amount of them. . . . Save yourself from them. If you have a desire to eat the large ones . . . let them not be red ones but white in appearance and with a good aroma. Of the Syrian mushrooms, consume those that have not even the slightest putrefaction and that have not grown below . . . nor below a fig [tree], nor below stones under which vipers, which are harmful reptiles, hide; nor those that grow in slippery mud which is putrefied.[107] The best of all is to leave over the vegetables; do not touch them. Pears have a unique property in that, if cooked in water and that water imbibed, they are beneficial against the harm of truffles, and people are saved from any danger to the body that might develop from them.

The forty-second section. Not one of the reptiles that crawl[108] on the roofs of houses is totally devoid of fatal poison. Therefore, in the house where you cook your food, be careful of the roofs and clean it well there because flies and lizards are constantly found on roofs and . . . woe if they fall into the cooked dishes. Prepare the following remedy which should always be with you to provide benefit against these fatal

---

[105] Fat meat?

[106] Apparently the "upper" pot was placed into another larger pot, perhaps an early double boiler.

[107] Alternate translation: has a stench.

[108] Literally: walks.

poisons. It should be with you when you sit [in your house], and when you are on a journey, and when you lie down, and when you get up, because it is very beneficial against fatal poisons. The following is its preparation: take three ounces of the milk of purified nuts and half an ounce of dried ruta and truffles and some *zedonar*, which is known as aristolochia, and *nantiyani* . . . the medicine known as myrrh in Arabic and grains of *lor* and *chinapli hanari* . . . and half [an ounce] of *rossia altiri* and grains of *balsam* and wood . . . and three parts by weight of good honey whose foam was removed . . . many figs, and strain them well and separate them; keep the myrrh by itself and strain it; and pulverize the figs very well together with the nuts in a mortar. Then add the honey to the mixture in the mortar and pulverize again and then add the other ingredients until it becomes like a cloudy remedy. . . . Then place it in a pot and conceal it in the pot in barley for six months. Then remove the mixture and the remedy is ready to work against all the fatal poisons in the world. Drink forty-two *zuzim*[109] thereof in one and a half [*zuz* portions], according to the strength of the patient, in hot water. The aforementioned ingredients should only be the best and choicest, fresh and without rot or putrefaction and without any bad odor. And if you are fearful that there is some fatal poison in your intestines, take this remedy and you will be immediately saved, with God's help.

The forty-third section. Do not believe in the foolishness of so-called wise physicians who, for every illness, prescribe purgative drinks such as scammony which is one of the most damaging remedies for the stomach. The next [most detrimental purgative] is the remedy called *sochram* in Arabic. Similarly, all purgatives are harmful whether taken in small or large amounts. If such [purgative] action is needed, use remedies that are not harmful[110] such as scammony or asparagus juice . . . as a drink or as a paste. There are other physicians who advise most people not to use purgatives except for great need. If you only suffer from the mild discomfort known as

---

[109]*Zuz* is a coin the size of a nut.
[110]Literally: which protect you from their harm.

alcham, which is a knot of the *chalgam* in the hips and the thighs, you can eliminate it with grains of *montiv*, if there is yellow humor[111] . . . or black humor which needs to be excreted, the above beverage that I recommended to you to drink will suffice to eliminate it.

The forty-fourth section. *Hiera picra* is one of the good things that God, blessed be He in His compassion, gave to the world. If in the cold season you suffer from white humor or from any other affliction in your intestines, seek it[112] out and drink therefrom with hot water at night before you go to sleep; and eat your meal early in the day before noon. Thus, you will be restored to health [and be cured] from your intestinal ailment. If you swallow it[113] as a peddler's powder, one *zuz* is sufficient but if you knead it with honey, take three *zuzim* thereof. If you feel heat or smoke in your head, consume [the remedy] with *isfanar juice* . . . according to this prescription; the *iyarig* is well known, I do not need to write to you thereof.

The forty-fifth section. Very often, a person develops scabs and boils because of the perspiration of his putrefaction and because of his eating moist, salty foods. It is from these that lice develop because of excessive eating. If you wish to prevent these illnesses from afflicting you, beware of the things that cause them. When you go to the bathhouse, rub your body before you leave there. If it is summertime or winter, rub your body with roses. If it is during the hot season, rub with oil of *safsig* and during the cold season, with oil of *kakotog* which is *masaklas*; and place this [material] on the body and you will never see scabs or boils on your flesh.

The forty-sixth section. . . . to the folly of those people who say that wine is beneficial for the illness of alcoholic intoxication, [I say] heal yourself[114] therefrom with an absynthium beverage and with juice of pomegranates which are lupines cooked in sugar . . . and wash yourself constantly

---

[111] See note 48.
[112] *Hiera picra.*
[113] *Hiera picra.*
[114] Literally: your soul.

THE BOOK OF REMEDIES

with hot water on your head in the bathhouse or in your home . . . the power of wine is to produce complete tranquility. Eat sour foods after vomiting, if you are able to vomit. If you cannot vomit, cleanse your intestines so that nothing remains therein.

The forty-seventh section. It is important[115] that you be careful when traveling . . . so that bad water not harm you, because many people die therefrom when traveling.[116] You can protect yourself by taking along a small skin bottle containing good and clean earth from your homeland from which you are traveling. At every camping stop, fill a pitcher of water and put some of that earth therein until it settles to the bottom of the water, thereby clarifying it.[117] Then drink it. Another purifying method is to put some water into a vessel and then place clean wool thereon. Place the vessel on the fire and squeeze the wool continuously.[118] The water that is extruded from the wool is suitable for drinking after it has cooled off and it will not harm you. There is another method and that is to add vinegar to the water and at every place that you set up camp, or to drink it with peels of gourds.

The forty-eighth section. For the maintenance of the strength of travelers, they should constantly eat meat, either a little or a lot. When a traveler enters the bathhouse, he should not tarry there. He should not eat until evening when he sets up camp and he should wash his head and his feet.

The forty-ninth section. For the maintenance of the strength and power and health of sea travelers, they should starve themselves for four or five days before they embark on the ocean [voyage] and should only eat a little. When they are on the high seas[119] they should use drying things and not look at the water for one or two days. If the traveler is a sensitive

---

[115]Literally: mostly.
[116]Literally: on most roads.
[117]Grossberg states in a footnote that earth cleanses water and removes from it foreign matter, thereby purifying it. He claims to have found such a statement in the book of Avicenna.
[118]Literally: every moment.
[119]Literally: when they enter there.

person,[120] he should vomit and then eat drying foods such as pears, asparagus types, and sour pomegranates. He should chew these well and drink their juices, discarding the residue. He should eat bread toasted over the fire and carry with him bundles of bags[121] containing *hordram* dust and pulverized *sandal*[122] and a little *bati* . . . Spread out constantly while still at sea and remove from yourself its bad odor and stench. If you suffer greatly from seasickness,[123] crush some of the drying and sour substances that I advised you to consume and place them on your abdomen and bind your legs well with a strong and firm binding.

The fiftieth section. Suppress[124] your desire and conquer your lust and in this way you will be the king of all kings and the master of all masters and let your brother live with you[125] but ensure your own well-being first.[126] The best thing for your soul is to teach it what it is and to educate it about its Creator, may He be praised and aggrandized. Let it delve into its God and His holy names.[127] You can achieve this [goal] by studying His deeds and His actions. And by reaching out to this goal, the good Father gives us permission and lets us go [in that path], with the help of God.

Blessed is the One who gives power to the faint and who increases the strength of those without might.[128]

---

[120]Hebrew: *istenis*.

[121]Literally: rags.

[122]A type of wood or tree.

[123]Literally: if you vomit a lot.

[124]Literally: destroy.

[125]Literally: and do good to your contemporaries.

[126]See the talmudic discussion (*Baba Metzia* 62a) concerning the concept that "thy life takes precedence over the life of thy fellow human being."

[127]In a lengthy footnote, Grossberg states that "the holy names" are explained in the book *Megillat Setarim* of Maimonides in a manuscript in the British Museum. They are published in the book *Chemdah Genuzah*. See also the language of Maimonides in his responsum to Rabbi Chasdai Halevi, published in Maimonides' letter to him. These are his words: "In the final analysis, the most fundamental thing is that there is nothing that stands forever and ever except the knowledge of the Creator, may He be blessed."

[128]Isaiah 40:29.

Completed are the fifty medical sections by the great sage, Moses Maimonides, who was physician to the sultan[129] of Egypt. All wise physicians today drink of his wisdom and his reputation spread widely throughout the world.[130]

Blessed is the One who gives power to the faint.[131] Completed and concluded [is this treatise], praise to the Lord of peace.

---

[129] Literally: king.
[130] Genesis 9:19.
[131] The quotation from Isaiah 40:29 is repeated.

BIBLIOGRAPHY

by Jacob I. Dienstag

א. מקור ותרגום
1900

1] **ספר רפואות** לרבינו משה מיימון ז"ל רופא למלך מצרים. יצא לאור ראשונה על פי כתב יד בריטיש מוזעאום בלונדון. עם הערות והגהות מאת מנשה גראסבערג מטרעסטינא... **ונלוה אליו ספר חבל מנשה** ...לונדון: בדפוס יצחק זאב מעציק, תר"ס/1900. 23 עמ'. ונלוה אליו ספר חבל מנשה עם שער מיוחד, עמ' (25)-64.

Added English title on left cover: *Sefer Rephuoth, The Book of Medicine*, by Maimonides. And a letter by the physician "Ali Hajishmaeli." From a hitherto unpublished manuscript in the British Museum, edited with a commentary by Menasseh Grossberg, to which is appended *Hevel Menasheh*. London: P. Meczyk, 1900.

1904

2] **ספר רפואות** לרבינו משה מיימון ז"ל רופא למלך מצרים יצא לאור בראשונה על פי כתב יד אשר הי' גנגז בבריטיש מוזעאום בלונדן עם הערות והגהות מאת מנשה גראסבערג מטרעסטינא... וכאשר הראשונים ספר גם תמו אמרתי להדפיסו שנית לתועלת האנושי. בהוצאת בית מסחר הספרים של יוסף מרדכי כהנא... מ. סיגעט תרס"ד. בדפוס זאב שווארץ. 12 עמ'. ונלוה אליו חבל מנשה עם שער מיוחד. תיאור מאת נ. בן־מנחם, **מספרות ישראל באונגאריה**. ירושלים: תשבי, תשי"ח, עמ' 158, מספר 75.

Not to be confused with a similar title in Ladino and printed in Salonica (about 1855) and Smyrna (1865).

3] Book of Remedies. In: *Six Treatises Attributed to Maimonides.* Translated by Fred Rosner. With Bibliographies by Jacob I. Dienstag. Northvale, NJ: Jason Aronson, p. 67.

ב. מאמרים ומחקרים

4] Pagel, J. 1851-1912.
Maimuni als medizinischer Schriftsteller. In W. Bacher, M. Brann, D. Simonsen, eds., *Moses ben Maimon*, vol. I. Leipzig: G. Fork, 1908, pp. 241-243.
Hebrew translation by Tuvia Preschel.

5] פגל, י., 1851־1912.
כתביו הרפואיים של הרמב"ם. **סיני**, 51 (תשכ"ב/1962), קכד־קכה.

6] מונטנר, 1897־1973.
משנה תפלה למשה. ירושלים: הוצאת "גניזה", תש"ו, עמ' 10.
"רוח הספר שונה תכלית השנוי מרוחם של שאר כתביו הרפואיים של הרמב"ם".

7] ריצ'לר, בנימין, 1940־
ספר החכמה או ספר ראמינוס ויחסו לחמשים שערים המיוחס לרמב"ם. **קרית ספר**, 58, חוברת ג' (תמוז תשמ"ג/יולי 1983): 624־625.
חמשים שערים אלו, זהים לחיבור בשם זה המיוחד לרמב"ם בכ"י לונדון 27089 Add. סי' 5769, ואשר נדפס ע"י מנשה גדוסברג ב"ספר רפואות לרבנו משה מיימון", לונדון, תר"ס. עדיין לא ברור אם ה"חמשים שערים" הם חלק מקורי של הספר או שנוספו ע"י אחד המעתיקים. עדות קדומה מצביעה על כך שכבר בסוף המאה הי"ג הם נחשבו לחלק מס' ראמינוס (או ספר החכמה) מהמאה הי"ג (מגנזי המכון ותצלומי כתבי־היד העבריים של בית הספרים הלאומי והאוניברסיטאי בירושלים).

ג. ציונים ביבליוגרפיים לכתבי־יד של ספר רפואות

8] Freimann, Aron, 1871-1948.
Union Catalog of Hebrew Manuscripts and their Location. Vol. 2. New York: American Academy for Jewish Research, 1964, no. 3261.

9] Kayserling, Meier, 1829-1905.
Bibliotheca Espanola-Portugueza-Judaica. Strasbourg: 1890, pp. 66-68; reprint: Nieuwkoop, 1961; New York: Ktav, 1971.

10] Margoliouth, George, 1853-1952.
Catalogue of the Hebrew and Samaritan Manuscripts in the British Museum. Part III, London, 1915 (reprint: 1965), no. 1076 (III).

Part III

TEFILAT HAROFÉ
THE PHYSICIAN'S PRAYER

INTRODUCTION

The Physician's Prayer attributed to Moses Maimonides is a lofty and beautiful prayer that first appeared in print in a German periodical in 1783.[1] The editor of this journal, Heinrich Christian Boie, and his associate, Christian Wilhelm Dohm, provide no notes or commentaries nor any indication as to who the author is. The prayer bears only the title "Daily prayer of a physician before he visits his patients: from the Hebrew manuscript of a renowned Jewish physician in Egypt from the twelfth century." A photostatic reproduction of this earliest version of the prayer appeared recently in a Hebrew medical journal.[2] Since the 1783 German edition, numerous versions, abbreviations, or excerpts thereof have been presented in English,[3] German,[4] Hebrew,[5] French,[6] Dutch,[7] and Spanish.[8]

---

[1] See ref. 1.
[2] See ref. 2.
[3] See ref. 3–16.
[4] See ref. 17–23.
[5] See ref. 21, 23, 24.
[6] See ref. 25–27.
[7] See ref. 28.
[8] See ref. 29.

There are undoubtedly others. Much heated debate exists among the various writers concerning the true authorship of the prayer. This controversy here is presented chronologically in an attempt to arrive at a reasonable conclusion as to whether Moses Maimonides actually wrote the "Prayer of Maimonides."

The first Hebrew version of the prayer was published by Isaac Euchel, editor of the Hebrew periodical *Ha-Maassef*, in 1790.[9] The title indicates that Marcus Herz was its author and that it was translated at his request from German into Hebrew. Half a century later, in 1841, the London newspaper, *The Voice of Jacob*, published the first English translation from the Hebrew, under the title "Daily Prayer of a Physician."[10] The writer, using the pen name of "Medicus," states:

> The composition of this prayer has erroneously been attributed to Maimonides, but it is the production of the late Dr. Marcus Herz, a celebrated physician of Berlin. It was published by him in the German language, and the Hebrew version, which is to be found in the *(Ha) maassef*,[11] owes its existence to the prolific pen of Itzig Eichel.

We next find the prayer, again in German, in a German-Jewish newspaper, the *Allgemeine Zeitung des Judenthums* for 1863.[12] The editor, Ludwig Philippson, makes no mention of authorship at all, but the title reads, "Daily prayer of a physician before the visits to his patients. From the Hebrew manuscript of a celebrated Jewish physician from the twelfth century." This title is nearly identical with that of the first German version that appeared eighty years earlier.[13] Philippson six years later, (1869) again reprinted the German version in his voluminous book, *Weltbewegend Fragen in Politik und Religion aus den letzten dreissig Jahren*.[14] In 1892, yet another German version ap-

---

[9] See ref. 24.
[10] See ref. 3.
[11] See ref. 24.
[12] See ref. 17.
[13] See ref. 1.
[14] See ref. 18.

INTRODUCTION

peared in the *Allgemeine Zeitung des Judenthums*,[15] this time by Julius Pagel and entitled "The Prayer of the Physician."

In 1899 Reverend Madison C. Peters, pastor of the Bloomingdale Church in New York City, published a short English version of the prayer[16] in his book, *Justice to the Jew*. This English version, in which authorship is not mentioned at all, later initiated heated debates among Jewish scholars.

In the same year, Moïse Schwab, the celebrated bibliographer, published his *Répertoire*,[17] in which he states that Marcus Herz authored the prayer published over a century earlier in *Ha-Maassef*.[18] At the turn of the century, Golden published excerpts of the prayer in English in an American medical journal.[19] His article, entitled "Maimonides' Prayer for Physicians," states that Maimonides composed the prayer. A later letter addressed to the *American Israelite* is evidence that he extracted the prayer from Peters' book.[20]

In 1902, the prayer appeared again in German[21] under the title, "Prayer of a Jewish physician in the Twelfth Century." The writer, Dr. Theodor Distel, specifically states that the prayer was published originally in 1783 in the *Deutsches Museum*[22] and that its importance prompted him to reprint it verbatim. Another quarter century was to pass before this 1783 version was again mentioned, in spite of the rather widespread interest in the prayer and its authorship, manifested by numerous articles on the subject during this period.

Again in 1902, it appeared in German in a Swiss newspaper,[23] using the same title. No commentary or discussion of authorship is to be found in this Swiss version. Rabbi Jules Wolff of La Chaux-de-Fonds, reading the prayer in the

---

[15] See ref. 19.
[16] See ref. 4.
[17] See ref. 30.
[18] See ref. 24.
[19] See ref. 5.
[20] See ref. 4.
[21] See ref. 20.
[22] See ref. 1.
[23] See ref. 21.

Swiss newspaper, was so impressed that he promptly translated it into French. In a letter dated February 26, 1903, to the editor of the periodical *L'univers israélite*, which was published the following day,[24] Wolff provides the first, excellent, French version of the prayer. He states that it is a "prayer composed by a famous Jewish physician from Egypt in the twelfth century (Maimonides?)." Thus, Wolff seems to assume, perhaps with a little doubt, that Maimonides is the true author of the prayer. Moïse Schwab, however, is quick to reply three weeks later, in a letter to the editor of the same periodical,[25] that the prayer could have been written by any Parisian physician. He further states that the prayer is definitely the work of Marcus Herz, friend and physician of Moses Mendelssohn, that Herz wrote it in German in Berlin, and that a Hebrew translation was published by Isaac Euchel in the *Ha-Maassef* in 1790.[26]

Although later authors state that German versions of the prayer appeared in the February 4 and August 21, 1904, issues of the periodical *Israelitisches Familienblatt*, this writer has been unable to locate copies of these journals in numerous libraries in the United States. I cannot, therefore, verify this for myself and must leave it in doubt, since numerous errors in bibliography have crept into various subsequent papers published on this subject.

In 1908, Dr. Gotthard Deutsch, professor of Jewish History and Literature at the Hebrew Union College of Cincinnati, wrote a letter to the editor of the journal *The American Israelite*,[27] vehemently denouncing those who believe Maimonides actually wrote the famous prayer. The first part of his letter, tracing the prayer from 1790[28] to 1903,[29] was reproduced in the miscellany section of the *Journal of the American Medical Association* in 1929.[30] The letter continues as follows:

---

[24]See ref. 25.
[25]See ref. 31.
[26]See ref. 24.
[27]See ref. 32.
[28]See ref. 28.
[29]See ref. 25, 31.
[30]See ref. 33.

INTRODUCTION

> God only knows into how many medical journals, textbooks of medicine, etc. this prayer found its way. The first source of the error is evidently Philippson. How he could commit this blunder is inconceivable to me. He could not have quoted from memory, for he gives a fairly accurate translation and he could not have translated from the original without seeing in his text that the prayer was written by Marcus Herz in German and translated into Hebrew by Euchel. Philippson, however, does not give Maimonides as the author, and I would like to know who was the author of this additional piece of historic information which I notice is stated by Wolff with a question mark. To me, this wandering hoax was a valuable piece of illustration of historic criticism.

Six years later, William W. Golden, superintendent of the Davis Memorial Hospital in Elkins, West Virginia, wrote a letter to the editor of *The American Israelite*. It was published in the June 25, 1914 issue as follows:

> Sir: Reverend Madison C. Peters in one of the editions of his book "Justice to the Jew" quotes a prayer for physicians by Maimonides. Can you tell me where the original can be found, or at least in what authoritative work on history, literature or medicine can it be found, and oblige?

Golden, who in 1900 had published excerpts of the prayer[31] and, in no uncertain terms, had attributed authorship to Maimonides, as described earlier, now seems to have had second thoughts on the matter. The reply to his letter came from Dr. Gotthard Deutsch in the same June 25, 1914, issue of *The American Israelite* and was subsequently reprinted in chapter 6 ("The Maimonides Prayer Myth") of Deutsch's *Scrolls*.[32]

Deutsch's reply begins: "This so-called prayer of Maimonides is an old hoax. It was actually written by Marcus Herz, a prominent physician of Berlin (1747–1803) who attended

---

[31]See ref. 5.
[32]See ref. 34.

Moses Mendelssohn in his last illness. . . ." Deutsch thus reiterates all the arguments expounded in his earlier letter of 1908.[33] He further states that

> . . . Haeser embodied it in his "Geschichte der Medizin" 1, p. 837, Jena 1875. Having thus been recognized by a standard publication, it was accepted by Julius Pagel, professor of the history of medicine at the Berlin University (1851–1912), also a Jew, in his essay on Maimonides as physician, which forms part of the memorial volume "Moses Ben Maimon," edited by the Gesellschaft zur Foerderung der Wissenschaft des Judentums, I, p. 244, Leipzig, 1908. Following all this, its authenticity could no more be doubted than the authenticity of the gospel of St. John. *The Israelite* (March 12, 1908) gave it its seal of approval, although I contested it in the subsequent issue, but repeatedly since, it has been proclaimed as being written in distinctly Maimonidean spirit. Recently I wrote a letter to the editor of "Ost und West," who had published it as Maimonidean. He thanked me, but preferred not to publish it. As the very popular "Medizinische Wochenschrift" of Berlin published it in 1902, and any number of medical journals reprinted it, no amount of argument will rob Maimonides of the credit for having written this typically sweet-lemonade prayer, characteristic of the rationalistic tendencies of the era of "Aufklaerung," and I still have hopes that one hundred years hence, somebody will credit Herodotus or at least Rabbi Jose Ben Halafta, the genuine author of *Seder Olam*, with my "Foreign Notes."

It seems quite evident that Deutsch was unaware of the 1783 edition of the prayer,[34] and thus he attributes the authorship of the prayer to Marcus Herz, whose version did not appear until 1790.[35] This ignorance of the 1783 edition of the prayer must have been shared by Schwab[36] and numerous later writers who also ascribe the prayer to Marcus Herz, in spite of the specific

---

[33]See ref. 32.
[34]See ref. 1.
[35]See ref. 24.
[36]See ref. 30, 31.

INTRODUCTION

mention by Distel in 1902[37] of the existence of the 1783 edition, antedating Herz by seven years.

Thus, Deutsch's criticism of Philippson seems unfounded. Philippson was probably aware of the *Deutsches Museum* edition of 1783, and in his own 1863[38] and 1869[39] versions of the prayer, he used the same title as in the 1783 original, namely "Daily prayer of a physician before he visits his patients: From a Hebrew manuscript of a renowned Jewish physician of the twelfth century." Deutsch further perpetuates the misconception,[40] later quoted by Friedenwald[41] that the prayer was embodied in Haeser's textbook of the history of medicine. In actuality, only a brief footnote exists in Haeser's text,[42] which, translated from the German, states: "Compare the beautiful morning prayer of a Jewish physician from the twelfth century in L. Philippson's *Weltbewegende Fragen.* . . ." In Haeser's discussion of Maimonides in the same work (pp. 595–597), no mention is made of the prayer. Nor is there any mention of the prayer in the two earlier editions of Haeser's textbook in 1845 and 1859 respectively. This indicates that Haeser, too, was unaware of the 1783 edition and first saw the prayer printed in Philippson's paper in 1863.[43]

Seeligmann in Holland[44] writes in 1928 that, in response to an inquiry regarding a Hebrew version of Maimonides' prayer, he remembers that it was probably not composed by Maimonides. He then states that Marcus Herz wrote it and traces its history from the *Ha-Maassef* in 1790,[45] through Philippson[46] and Haeser.[47] Seeligmann further writes that the first Dutch version is

---

[37] See ref. 20.
[38] See ref. 17.
[39] See ref. 18.
[40] See ref. 32, 34.
[41] See ref. 14.
[42] See ref. 35.
[43] See ref. 17.
[44] See ref. 28.
[45] See ref. 24.
[46] See ref. 17, 18.
[47] See ref. 35.

by Hektor Treub, which Dr. M. J. Premsela published in his brochure *Medische Fastoensleer* (Amsterdam 1903, pp. 52–53).

Emil Bogen,[48] in response to the reprinting of part of one of Gotthard Deutsch's letters[49] in the *Journal of the American Medical Association*,[50] correctly points out the existence of the 1783 version, which was not known to Deutsch. Bogen agrees with Kroner,[51] who shows the harmony that exists between the other writings of Maimonides and the so-called "Prayer of Maimonides" in both form and spirit.

Bennigson and his colleagues[52] reprinted the German version in Leipzig in 1931; they briefly trace the history of the prayer from its origin in the *Deutsches Museum*.[53] They erroneously state that it was reprinted in German by Distel in the *Deutsche medizinische Wochenschrift* in August 1904, when they probably mean 1902.[54] This error has been perpetuated by Kagan[55] and Muntner,[56] neither of whom probably had access to the periodical in question. Another, probably typographical, error in Bennigson's paper[57] is the June 1893 date given for Pagel's[58] version of the prayer, an error again perpetuated by Kagan.[59] The correct date is June 1892.

Keller,[60] in 1931, in an essay entitled, "The Ideal Practice of Medicine from the Rabbinical Point of View," compares the Prayer of Maimonides to the Hippocratic Oath and quotes excerpts from both. Maimonides, he says, considers the patient important because he is the creation of the Almighty, so that the

---

[48]See ref. 7.
[49]See ref. 32.
[50]See ref. 33.
[51]See ref. 36.
[52]See ref. 22.
[53]See ref. 1.
[54]See ref. 20.
[55]See ref. 13
[56]See ref. 23.
[57]See ref. 22.
[58]See ref. 19.
[59]See ref. 13.
[60]See ref. 8.

INTRODUCTION 111

responsibility for the outcome of our treatment rests partly with us as an instrument of the Almighty. Hippocrates, on the other hand, considers the preciousness of a human being from the sociological viewpoint.

To commemorate the 800th anniversary of the birth of Maimonides, in 1935, numerous articles on all aspects of Maimonides appeared in various periodicals, newspapers, journals, and books around the world. Among these are several references to the prayer. Gershenfeld[61] provides excerpts of the English version. Illevitz[62] and Meyerhof[63] emphatically state that Maimonides did not write the prayer. A Spanish version of the prayer[64] also appeared in 1935. The author, E. Singer, states that it was previously published in the *Allgemeine Zeitung des Judenthums* in 1863,[65] in *Sulamit* in 1842, in *Abend Zeitung* in 1840, and in the *Medizinischer Almanach*.

An interesting inquiry by Sir William Osler concerning the authorship of the prayer was answered by the Chief Rabbi of the British Empire, Dr. Joseph H. Hertz, in a letter dated May 23, 1917, but published in the *Canadian Jewish Chronicle* in 1935.[66] The letter reads as follows:

> Dear Sir William:
>
> Some 2 years ago you inquired of me as to the "Physician's Prayer" attributed to Maimonides. I can now give you the following information on the subject:
>
> This prayer is the production of Dr. Markus Herz (1747–1802), a friend and pupil of Immanuel Kant and of Moses Mendelssohn. He was a physician to the Jewish Hospital in Berlin. The prayer was composed by him in the German language and was published in a Hebrew translation in the periodical *Ha-Maassef*. The current English version seems to be

---

[61]See ref. 10.
[62]See ref. 37.
[63]See ref. 38.
[64]See ref. 29.
[65]See ref. 17.
[66]See ref. 39.

from this Hebrew translation and first appeared in the London paper *Voice of Jacob* on the 24th December, 1841.

Sincerely yours,
J. H. Hertz

Also in 1935, Münz, in his book on Maimonides,[67] ascribes the prayer to the great medieval physician, although the earlier German edition of his book[68] questions the true authorship.

In 1938, Kagan reprinted excerpts of the English version of the prayer[69] and traced its history. He based his article mainly on two previous papers, those of Bogen[70] and Bennigson *et al.*,[71] as evidenced by Kagan's incorporation of the bibliographical errors in Bennigson's article into his own paper as described above. Kagan concludes with six arguments favoring Maimonides as the true author of the prayer. These arguments can be summarized as follows:

1. The medieval form and style of the prayer conform with Maimonides' other writings.
2. If Marcus Herz was the author, he would have laid claim to its authorship.
3. Herz, a master of the German language, would have published the original prayer in German and only later would have arranged for a Hebrew translation.
4. If the later German version omitted Herz's name at his request, he would not have requested Euchel, editor of the *Ha-Meassef*, to mention his name in the Hebrew translation.
5. Herz probably knew of the 1783 German version and sent the document for Hebrew translation to Euchel, who erroneously ascribed the German text to Herz. Herz did not know Hebrew, since he did not translate it himself, and probably was unaware of the Hebrew editor's note making him the author.
6. All the professional ethics expressed in the prayer are also expressed in some of Maimonides' letters and books.

---

[67] See ref. 40.
[68] See ref. 41.
[69] See ref. 13.
[70] See ref. 7.
[71] See ref. 22.

INTRODUCTION

In 1939, Levinson reprinted the prayer in English[72] as part of a larger review of Maimonides' medical contributions. In 1944, Friedenwald, in his two volume classic *The Jews and Medicine*,[73] also reprinted the prayer in English.

A most interesting booklet comparing the prayer of Maimonides with the Oath of Asaph[74] and the physician's prayer of Jacob Zahalon[75] was published by Muntner in 1946.[76] In addition to publishing both the Hebrew and German versions, Muntner provides us with a brief bibliographical sketch tracing the background of the prayer, a sketch which he found in a 1928 Berlin version of the prayer by Professor Heinrich Levy. The August 1904 date quoted for Distel's version in the *Deutsche Medizinische Wochenschrift* is incorrect and should properly be August 1902.[77] Muntner calls attention to the existence of a Hebrew manuscript in the Bibliothèque Nationale de Paris which is entitled "The Prayer of Moses Maimonides." It is Hebrew manuscript 837, part 7, fol. 98V°, described in the catalog[78] as: "Prayer of Rabbi Moses Maimonides, beginning with *Tefila Lisegulas Eeshim* and terminating by the piece of verse Galgal Soveiv." The great bibliographer Moritz Steinschneider[79] describes an identical Hebrew work as manuscript Warner 41, part 11, folio 150 and refers to the Paris Hebrew manuscript as 285 (perhaps an error or perhaps an earlier different numbering system). In addition, this medieval Hebrew manuscript version of the "Prayer of Maimonides" was published in 1867 in the weekly Hebrew newspaper *Hacarmel*.[80]

Muntner[81] correctly points out that this manuscript version

---

[72]See ref. 12.
[73]See ref. 14.
[74]See ref. 42.
[75]See ref. 14, 43, 44.
[76]See ref. 23.
[77]See ref. 20.
[78]See ref. 45.
[79]See ref. 46.
[80]See ref. 47
[81]See ref. 23.

of the prayer is a forgery and could not possibly have been written by Maimonides, since its numerous references to astrology are not in keeping with Maimonides' vehement opposition to the "pseudoscience" of astrology.[82] Muntner further claims that the versions of the prayer, beginning with the 1783 German edition,[83] although written in the spirit and form of Maimonides, omitting any reference to astrology, are also forgeries and can all be traced back to Marcus Herz.

Probably the most comprehensive review of the subject to date is the one published in Hebrew by Leibowitz in 1954.[84] A photocopy of the 1783 original German version[85] is presented, as well as the first page of the 1790 Hebrew version.[86] Leibowitz must have consulted the original sources, since the bibliographical errors described above first made by Bennigson et al.[87] and later perpetuated by Kagan[88] and others are absent from Leibowitz's paper. A new Hebrew translation, made directly from the 1783 German version, is also provided in this article.

A second French edition of the prayer appeared in 1956[89] and a short English version was reprinted in 1957.[90] A brief version of "The oath and prayer of Maimonides" was published in the *Journal of the American Medical Association* in 1955,[91] in which Maimonides is erroneously described as an Islamic philosopher, an error that was corrected by Lanzkron and Berner in two separate letters to the editor.[92]

The most recent version of the prayer that I have been able

---

[82] See ref. 48.
[83] See ref. 1.
[84] See ref. 2.
[85] See ref. 1.
[86] See ref. 24.
[87] See ref. 22.
[88] See ref. 13.
[89] See ref. 26.
[90] See ref. 16.
[91] See ref. 15.
[92] See ref. 49.

INTRODUCTION

to find is a French one in 1962.[93] Only parts of the prayer have been translated into French, according to the author Dr. J. Pines, from the Paris Hebrew manuscript 837[94] described already.

I have been fortunate in obtaining copies of every reference enumerated in the bibliography. There are undoubtedly other versions, editions, and printings of the prayer in numerous languages in various newspapers, periodicals, and books throughout the world. The popularity of the prayer is attested to by its frequent quotation and publication. Whether Maimonides actually wrote the prayer or not remains an open question. Certainly most of those who are of the opinion that Maimonides did not write it, including Illevitz,[95] Meyerhof,[96] Simon,[97] Hertz,[98] Seeligmann,[99] and others, base their remarks on the statements of Deutsch[100] and Schwab,[101] although "Medicus" had already attributed authorship of the prayer to Marcus Herz in 1841.[102] As has already been pointed out, both Deutsch and Schwab were probably unaware of the 1783 German version of the prayer, which antedated Herz by seven years, and thus they have perpetuated the concept that Marcus Herz wrote the prayer. This thesis may not be valid.

Other writers such as Bogen,[103] Kagan,[104] and perhaps Wolff[105] agree with Kroner[106] that the prayer was probably truly composed by Maimonides, since it conforms completely with the ideals, medical ethics, and spirit of Maimonides; they

---

[93]See ref. 27.
[94]See ref. 45.
[95]See ref. 37.
[96]See ref. 38.
[97]See ref. 26.
[98]See ref. 39.
[99]See ref. 28.
[100]See ref. 32, 34.
[101]See ref. 30, 31.
[102]See ref. 3.
[103]See ref. 7.
[104]See ref. 13.
[105]See ref. 25.
[106]See ref. 36.

believe that the original will yet be found. Pagel[107] also supports this viewpoint. Certainly, at this point in history, such a suggestion is no more than wishful thinking. However, it is conceivable that Marcus Herz saw an original manuscript in Hebrew; he may have based his version, in which he does not claim authorship, on such an original. This proposal seems unlikely. Alternatively, Herz may have seen the 1783 German version and asked his friend Isaac Euchel to translate it into Hebrew. The latter may have erroneously ascribed the German to Herz, as Kagan postulates.[108] This theory, too, seems unlikely. It is also possible that neither Maimonides nor Herz wrote the prayer, but that a twelfth-century astrologer wrote what became the Paris Hebrew manuscript, from which was extracted an abbreviated German version. A further possibility is that Maimonides did indeed write the prayer, but that an astrologer amended it and only the amended versions are extant today. These two latter possibilities are extremely remote.

It seems clear that the manuscript version of the prayer in Paris[109] and Oxford[110] mentioned previously is a forgery and was not written by Maimonides. This is proved by Muntner,[111] who states that the numerous references to astrology in this work make it impossible to ascribe authorship to Maimonides, who was vehemently opposed to this "pseudoscience."[112]

The question remains whether the 1783 *Deutsches Museum* edition[113] of the prayer, upon which many versions in numerous languages[114] are based, was truly written by Maimonides or not. As already mentioned, Kroner,[115] Pagel,[116] Wolff,[117]

---

[107]See ref. 50.
[108]See ref. 13.
[109]See ref. 45, 46.
[110]See ref. 47.
[111]See ref. 23.
[112]See ref. 48.
[113]See ref. 1.
[114]See ref. 1–29.
[115]See ref. 36.
[116]See ref. 50.
[117]See ref. 25.

INTRODUCTION

Bogen,[118] and Kagan[119] support the former view, whereas Leibowitz,[120] Muntner,[121] Schwab,[122] Deutsch,[123] Illevitz,[124] Meyerhof,[125] Seeligmann,[126] "Medicus,"[127] and Hertz[128] believe the prayer to be spurious.

The most potent arguments favoring the rejection of Maimonides as the author come from Professor Leibowitz,[129] who states that no prominent medical historian supports such authorship. Furthermore, in Euchel's Hebrew version of 1790,[130] it is specifically stated that the prayer was composed by Marcus Herz and translated from German into Hebrew at his request. The confusion arose from the discovery of an earlier German edition[131] bearing the unfortunate title ". . . From the Hebrew manuscript of a renowned Jewish physician in Egypt from the twelfth century." This title leads logically to the supposition that Maimonides is the renowned physician referred to. However, a careful reading of the 1783 text shows that contrary to what Kagan states,[132] style, phrasing, and concepts are not compatible with a medieval dating. A phrase such as ". . . art is great, but the mind of man is ever expanding . . ." is typical and characteristic of eighteenth-century Europe and is at variance with Maimonidean medieval thinking. Here, according to Leibowitz,[133] is the idea of

---

[118]See ref. 7.
[119]See ref. 13.
[120]See ref. 2.
[121]See ref. 23.
[122]See ref. 30, 31.
[123]See ref. 32, 34.
[124]See ref. 37.
[125]See ref. 38.
[126]See ref. 28.
[127]See ref. 3.
[128]See ref. 39.
[129]See ref. 2.
[130]See ref. 24.
[131]See ref. 1.
[132]See ref. 13.
[133]See ref. 51.

progress, which became even more popular in the nineteenth century.

Further evidence for an eighteenth-century author lies in the phrase ". . . that act unceasingly and harmoniously to preserve the whole in all its beauty. . . ." This concept of "beauty" or "das Schöne" is characteristic of German literature of the Enlightenment. Moreover, a phrase such as ". . . ten thousand times ten thousand organs hast thou combined . . ." presupposes knowledge of the newer sciences of anatomy, biology, and microscopy. The tensions among colleagues discussed in the prayer are also products of a more modern period and dictated by the new academic hierarchy.

Leibowitz further writes[134] that:

> Markus Herz probably wrote the Prayer as a contribution to medical ethics and as a comment on prevailing low standards of the practice. It was usual to insert in almanachs anonymous short contributions. Markus Herz was a warm Jew, proud of the history of his people; he clad his literary piece into the colorful frame indicated in the caption, probably indeed meaning Maimonides, but not based on a manuscript, which did not exist, but as belonging to the belles-lettres. Editions of Hebrew medical manuscripts began only in 1867 (Steinschneider's Donnolo). . . .

Probably the greatest recent authority on the medical writings of Maimonides is Süssman Muntner. His book on the subject of Maimonides' prayer[135] has been mentioned earlier. Muntner also believes strongly[136] that Marcus Herz composed this prayer in beautiful German and that a very poor translation into Hebrew was produced by Euchel.[137] Furthermore, an anonymous or unknown writer added the confusing caption to this earliest (1790) Hebrew version. Muntner further states that Herz based his version of the prayer on the earlier Prayer of

---

[134]See ref. 51.
[135]See ref. 23.
[136]See ref. 52.
[137]See ref. 24.

INTRODUCTION

Jacob Zahalon,[138] which was written in the seventeenth century, and was greatly influenced and stimulated by it.

From all the foregoing discussion, the evidence overwhelmingly favors the concept that the physician's prayer attributed to Maimonides is a spurious work, not written by Maimonides but composed by an eighteenth-century writer, probably Marcus Herz. Absolute proof is, however, lacking and may never be discovered.

Recently, in a comparative and historical study of Jewish religious attitudes to medicine and its practice,[139] Lord Immanuel Jakobovits, Chief Rabbi of the British Commonwealth, emphasized the ethical and moral responsibilities of the physician as a divine agent in the alleviation of human suffering. Deeply pious and moving prayers of gratitude for divine help, such as those of Asaph,[140] Judah Halevy,[141] Jacob Zahalon,[142] and Abraham Zacutus,[143] as well as the physician's prayer attributed to Maimonides,[144] says Jakobovits, all recognize God as the ultimate healer of disease, while also asserting "the indispensable part played by the physician, his art and his medicines" in the preservation of health.

The Physician's Prayer attributed to Maimonides contains moral and ethical standards by which a physician should conduct his professional life. The daily recitation of this prayer serves to remind the physician of these standards that have been set for him and that he should attempt to live by. Physicians should constantly carry with them the highest code of medical philanthropy and professional ethics. Such noble philosophy and high aspirations of the profession are embodied in the Physician's Prayer.

---

[138]See ref. 14, 43, 44.
[139]See ref. 53.
[140]See ref. 42.
[141]See ref. 14.
[142]See ref. 14, 43, 44.
[143]See ref. 43.
[144]See ref. 1–29.

References

(Hebrew titles have been translated into English.)

1. Tägliches Gebet eines Arztes bevor er seine Kranken besucht—Aus der hebräischen Handschrift eines berühmten jüdischen Arztes in Egypten aus dem zwölften Jahrhundert. *Deutsches Museum*, 1783, *1*:43–45.
2. Leibowitz, J. O., "The physician's prayer ascribed to Maimonides." *Dapim Refuiim*, 1954, *13*:77–81.
3. Medicus, "Daily prayer of a physician." *Voice of Jacob* (London), 1841, *1*(7): 49–50.
4. Peters, M. C., *Justice to the Jew. The story of what he has done for the world.* London and New York: Neely, 1899, pp. 173–175.
5. Golden, W. W., "Maimonides' prayer for physicians." *Transactions of the Medical Society of West Virginia*, 1900, *33*:414–415.
6. Friedenwald, H., "The ethics of the practice of medicine from the Jewish point of view." *Bulletin of the Johns Hopkins Hospital*, 1917, *28*:256–261.
7. Bogen, E., "The daily prayer of a physician." *Journal of the American Medical Association*, 1929, *92*:2128.
8. Keller, H., Comparison between Hippocratic Oath and Maimonides' Prayer, in "The Ideal Practice of Medicine from the Rabbinical Point of View," in *Modern Hebrew Orthopedic Terminology and Jewish Medical Essays*. Boston: Stratford Co., 1931, pp. 142–146.
9. Roman, D., "Maimonides' prayer." *Hahnemannian Monthly*, 1932, *67*: 244–250.
10. Gershenfeld, L., "The medical works of Maimonides and his Treatise on personal hygiene and dietetics." *American Journal of Pharmacy*, 1935, *107*: 14–28.
11. "Physician's prayer by Maimonides." *Medical Leaves*, 1937, *1*:9.
12. Levinson, A., "Maimonides, the physician." *Medical Leaves*, 1939, *2*:96–105.
13. Kagan, S. R., "Maimonides' prayer." *Annals of Medical History*, 1938, *10*: 429–432.
14. Friedenwald, H., *The Jews and Medicine*. Baltimore: Johns Hopkins Press, 1944, vol. I, pp. 28–30.
15. "The oath and prayer of Maimonides." *Journal of the American Medical Association*, 1955, *157*:1158.
16. Minkin, J. S., *The World of Moses Maimonides with Selections from his Writings*. New York: Yoseloff, 1957, pp. 149–150.
17. Philippson, L., "Tägliches Gebet eines Arztes vor dem Besuch seiner Kranken. (Aus der hebr. Handschrift eines berühmten jüdischen Arztes aus dem zwölften Jahrhundert.)" *Allgemeine Zeitung des Judenthums*, 1863, *27*(4):49–50.
18. Philippson, L., *Weltbewegende Fragen in Politik und Religion aus den letzten*

dreissig Jahren. Zweiter Theil: Religion. Leipzig: Baumgärtner, 1869, pp. 159–160.
19. Pagel, J., "Das Gebet des Arztes." *Allgemeine Zeitung des Judenthums,* 1892, *56*(25):294–295.
20. Distel, Th., "Gebet eines jüdischen Arztes im 12. Jahrhundert." *Deutsches Medizinische Wochenschrift,* 1902, *28*(32):580.
21. "Gebet eines jüdischen Arztes im 12. Jahrhundert." *Correspondenz-Blatt für Schweizer Aerzte,* 1902, *32*(19):611–613.
22. Bennigson, W., et al., Des Moses Maimonides Morgengebet bevor er seine Kranken besuchte. Leipzig, 1931, p. 6.
23. Muntner, S., *The Deutero Prayer of Moses*; with an Introduction about the history of the prayer, attributed to the physician Maimonides and a contemplation on the state of the praying and on the valour of the prayer in general. Jerusalem: Geniza, 1946, p. 57.
24. Euchel, I., "Prayer for the physician as he pours out his anxieties before God prior to visiting the sick. Composed by Sir Hofrat Professor Herz." *Ha-Maassef,* 1790, *6*:242–244.
25. Wolff, J., "Prière d'un médecin juif à l'usage de ses confrères." *Univers israélite,* 1903, *58*:753–755.
26. Simon, I., "L'oeuvre médicale de Maïmonide." *Revue d'Histoire de la Médecine Hebraique,* 1956, no. 31:107–120.
27. Pines, J., "La contribution juive à la médecine arabe au moyen âge." *Scalpel* (Bruxelles), 1962, *115*:207–218.
28. Seeligmann, S., "Morgengebed van den arts naar Maimonides." *Vrijdagavond,* 1928, *5*(1): 404–406.
29. Singer, E., "Maimonides, medico." *Semana Medical,* 1935, *2*: 1960–1965.
30. Schwab, M., *Répertoire des articles relatifs à l'histoire et á la littérature juives parus dans les périodiques de 1783 à 1898.* Paris: Durlacher, 1899, p. 167.
31. Schwab, M., "La priére d'un médecin juif." *Univers israélite,* 1903, *58*: 818–819.
32. Deutsch, G., "Maimonides' prayer." *American Israelite,* March 19, 1908, p. 5, cols. 5, 6.
33. "The 'Prayer of Maimonides' and its true author." *Journal of the American Medical Association,* 1929, *92*:836.
34. Deutsch, G., *Scrolls,* vol. III: *Jew and Gentile.* Essays on Jewish apologetics and kindred historical subjects. Boston: Stratford Co., 1920, pp. 93–95.
35. Haeser, H., *Lehrbuch der Geschichte der Medizin und der epidemischen Krankheiten.* 3rd ed. Jena: Dufft, 1875, vol. I.
36. Kroner, H., "Arzt und Patient in der Medizin des Maimonides." *Ost und West, Illustriertes Monatsschrift für modernes Judenthums,* 1912, *12*:745–750.
37. Illevitz, A. B., "Maimonides the physician." *Canadian Medical Association Journal,* 1935, *32*:440–442.
38. Meyerhof, M., The Medical Work of Maimonides, in *Essays on Mai-*

monides, An Octocentennial Volume, ed. S. W. Baron. New York: Columbia University. Press, 1941, pp. 265–299.
39. Hertz, J. H., Letter to Sir William Osler. *Canadian Jewish Chronicle*, 1935, *22*:7 (April 12).
40. Münz, I., *Maimonides (The Rambam)*. The story of his life and genius. Trans. from German. Introduction by H. T. Schnittkind. Boston: Winchell-Thomas, 1935, p. 191.
41. Münz, I., *Moses ben Maimon (Maimonides)*; sein Leben und seine Werke. Frankfurt a. M.: Kauffmann, 1812, pp. 267–268.
42. Rosner, F. and Muntner, S., "The oath of Asaph." *Annals of Internal Medicine*, 1965, *63*:317–320.
43. Savitz, H., "Jacob Zahalon and his book, 'The Treasure of Life.'" *New England Journal of Medicine*, 1935, *213*:167–176.
44. Simon, I., "La prière des médecins. 'Tephilat Harofim,' de Jacob Zahalon, médecin et rabbin en Italie (1630–1693)." *Revue d'histoire de la Médecine Hebraique*, 1955, no. 8:38–51.
45. Bibliothèque nationale—*Catalogues des manuscrits hébreux et samaritains de la Bibliothèque impériale*. Paris, 1866, p. 142.
46. Steinschneider, M., *Catologus codicuin hebraeorum Bibliothecae academiae Lugduno Batavae*. Leiden: E. J. Brill, 1858, p. 188.
47. Steinschneider, M., "The prayer of Rabbi Moses attributed to Rabbi Moses ben Maimon (Maimonides)." *Hacarmel*, 1867, *6*:350.
48. Marx, A., "The correspondence between the rabbis of southern France and Maimonides about astrology." *Hebrew Union College Annual*, 1926, *3*: 311–358, and 1927, *4*:493–494.
49. Lanzkron, J. and Berner, H., "Maimonides—physician, astronomer, philosopher, talmudist." *Journal of the American Medical Association*, 1955, *157*: 1637.
50. Pagel, J., *Maimuni als medizinischer Schriftsteller*. Frankfurt a. M.: Kauffmann, 1908, p. 17.
51. Leibowitz, J. O., personal communication.
52. Muntner, S., personal communication.
53. Jakobovits, I., *Jewish Medical Ethics*. New York: Bloch, 1959, pp. 15–18.

THE PHYSICIAN'S PRAYER

Almighty God, Thou hast created the human body with infinite wisdom.[1] Ten thousand times ten thousand organs hast Thou combined in it that act unceasingly and harmoniously to preserve the whole in all its beauty—the body which is the envelope of the immortal soul. They are ever acting in perfect order, agreement and accord. Yet, when the frailty of matter or the unbridling of passions deranges this order or interrupts this accord, then forces clash and the body crumbles into the primal dust from which it came. Thou sendest to man diseases as beneficent messengers to foretell approaching danger and to urge him to avert it.

Thou hast blest Thine earth, Thy rivers, and Thy mountains with healing substances; they enable Thy creatures to alleviate their sufferings and to heal their illnesses. Thou hast endowed man with the wisdom to relieve the suffering of his brother, to recognize his disorders, to extract the healing substances, to discover their powers, and to prepare and to apply them to suit

---

[1] This English version of the "Daily Prayer of a Physician" by Dr. Harry Friedenwald is reprinted from the *Bulletin of the Johns Hopkins Hospital* (1917) 28:256–261, with kind permission of the editors and publishers.

every ill. In Thine Eternal Providence Thou hast chosen me to watch over the life and health of Thy creatures. I am now about to apply myself to the duties of my profession. Support me, Almighty God, in these great labors that they may benefit mankind, for without Thy help not even the least thing will succeed.

Inspire me with love for my art and for Thy creatures. Do not allow thirst for profit, ambition for renown and admiration, to interfere with my profession, for these are the enemies of truth and of love for mankind, and they can lead astray in the great task of attending to the welfare of Thy creatures. Preserve the strength of my body and of my soul that they ever be ready to cheerfully help and support rich and poor, good and bad, enemy as well as friend. In the sufferer let me see only the human being. Illumine my mind that it recognize what presents itself and that it may comprehend what is absent or hidden. Let it not fail to see what is visible, but do not permit it to arrogate to itself the power to see what cannot be seen, for delicate and indefinite are the bounds of the great art of caring for the lives and health of Thy creatures. Let me never be absent-minded. May no strange thoughts divert my attention at the bedside of the sick, or disturb my mind in its silent labors, for great and sacred are the thoughtful deliberations required to preserve the lives and health of Thy creatures.

Grant that my patients have confidence in me and my art and follow my directions and my counsel. Remove from their midst all charlatans and the whole host of officious relatives and know-all nurses, cruel people who arrogantly frustrate the wisest purposes of our art and often lead Thy creatures to their death.

Should those who are wiser than I wish to improve and instruct me, let my soul gratefully follow their guidance; for vast is the extent of our art. Should conceited fools, however, censure me, then let love for my profession steel me against them, so that I remain steadfast without regard for age, for reputation, or for honor, because surrender would bring to Thy creatures sickness and death.

Imbue my soul with gentleness and calmness when older

THE PHYSICIAN'S PRAYER

colleagues, proud of their age, wish to displace me or to scorn me or disdainfully to teach me. May even this be of advantage to me, for they know many things of which I am ignorant, but let not their arrogance give me pain. For they are old and old age is not master of the passions. I also hope to attain old age upon this earth, before Thee, Almighty God!

Let me be contented in everything except in the great science of my profession. Never allow the thought to arise in me that I have attained to sufficient knowledge, but vouchsafe to me the strength, the leisure and the ambition ever to extend my knowledge. For art is great, but the mind of man is ever expanding.

Almighty God! Thou hast chosen me in Thy mercy to watch over the life and death of Thy creatures. I now apply myself to my profession. Support me in this great task so that it may benefit mankind, for without Thy help not even the least thing will succeed.

BIBLIOGRAPHY

by Jacob I. Dienstag

1783

1] Tagliches Gebet eines Arztes bevor er seine Kranken besucht. Aus der hebraischen Handschrift eines beruhmten judischen Arztes in Egypten aus dem zwolften Jahrhunderts. *Deutsches Museum*, 1 (1783), 43-45.

The prayer appeared for the first time in this German periodical. Scholars now agree that its true author is the physician Marcus Herz (1747-1803), a friend of the philosophers Immanuel Kant and Moses Mendelssohn. Photostatic reproduction of this earliest version appeared in Joshua O. Leibowitz's study on this theme (1954), and in G.A. Lindeboom's Dutch translation (1971); reprinted in S. Muntner's *The Deutro Prayer of Moses* (1943, 1946), p. 14.

1790

תפלה לרופא, כי ישפוך לפני ה' שיחו טרם בקרו את החולים. חברה האדון האפֿראטה ופראאפֿעסר הערץ ונעתקה על פקודתו ללשון עבר. **המאסף**, 6 (תק"ן/1790), רמב-רמה. הופיע שוב **במשנה תפלה למשה** מאת זיסמן מונטנר, ירושלים, תש"ג/1943 ותש"ו/1946. צלום מעמוד הראשון ע"י זקן (1973).
התרגום הוא מאת איצק אייכל, עורך **המאסף**.

Hebrew translation by I. Euchel from this German edition (1783).

1841

3] Tarnowsky, Ladislas, 1811-1847.

La Priere du Medecin. Episode de la vie de Maimonides, imitee de l'allemand. *Archives Israelites de France*, 2 (1841), 148-160.

"Cet episode de la vie du celebre Maimonides, que nous donnons ici, n'est qu'un fragment extrait d'une nouvelle historique de M. Ladislas Tarnowsky, inseree dans un journal litteraraire allemand *(Abendzeitung)* de Juin [1840] dernier. L'auteur a embrasse dans son recit un espace de temps plus grand, et a suivi Maimonides jusqu'a sa mort, en y inserant plusieurs anecdotes et traditions plus ou moins romantiques et meme merveilleuses, mais qu'on ne trouve nulle part garanties. Nous ne donnons ici que l'imitation, ou si l'on aime mieux, la traduction libre de la partie de son recit qui se rapporte le plus directement a la *priere* qui en est l'objet principal."

Pp. 155-157: Priere quotidienne d'un medecin avant de visiter ses malades, Translation of this story in which the *Prayer* appeared was made by H. Somerhausen. At this writing, I could not locate the above noted *Abendzeitung* in which the original German appeared.

4] "Medicus"

Daily Prayer of a Physician. *Voice of Jacob* (London), 1, no. 7 (Dec. 24, 1841) 49-50.

"A friend under the signature of "Medicus" has obliged us with a translation of this beautiful prayer from the Hebrew of the celebrated periodical המאסף."

1861

5] Bedarride, Jassuda, 1804-1882.

Les Juifs en France en Italie et en Espagne. Paris: Michel Levy, 1861, pp. 489-490, reprinted there, 1867.

1863

6] Philippson, Ludwig, 1811-1889.

Tagliches Gebet eines Arztes vor dem Besuch seiner Kranken (aus der hebr. Handschrift eines berumten judischen Arztes aus dem zwolften Jahrhunderts). *Allgemeine Zeitung des Judenthums,* 27, no. 4 (Jan. 20, 1863, 49-50; reprinted in his *Weltbewegende Fragen,* 2. Theil. Leipzig: Baumgartner, 1869, pp. 159-160. Reprint of Marcus Herz's composition (1783).

1867

7] Bedarride, Jassuda, 1804-1882.

Etude sur le Guide des Egares. *Memoires de l'Academie des Sciences et Lettres de Montpellier,* 4 (1867): 409-436. p. 431: Physician's Prayer.

1875

8] Haeser, Heinrich, 1811-1884.

Lehrbuch der Geschichte der Medizin und der epidemischen Krankheiten, vol. 1, Jena: Fischer, 1875, p. 837.

1887

9] Philipson, David, 1862-1949.

Jews as physicians. *Menorah,* III, no. 6 (Dec. 1887); 388-389.
English translation.

1892

10] Pagel, Julius Leopold, 1851-1912.
Das Gebet des Arztes. *Allgemeine Zeitung des Judenthums*, 56, no. 25 (1892) 294-295.

1895

11] La Preghiera del Medico. *Il Corriere Israelitico*, 32, no. 10 (1895), 222-224.

1899

12] Kahan, Hermann
Hat Moses Maimonides dem Krypto-Mohammedanismus gehuldigt? M. Sziget: Blumenfeld and David, 1899, pp. 57-58.

13] Peters, Madison C., 1859-1918.
Justice to the Jew. London and New York: Neely, 1899, pp. 173-175.

1900

14] Golden, William W.
Maimonides' Prayer for Physicians. *Transactions of the Medical Society of West Virginia*, 33 (1900) 414-415.

1902

15] Distel, Theodor
Gebet eines judischen Arztes im 12. Jahrhundert. *Deutsche Medizinische Wochenschrift*, 28, no. 32 (Aug. 7, 1902) 580. Reprinted from 1783 edition.
Gebet eines judischen Arztes im 12. Jahrhundert. *Correspondenz-Blatt fur Schweizer Aerzte*, 32, no. 19 (Oct. 1, 1902) pp. 611-613. Reprinted from 1783 edition.

16] Rightman, W.
Maimonides the physician. *Plexus*, (1902) pp. 245-248. Includes Prayer for Physicians.

17] Toeplitz, Peter
Das Gebet eines judischen Arzte. *Israelitisches Familienblatt*, V, no. 36 (Feb. 4, 1902). (Listed in M. Meyerhof's study "The Medical Works of Maimonides," in *Essays on Maimonides*, Salo W. Baron, ed., New York: Columbia Univ. Press, 1941, p. 299 and J. Pagel in W. Bacher, M. Brann and D. Simonsen, eds., *Moses ben Maimon*, Band I, Leipzig, 1908, p. 244, note 1).

1903

18] Wolff, Jules, 1862-1955.
Priere d'un medecin juif a l'usage de ses confreres. *Univers Israelite*, 58 (Feb. 27, 1903) 753-755. Translated from the German published by Distel (1902). Attributes the *Prayer* to Maimonides; criticized by Schwab.

19] Schwab, Moise, 1839-1918.
La Priere d'un Medecin Juif. *L'Univers Israelite*, 58, no. 26 (Mar. 20, 1903) 818-819. Criticizes Wolff and attributes the *Prayer* to Herz.

20] * Treub, Hektor
[Dutch translation of the Prayer]. In M.J. Premsela's *Medische Fastoensleer*. Amsterdam, 1903, pp. 52-53. According to S. Seeligmann (1928).

1908

21] Grossman, Louis, 1863-1926.
The Jew in Medicine. *American Israelite*, 54, no. 37 (Mar. 12, 1908), 1. Attributes the prayer to Maimonides. Criticized by Deutsch.

22] Deutsch, Gotthard, 1859-1921.
Maimonides' Prayer. *American Israelite*, 54, no. 38 (Mar. 19, 1908):5. Reprinted in his *Jew and Gentile*, Vol. III: Scrolls. Boston: Stratford, 1920, pp. 93-95. Refutes Grossman and attributes the *Prayer* to Herz.

1912

23] Kroner, Hermann, 1870-1930.
Arzt und Patient in der Medizin des Maimonides. *Ost und West*, 12, no. 8 (Aug. 1912), 745-750. Suggests an affinity between the *Prayer* and the other writings of Maimonides.

24] Munz, I. 1857-
Moses ben Maimon (Maimonides). Frankfurt a.M.: J. Kauffmann, 1912, pp. 267-268. Questions the authenticity of the Prayer.

1913

25] Golden, William G.
Prayer for Physicians. Paper read before the West Virginian Medical Society. [Elkins, W. Va. ? 1913 ?]. 2 Leaves.

26] * Haupt, Paul, 1858-1926.
Morgengebet des Arztes. Wandspruch in kunstlerischer Umrahmung. Bern (c. 1913).
Wall edition distributed by Haupt (G. Sarton, *Introduction to the History of Science*, vol. 2 (1931), p. 378).

1914

27] Golden, William W.
Letter to the Editor. *American Israelite*, 52, no. 60 (June 25, 1914). Inquires about the authorship of the Prayer. See reply by Deutsch.

28] Deutsch, Gotthard, 1859-1921.
The Maimonides Prayer Myth. *American Israelite*, 52, no. 60 (June 25,

---
* An asterisk means that the information is taken from a secondary source.

1914) p. 4; reprinted in his *Jew and Gentile (Scrolls,* vol. 3), Boston: Stratford, 1914, pp. 93-95.
Suggests Marcus Herz is the author of the *Prayer.*

1917

29] The Physician's Prayer. *The Medical Critic and Guide,* 10 (1917), 443.

30] Friedenwald, Harry, 1864-1950.
The Ethics of the Practice of Medicine from the Jewish Point of View. *Bulletin of the Johns Hopkins Hospital,* 28, no. 318 (Aug. 1917), pp. 256-261; reprinted in his *The Jews and Medicine: Essays,* vol. 1, Baltimore: Johns Hopkins Press, 1944, pp. 18-30. Pp. 28-30: Daily Prayer of the Physician. (Reprint, New York: Ktav, 1967, reprinted in *Encyclopedia of Bioethics,* ed. W. T. Reich), IV. New York: The Free Press, 1978, pp. 1737-1738.
Takes no side in the controversy.

1919

31] Keller, Henry, 1877-1944.
The ideal practice of medicine from the rabbinical point of view. *Jewish Forum,* II, no. 8 (Aug. 1919), pp. 1118-1121; reprinted in his *Modern Hebrew Orthopedic Terminology and Jewish Medical Essays.* Boston: Stratford (c. 1931), pp. 128-146.
Includes a section entitled "Comparison between Hippocratic *Oath* and Maimonides' *Prayer.*" Keller was criticized by B. Rozos (1982).

1926

32] Remington Practice of Pharmacy. 7th ed., Philadelphia: J. B. Lippincott, 1926, pp. 5-6; 8th ed. (c. 1936), pp. 5-6; 9th ed. Easton, Pa.: Mack (c. 1948), p. 7; 10th ed. (c. 1951), p.8; 11th ed. 1956, p. 8; 15th ed., 1975, p. 15.
English translation.

1927

33] La Wall, Charles H.
Four Thousand Years of Pharmacy. Philadelphia: J.B. Lippincott Co. (c. 1927), pp. 112-113.
English translation.

1928

34] Seeligmann, Sigmund, 1873-1940.
Morgengebed van den Arts Naar Maimonides. *De Vrijdagavond,* 5, no. 26 (28 Sept. 1972) pp. 404-406.
Dutch translation.

35] מארגענגעבעט פון א דאקטאר לויט'ן רמב"ם ז"ל. **אונזער גייסט** (זאמאשטץ), 1, העפט 1 (אלול תרפ"ח/1928), [נב].
Yiddish translation.

1929

36] [Deutsch, Gotthard, 1859-1921.]

The "Prayer of Maimonides" and its True Author. *Journal of the American Medical Association*, 92, no. 10 (Mar. 9, 1929) 836.

Extract by the editor from Deutsch's article in this journal, vol. 54, no. 38 (Mar. 19, 1908) p. 5 in which he attributes the *Prayer* to Marcus Herz.

37] Osler, William, 1849-1919.

Maimonides' Prayer for Physicians. In his *Bibliotheca Osleriana*. Oxford: Clarendon Press, 1929, pp. 459-460 (no. 5114).

38] Bogen, Emil, 1896-

The Daily Prayer of a Physician. *Journal of the American Medical Association*, 92 (June 22, 1929), 2128.

Agrees with Kroner (1912) who shows that there is a harmony between the Prayer and the other writings of Maimonides.

39] Lucia, Salvatore Pablo, 1901-

Invocatio Medici: Code of Fushi Ikai No Ryaku, Oath of Hippocrates, and Supplication of Maimonides. *California and Western Medicine*, no. 2 (Feb. 1929) pp. 117-120. Includes "Invocation of Maimonides."

1930

40] Marconi, E.

Mosheh ben Maimon. *Illustrazione Medica Italiana*, 12 (1930) 11-18. Pp. 13-14: *Physician's Prayer*.

1931

41] *Des Moses Maimonides Morgengebet bevor er seine Kranken besuchte.* Berlin, (Officina serpentis, 1931). [8] p.

"...als Spende der Mediziner zur Jahresversammlung 1931 der Soncino Gesellschaft uberreicht..."

"Vorstehendes Gebet findet sich in der in Leipzig erschienenen Zeitschrift *Deutsches Museum* vom Jahre 1783, Bd., pp. 143-45." P. [6]. Reviewed by Esriel Carlebach, *Israelitisches Familienblatt* (Hamburg), 33, no. 39 (Sept. 24, 1931) who points to Marcus Herz as the author of the *Prayer*. Carlebach and Heinrich Lowy's views are cited, ibid., Nov. 19, 1931.

1932

42] Roman, Desidric

Maimonides' Prayer. *Hahnemannian Monthly*, 67 (Apr. 1932) 244-250. An appraisal.

1933

43] Kramer, John E.

The Apothecary in the Bible and Religious Lore. *American Journal of Pharmacology* 105 (Nov. 1933): 555-556.

1934

44] Gorfinkle, Joseph I. 1880-1950.
The Daily Prayer of a Physician before Visiting his Patients from a manuscript of a celebrated Jewish physician of the 12th century, attributed to Maimonides. Translated from the original. *Jewish Advocate*, Feb. 13, 1934, p. 2.

45] Kagan, Solomon R., 1889-1955.
Jewish Contributions to Medicine in America. Boston, Mass.: Boston Medicine Publishing, 1934, p. XXIX-XXX; 513-514; 2nd ed., 1939.
Repeats the thesis that Maimonides was the author of the *Prayer*.

1935

46] Castiglioni, Arturo, 1874-1953.
Mose Maimonide, medico e filosofo; nell'ottavo centenario della sua nascita (1135-1935). *Rassegna Clinico Scientifica*, 13, no. 4 (April 1935), 169-175.
Pp. 174-175: Prayer for Physicians.
Italian translation.

47] Castiglioni, Arturo, 1874-1953.
Mose Maimonide, Medico e Filosofo nell'ottavo centenario della sua nascita (1135-1935). Estratto dalla "Rassegna Clinico Scientifica" dell'Istituto Biochimico Italiano no. 4 anno xiii, Milano [1935]. 23 p. Pp. 19-22: Prayer for Physicians.

48] Edgar, Irving Iskowitz, 1902-
Maimonides and his contributions to medicine. *Phi Delta Epsilon News* (Menasha), 28 (1935) 163-165.

49] Feldman, Joseph
Maimonides as physician. *Brooklyn Jewish Center Review*, XV, no. 29 (March 1935), 5-6, 16-17. P. 17: Prayer.

50] Fishcher, Isidor, 1868-1942.
On the ethics of the Jewish physician. *Medical Life*, 42 (1935); 38-39.

51] Gershenfeld, Louis, 1895-
Moses Maimonides, Cordova 1135, Cairo 1204. *Medical Life*, 42 (January 1935), 1-34. Includes English translation of Physician's Prayer.

52] Gershenfeld, Louis, 1895-
The medical works of Maimonides and his treatise on personal hygiene and dietetics. *American Journal of Pharmacy*, 107 (January 1935) 14-28. Pp. 19-20: Summary of the above prayer.

53] Hertz, Joseph H., 1872-1946.
Letter to Sir William Osler. *Canadian Jewish Chronicle*, 22 (April 12, 1935) 7; reprinted in F. Rosner's "The Physician's Prayer attributed to Moses Maimonides." *Bulletin of the History of Medicine*, 41 (1967) 445 and in his *Medicine in the Bible and the Talmud*, New York: Ktav, 1977, p. 131. States that the *Prayer* was written by Marcus Herz.

54] Keller, Henry, 1877-1944.
Maimonides the physician. *Jewish Forum*, 18, no. 9-10 (September/November 1935), p. 247.
English translation.

55] Macht, David I., 1882-1961.
Moses Maimonides, Physician and Scientist; the William Osler of Medieval Arabic and Hebrew Medicine. *Bulletin of the Institute of History of Medicine*, 3 (July 1935), pp. 585-598; reprinted in *Jews in the Arts and Sciences; Jubilee Volume Jewish Academy of Arts and Sciences*. New York: Harold Square Press, [1955], pp. 107-119; reprinted in *Maimonides as Physician and Scientist; a Tribute*. New York: Jewish Pharmaceutical Society of America, 1963. Offset reproduction. Unpaged. [14] P. Last two pages: Macht's metrical translation of Physician's Prayer.
Summary in *Scientific Monthly*, 41 (August 1935), 184-187. *Physician's Prayer* at the end of the study.

56] Perel, Leon, 1910-
Maimonide, Medecin Humaniste. *Hippocrate*, 3, no. 10 (December 1935), 880-888. P. 883: Prayer of Physician.

57] Robinson, Victor, 1866-1947.
Maimonides. *Medical Review of Reviews*, 41 (1935) 362-375. Pp. 373-374: Physician's Prayer.

58] Singer, Elias, 1896-1959.
Maimonides Medico. *Maimonides (Moises ben Maimon) 1135-1935*. Buenos Aires: Sociedad Hebraica Argentina, 1935, pp. 269-271: Physician's Prayer.
Spanish translation.

59] Singer, Elias, 1896-1959.
Maimonides, Medico. *Semana Medica* 42 (Dec. 19, 1935), pp. 1960-1961. Physician's Prayer. See also his Yiddish version (1954).

60] Solis-Cohen, Solomon, 1857-1943.
"The Prayer of Maimonides" and its true author. *Jewish Exponent*, 95 (March 15, 1935), p. 7.

BIBLIOGRAPHY

The Physician's Prayer. *Maimonides' Eighth Centenary.* Commemorative Supplement to the *Zionist Record.* Johannesburg: Maimonides' Committee of the South Africa Board of Jewish Education, April 17, 1935, p. 16.

61] *Prayer for Physicians* by Maimonides. *Medical Times,* 63, no. 5 (May 1935) p. 165.

62] The Oath and Prayer of Maimonides. *Phi Lambda Kappa Quarterly,* IX, no. 4 (April 1935), back cover.

63] The Invocation of Maimonides. *Rambam Golden Book.* New York Maimonides Hygienic Ass'n, 1935, p. 27.

‎64] וויינינג, נפתלי, 1897־1943 או: 1944.
‎די תפילה פון רמב"ם אלס געצייג אין קאמף קעגן אנטיסעמיטיזם. **סאציאלע מעדיצין** (ורשה), 8, חוברת 3־4 (מערץ־אפריל 1935), 54־57.
‎עמ' 56־57: תפילת הרופא ביודית. שתפילת הרופא שרתה כתעמולה נגד עלילות האנטישמיים על הרופאים היהודים.

‎65] מזיא, אהרן מאיר, 1858־1930.
‎הרמב"ם בתור רופא. **הארץ**, גליון 4788 (קובץ הרמב"ם, למלאות 800 שנה להולדתו, ערב פסח, תרצ"ה/1935) 85־98. עמ' 94: **תפילת הרופא**.
‎נדפס שוב **המורה לדורות**, מאת מ. אוריין ירושלים: מוסד הרב קוק, תשט"ז, עמ' 182־183.

‎66] קלר, חנוך הנרי, 1877־1944.
‎הרמב"ם בתור רופא ומרפא. **ברבנו משה בן מיימון**; קובץ תורני־מדעי, חלק ב' בעריכת י.ל. פישמן. ירושלים, תרצ"ה/1935, עמ' רכח־רם. עמ' רלח: **תפילת הרופא**.

‎תפילת הרמב"ם. **בריאות**, 3, חוברת 10־11 (אייר תרצ"ה/1935), 84.

1936

67] Baras, E.
La Circoncision, son historique, son importance au point de vue hygienique; avec la traduction integrale de la *Priere de Maimonide.* Paris: Lipschutz, 1936.

1937

68] Physician's Prayer by Maimonides. *Medical Leaves* I (1937), 9.

‎69] * **תפלת הרופא** בתרגום א. ז. רבינוביץ. **דבר**, מוצאי יום כפור, תרצ"ח/15 לספטמבר, 1937.

1938

70] Kagan, Solomon R., 1889-1955.
Maimonides' Prayer. *Annals of Medical History*, n.s. 10 (September 1938), 429-432. English translation of the Prayer; states that Maimonides was its author.

1939

71] Bookstaber, Philip David, 1892-
Judaism and the American Mind. New York: Bloch, 1939. P. 214: Prayer for Physicians.

72] Levinson, Abraham, 1885-1955.
Maimonides the Physician. *Medical Leaves* [2] (1939): 96-105. Pp. 104-105: Physician's Prayer.

73] *Daily Prayer of a Physician Before Visiting a Sick Man.* [Chicago]: Northwestern University Medical School, 1939. 1 leaf.

1942

74] די תפילה פון רמב"ם דעם דאקטאר. נאכריכטען פון אלגעמיינעם פארבאנד פון די יידן אין פראנקרייך/"יידישע נאכריכטן" (באזעצטע זאנע), נומער 4. פרייטיק 13 פעברואר 1942.
This periodical was published by the Union Generale des Israelites during the German occupation of France. This issue is found in the Jewish Division of the New York Public Library.

75] * Aron, Willy
Maimonides, Physician and Pharmacist. I. P. A. Voice, Feb. 1942.

1943

76] מונטנר, זיסמן, 1897־1973.
משנה תפלה למשה, עם מבוא לתולדות התפלה המיוחסת לרופא ר' משה בן מיימון, ובו השקפות על מצב המתפלל ועל השפעת התפלה האמיתית בכלל... בצרוף סקירה מקיפה על תוכן החיבור "עולם התפלה". ירושלים, "גניזה", (דפוס "המערב"), תש"ג. 46 [2] ע. °8. שער נוסף באנגלית. הוצאה מורחבת של מאמר שי"ל בסיני כרך י"ב, תש"ג. כוונת המחבר "לכתוב מחדש את תפלת הרמב"ם בהתאם לרוחו". — ע' 15.
שער נוסף באנגלית:

The Deutero Prayer of Moses, with an introduction about the history of this prayer, attributed to the physician Moses Maimonides connected with a contemplation on the state of the praying and on the genuine prayer in general. Jerusalem: Geniza, 1943.

1946

77] מונטנר, זיסמן, 1897-1973.
משנה תפלה למשה, עם מבוא לתולדות התפלה המיוחסת לרופא ר' משה בן
מימון... בצרוף... סקירה על תוכן החיבור "עולם התפילה" (טרם יצא לאור)...
מהדורה שניה. ירושלים, "גניזה", (דפוס המערב), תש"ו. [2], 57, [4] ע'. שער נוסף
באנגלית. הוצאה מורחבת של מאמר שיצא לאור ב"סיני", תש"ג, עמ' קכ. כוונת
המחבר "לכתוב מחדש את תפילת הרמב"ם... בהתאם לרוחו". — ע' 15.

1947

78] Etziony, Mordecai, 1905-1976.
The Prayer of a Physician (dedicated to the memory of Rabbeinu Moses-ben-Maimon) translated from the Yiddish by A. M. Klein. *Canadian Medical Association Journal*, 56 (1947): 100-101.

1949

79] Aron, William
The Oath of Maimonides or a Misrepresentation of Facts. *I.P.A. Voice*, 16, no. 10-11 (Oct.-Nov. 1949): 4.

80] Nunez Mata, Efren
La Plegaria de Maimonides. *Tribuna Israelita*, 5, no. 56 (July 1949): 12-13.

1951

81] Kagan, Solomon R.
The medical ethics of Maimonides. *The Medical Way*, 13, no. 5 (May 1951), p. 5. Includes English translation of *Physician's Prayer*.

82] Simon, Isidore, 1906-1985.
Le Serment Medical d'Assaph, Medecin Juif du Septieme Siecle. Avec une etude comparative du Serment d'Hippocrate, de "la Priere Medicale" de Maimonide, et du Serment de Montpellier. *Revue d'Histoire de la Medecin Hebraique*, no. 9 (July 1951): 36-45.

83] תפלת הרופא. במבוא ל**אגרות הרמב"ם**, כרך א', ערוכות ומבוארות ע"י מ.ד.
רבינוביץ. תל-אביב: הוצאת "ראשונים", תשי"א/1951, עמ' רנג; הדפסות חדשות:
ירושלים: מוסד הרב קוק, תש"ך/1960; תשכ"ד/1964; תשל"ד/1974, נדפס שוב ב**אוצר
הרמב"ם** לנחום אריאלי, כרך ב'. תל-אביב: דביר, תשי"ז/1957, עמ' 380.

1952

84] Rapport, Samuel, 1903- and Helen Wright, 1914-
The Oath and Prayer of Maimonides. In *Great Adventures in Medicine*, New York: Dial Press, 1952, pp. 7-8, revised ed. 1961.

1953

85] Ausubel, Nathan, 1899-
Pictorial History of the Jewish People. New York: Crown Publishers (c. 1953), p. 161.

1954

‎[86 מרגלית, דוד, 1888-1977.
הרמב"ם כרופא וכסופר רפואי. **דפים רפואיים**, 13, חוברת א' אדר ב' תשי"ד/מארס 1954): 82-89; נדפס שוב בספרו "חכמי ישראל כרופאים". ירושלים: מוסד הרב קוק, תשכ"ב, עמ' 100-110.
תפילת הרופא בסוף המאמר.

87] Kohenov, David
Etude Historique et Critique des Serments Medicaux et des Prieres Medicales, depuis Hippocrate jusqu' a nos Jours. Thesis, Paris, May 1954. 104 pp. Cited in *Revue d'Histoire de la Medecine Hebraique*, March 1955, p. 40.

88] *The Oath and Prayer of Maimonides.* [Boston: E.L. Parch, 1954?]. [1] leaf. Hebrew Union College Catalogue, Cincinnati.

‎[89 דבורז'צקי, מ', 1908-1975.
הרמב"ם והפילוסופיה של המוסר הרפואי. **ניב הרופא**, 4, חוברת ג-ד (אב תשי"ד / 1954), 8-13.

‎[90 דבורז'צקי, מ, 1908-1975.
דער רמב"ם און די פילאזאפיע פון דער מעדיצינישער עטיק. **פאלקסגעזונט**, גליון 4-3 [48-49] (מאי-יולי 1954) 18-21.

‎[91 **פארן פאלקסגעזונט**, 20 (סעפט. 1954), 166-167.

‎[92 זינגער, יואל, 1896-1959.
דער רמב"ם ווי א מעדיקער. **דווקא**, 5, חוברת 18-19 (יאנואר-יוני 1954), 104-105.
ראה גם מאמרו בספרדית למעלה (1935).

‎[93 ליבוביץ, יהושע, -1895
התפילה המיוחסת לרמב"ם. **דפים רפואיים**, 13 (1954): 77-81; נדפס שוב במאמרו של דוד מרגלית וספרו, "חבוריו רפואיים שיוחסו לרמב"ם ולרמב"ן", **קורות**, 5, חוברת 3-4 (סיון תשכ"ז), 228-231; "דרך ישראל ברפואה". ירושלים: הוצאת האקדמיה לרפואה, תש"ל, עמ' 522-524. תרגום עברי חדש.

‎[94 א טעגליכע תפילה פון א דאקטאר איידער ער באזוכט זיינע קראנקע.
פאלקקסגעזונט, גליון 3-4 [48-49] (יאנואר-יוני 1954), 14-15.
תרגומיהם השונים של מ. דבורז'צקי ול. קורלאנד.

‎[95 תפילה לרופא מיוחסת לרמב"ם. **ידע-עם**, ב, חוברת ד-ה (תשרי תשט"ו — 1954), 219.

1955

96] Conrad, Robert
Moses Maimonides. *Ohio State Medical Journal* 51 (1955): 243-246.

97] Dujovich, Adolfo, 1907-
Maimonides. *Revista de la Associacion Medica Argentina*, 69 (1955): 439-443. P. 441: Physician's Prayer.

98] d'Esaguy, Augusto, 1889-
Oraoao e Juramente Medico de Moises Maimonides e Amato Lusitano. Lisboa: [Soc. Ind. de Tipografia...], 1955. 27 p.
Pp. 7-19: Discussion of the *Physician's Prayer* and translation of it (pp. 12-14).

99] Macht, David I., 1882-1961.
Maimonides as physician and scientist. *Jews in the Arts and Sciences*-Jubilee volume. Jewish Academy of Arts and Sciences. New York, 1955, pp. 107-119. Prayer of Maimonides in metrical translation by the author. Reprint from 1935 edition.

1956

100] אואריין, מאיר, 1910-1979.
המורה לדורות — רבנו משה בן מימון. ירושלים: מוסד הרב קוק, עמ' 179-183.
עמ' 182-183: **תפילת הרופא** לפי התרגום המובא אצל ד"ר א.מ. מזיא בקובץ הרמב"ם של **הארץ**, ערב פסח תרצ"ה.

101] Physician's Prayer. In: Max Felshin, *Moses Maimonides (Rambam)*. New York: Book Guild, 1956, pp. 159-160.

1957

102] Minkin, Jacob J., 1885-1962.
The World of Moses Maimonides. New York: Yoseloff, 1957, pp. 149-150; reprinted in 1987 edition under new title: *The Teachings of Maimonides*. Northvale, NJ: Jason Aronson.

103] אריאלי, נחום, -1930.
אוצר הרמב"ם; דברי מחשבה ואגדה. כרך ב', תל-אביב: דביר, תשי"ז/1957, עמ' 380.
לפי תרגום מ.ד. רבינוביץ (1951).

1958

104] Baron, Salo W., 1895-1989.
A Social and Religious History of the Jews, vol. 8. New York: Columbia Univ. Press, 1958, p. 391, note 23.
Bibliographical.

105] מונטנר, זיסמן, 1897-1973.
יעקב צהלון. במחקרו "הרניסאנס (התחייה) של מדעי הטבע והרפואה נוכח השמדת הגניוס היהודית באותה התקופה". **קורות** 7, כרך ב', חוברת א-ב (אייר תשי"ח/1958), 36.
שר' יעקב צהלון הוא המחבר של **תפילת הרופא** שתורגמה אחר כך לגרמנית ע"י מרקוס הרץ בלי ציון מדויק אל המקור ושנתפרסמה, כתפילתו של הרמב"ם.

106] The Oath and Prayer of Maimonides (Maimonides—Islamic [sic] philosopher and sage of Cordova, 1135-1204 A.D.). *Journal of the American Medical Association*, 157, no. 13 (Mar. 26, 1958), 1158.

1959

107] Gordon, Benjamin Lee, 1875-1965.
Medieval and Renaissance Medicine. New York: Philosophical Library (c. 1959), pp. 225-226.

108] Polsky, Morris, 1908-
Maimonides — Master Physician. *Texas State Journal of Medicine*, 55 (June 1959), 457.

109] Schwartz, Stephen C.
"Maimonides: Portrait of a Man." *Philadelphia Medicine*, 55 (1969), 166-168. *Physician's Prayer.*

110] Zakon, Samuel J., 1898-
Maimonides. *Quarterly Bulletin of North Western University Medical School*, 33, no. 1 (Spring 1959), 71-76. P. 74: *Physician's Prayer.*

1959

111] דינגאל, ש. 1887־1961.
טעקס פון דעם רמב"ם'ס תפלה פאר א דאקטאר. בתוך מאמרו "די װאך אין אידישען לעבען". **טאג** 13 יוני, 1959, עמ' 3.

112] מלאכי, אליעזר רפאל, 1895־1980.
מי חבר את ה"תפלה לרופא"?. **הדואר,** 38, גליון ל' (כ' סיון תשי"ט/1959): 566־571.
שמרקוס הרץ חיבר את התפילה.

113] צייטלין, אהרן, 1875־1962.
דער וויכוח ארום דער רמב"ם שבועה. **טאג־מארגען זשורנאל,** 21 אויגוסט, 1959, עמ' 6־7.

1960

114] מימון, יהודה ליב, 1898־1962.
רבי משה בן מיימון. ירושלים: מוסד הרב קוק, תש"ר/1960, עמ' קנא־קנג. לקוח (בקצת שינויים) ממאמרו של חנוך הנרי קלר (עיין למעלה: 1935).

1961

115] Besso, Henry V.
Oracion Cuotidiana de un Medico Pronunciada antes de Visiter a sus Enfermos (attribuida a Moses Maimonides). *Le Judaisme Sephardi*, n.s. 22 (Aug. 1961): 953-954.

1962

116] מרגלית, דוד, 1888־1977.
הרמב"ם — רופא וסופר רפואי. בספרו חכמי ישראל כרופאים, ירושלים: מוסד
הרב קוק, תשכ"ב, עמ' 100־110.

1963

117] Aguinis, Marcos
Maimonides. Un Sabio de Avanzada. Buenos Aires: Institutio Cientifico Judio (IWO), 1963, pp. 67-69.

Macht, David I. (See 1935).

1965

118] Zao, Sylvain
Maimonide. Presentation, choix de textes, biographie et bibliographie. [Paris ?]: Editions Seghers [1965]. P. 185: *Priere d'un Medecin*.

1966

119] Hausdorff, David M.
The Golden Heritage. New York: Feldheim, 1966, pp. 168-169.

1967

120] Rosner, Fred, 1935-
The Physicians Prayer Attributed to Maimonides. *Bulletin of the History of Medicine*, 41, no. 5 (Sept.-Oct. 1967); pp. 440-454; in *Medicine in the Bible and the Talmud*. New York: Ktav, 1977, pp. 125-140; in *Legacies in Ethics and Medicine*, Chester R. Burns, ed., New York: Science History Publications, 1977, pp. 158-172.

121] Hertz, Joseph H., 1872-1946.
Letter to Sir William Osler. *Revue d'Histoire de la Medecine Hebraique*, no. 81 (October 1968), p. 115. French translation of letter published in *Canadian Jewish Chronicle* (1917).

122] Pelner, Louis, 1907-
Maimonides the physician. *New York State Journal of Medicine* 68 (1968): 2093-2098.

123] Rosner, Fred, 1935-
La Priere du Medecin attribuee a Moise Maimonide. *Revue d'Histoire de la Medecine Hebraique*, no. 81 (Oct. 1968), pp. 109-124. Translation from English study (1967).

124] Simon, I., 1906-1985.
Texts abrege de la "Priere Medicale." *Revue d'Histoire de la Medecine Hebraique*, no. 81 (October 1968), p. 107.

125] מרגלית, דוד, 1888-1977.
חבורים רפואיים שיוחסו לרמב"ם ולרמב"ן. **קורות** 4, חוברת ג-ד, סיון תשכ"ז(1967): 208-231.
עמ' 228-231: תפילת הרופא (בתרגום יהושע ליבוביץ-שפרסם אותה בדפים **רפואיים**, 13 (1954), 77-81) [= ד. מרגלית, דרך ישראל ברפואה ירושלים: הוצאת האקדמיה לרפואה, תש"ל, עמ' 522-524].

1970.

126] Juramintul Lui Maimonide.
Revista Cultului Mozaic (Bucarest), 15, no. 227 (April 1, 1970).

1971

127] תפלת הרופא (נוסח קצר). בספר **לב אברהם**; הלכות רפואה לחולה, חלק ב' מאת ד"ר אברהם-סופר אברהם. ירושלים: הוצאת ספרים פלדהיים תשל"א, עמ' ו'.
"נעתק מח" **הרמב"ם, ספריו ופעולותיו**" (תרצ"ה).

128] Goodhill, Victor, 1911-
Maimonides — Modern medical relevance. *Transactions of the American Academy of Ophthalmology and Otolaryngology*, 75 (1971), 463-491. Pp. 486-487: Prayer for Physicians.

129] Lindeboom, G.A.
Het (aan Maimonides toegeschreven) Ochtendgebed van een ars. *Nederlands Tijdschrift voor Geneeskunde*, 15, no. 21 (May 22, 1971), pp. 924-927. Facsimile of Prayer by Marcus Herz of the German edition of 1783 in Dutch translation.

130] *New York Times*, July 11, 1971, p. 71:5.
Graduate shift on Medical Oath: U[niversity] of Miami doctors shun Hippocratic version.
"For the second consecutive year, graduates of the University of Miami Medical School have recited the *Oath of Maimonides* instead of the traditional *Oath of Hippocrates* upon receiving their medical degrees."

1973

131] Etziony, Mordecai B., 1905-1976.
The Prayer of Moses Maimonides. In his *The Physician's Creed*. An Anthology of medical prayers, oaths and codes of ethics written by medical practitioners through the ages. Springfield, Ill.: Charles C Thomas, 1973, pp. 28-31.

1974

132] Adise, Herbert H.
Looking back to the future. *Reconstructionist* XL, no. 6 (September 1974),

pp. 24-26. Comparison between Hippocratic Oath and Prayer for the Physician, attributed to Maimonides.

133] Goodhill, Victor, 1911-
Address by Victor Goodhill, second recipient of the Maimonides Award of Wisconsin, October 24, 1974. Wisconsin Society for Jewish Learning, Mount Sinai Medical Center, Milwaukee, 1974, pp. 15-16. Physician's Prayer.

134] Goodhill, Victor, 1911-
Maimonides on Moral Deafness. Milwaukee: Wisconsin Society for Jewish Learning; Mount Sinai Medical Society [1974], pp. 15-16; reprinted in *Jewish Spectator*, 40 (Winter 1975): 23-24.

135] Le Porrier, Herbert
Le Medicin de Cordoue. Roman. Paris: Editions du Seuil, 1974. P. 284: "Invocation."

1975

136] Adise, Herbert H.
Hipocrates vs. Maimonides. Mirando enel parado en pos di un future. *Majshhavot/Pensamientos*, XIV, no. 2 (April-June 1975), pp. 43-45. Translation from the English (1974) by Sau Voloschin.

137] Goodhill, Victor, 1911-
Maimonides on moral Deafness. *Jewish Spectator*, 40 (Winter 1975), 20-24. Pp. 23-24: Physician's Prayer. Abbreviated text, originally published in 1974.

1976

138] Csillag, Istvan
Maimonidesz, Mozes. *Orvosi Hetilap*, 117, no. 48 (Nov. 28, 1976), pp. 2926-2927: Physician's Prayer in Hungarian translation.

139] תפילת הרופא של הרמב"ם. תרגום יהושע ליבוביץ. **ספר אסיא**, נערך ע"י אברהם שטינברג. ירושלים: הוצאת המכון ע"ש ד"ר פלק שלזינגר ז"ל לחקר הרפואה עפ"י התורה ליד בית החולים "שערי צדק", תשל"ו, עמ' 258-259.

140] The Prayer of Maimonides. *Voice of the Vaad* (Organ of the Jewish community council of Montreal), March 1976, p. 8.

1977

141] Rosner, Fred, 1935-
The Physician's Prayer attributed to Moses Maimonides (with text in English). In, Chester R. Burns, ed., *Legacies in Ethics and Medicine.* New York: Science History Publications, 1977, pp. 158-172.

1979

142] Le Perrier, Herbert
The Doctor from Cordova. A biographical novel about the great philosopher Maimonides. Translated from the French by Barbara Wright. New York: Doubleday. P. 277: Prayer.

143] Savitz, Harry A.
The Oath and Prayer of Maimonides. In his *A Jewish Physician's Harvest.* New York: Hebrew College Press, 1979, p. 196-197.

1982

144] Rozos, B, N. Degleris; C. Tsolis; I. Papayannopoulos
The Hippocratic Oath and Maimonides' Prayer. *Koroth*, 8 no. 5-6 (Fall 1982), pp. 248-258.
Criticism of H. Keller's "Comparison between Hippocratic Oath and Maimonides' Prayer" (1919, 1931).

145] תפילת יום יום של רופא. **בהרפואה לאור ההלכה**, בעריכת הרב זאב מצגר. ירושלים: המכון לחקר הרפואה בהלכה, תשמ״ב, עמ' כז-ל.

ונראה שהתרגום הוא מאת יהושע ליבוביץ.

1983

146] תפילת יום יום של רופא. בספרו של ברוך שטרסבורגר, **הרמב״ם — האיש ופועלו**. תל-אביב: הוצא לאור בסיוע מוזיאון "בית התפוצות", 1983. (בלי עימוד). תרגום של יהושע ליבוביץ.

1984

147] Orian, Meir, 1910-1979.
Maimonides. Vida, Pensamiento y Obra. Traducido del hebreo por Zeev Zvi Rosenfeld. Barcelona: Riopedras [1984?]. P. 270: La Plegaria.

1985

148] [Mangel, Nissen]
The Rambam; a brief biography. Brooklyn, NY: Merkos Linyonei Chinuch, 1985. Pp. 51-53: Oath for Physicians.

149] Unesce (Paris)
850e Anniversaire de la Naissance de Maimonide (1135-1204). Paris: 1985. P. 7: Priere de Moise Maimonide.

150] בעלענקי, משה, 1910-
דער רמב״ם (צום 850-סטן געבוירטס-טאג). **פאלקס-שטימע** (ורשה), נומער 11 (4718), מארץ 16, 1985, ז״י 6-7.
עמ' 6: תפילת הרופא ביודית.

1987

151] Minkin, Jacob J., 1885-1962.

The Teachings of Maimonides. Northvale, NJ: Jason Aronson, 1987, pp. 149-150. Reprinted from the 1957 edition under the title: *The World of Moses Maimonides*.

1991

152] The Physician's Prayer. In: *Six Treatises Attributed to Maimonides*. Translated by Fred Rosner. With Bibliographies by Jacob I. Dienstag. Northvale, NJ: Jason Aronson.

Part IV

SHA'ARE HAMUSAR
THE GATES OF MORAL INSTRUCTION

INTRODUCTION

The first mention I found of a "Last Will and Testament" of Moses Maimonides was in an appendix to the 1802 (5562) book *Lekach Tov* by Abraham Yagal, published in Warsaw. The title of the will is "A very beautiful moral instruction by Moses Maimonides to his son the Sage Rabbi Abraham." The same title was used in a collection of responsa and letters of Maimonides published in 1859 in which the will was reprinted.[1]

In 1852, Tzvi Hirsh Edelman published the last will of Rabbi Judah ibn Tibbon in a book entitled *Derech Tovim* ("The Path of Good Men"). That book also contains "The Last Will of Rabbi Moses Maimonides, addressed to his son Rabbi Abraham" in both Hebrew and English.[2] The editor's preface indicates that the English translation is by M. M. Bresslau. It was also reprinted in a New York publication, the *New Era*, in 1873.[3] The

---

[1]*Kovetz Teshuvot HaRambam VeIggrotav*, Leipzig, 1859 (5619) pp. 38–40. Reprinted in Jerusalem in 1967 (5727).

[2]T. H. Edelman, *The Path of Good Men*, London, 1852, pp. 25–33 (English) and pp. 16–19 (Hebrew).

[3]M. M. Bresslau, The Last Will of Rabbi Moses Maimonides, addressed to his son, Abraham (from *The Path of Good Men*). *New Era*, Vol. 3, pp. 446–447.

wills of Maimonides and of Rabbi Judah ibn Tibbon were also published in Zhitomir in 1865 by Eliezer Tzvi Tzvifel.[4]

In 1926, Israel Abrahams included "The Gate of Instruction Attributed to Maimonides" (*Sha'are HaMusar HaMeyuchas LehaRambam*) in his collection of Hebrew Ethical Wills[5] in Hebrew and English, although he had previously included an extract in 1891.[6] Abrahams points out that there are two testaments attributed to Maimonides. One, often described as Maimonides' Testament, is found in many libraries in manuscript form, and has often been reprinted since the first edition appeared in Venice in 1544.

> It is of polemical rather than of ethical interest, for it culminates in an ungracious, not to say abusive, denunciation of the French school of Jewish scholars. It is true that in other letters ascribed to Maimonides a similar tone is sometimes heard. Here and there, too, there are touches worthy of Maimonides, as this: "The perfect rest of the Sabbath is the attuning of the heart to the comprehension of God." Then, again, there is a circumstantial statement in a Bodleian Ms. (Cat. Neubauer No. 2386) to the following effect. The Testament was written in Arabic on two leaves by Maimonides; the said leaves were detached from the book containing them, soon after the philosopher's death; and the Testament was thereupon translated into Hebrew. There is no probability in the story. The most that can be urged for the document is that it may contain some authentic points. [*Steinschneider, Die Hebraeischen Uebersetzungen des Mittelalters*, Berlin, 1893 p. 931].

Because of this, Abrahams omits the document from his collection of *Hebrew Ethical Wills*. However, he did include the other version of Maimonides' last will and testament, even

---

[4] E. T. Tzvifel, *Mussar Av, Shney Michtavim* . . . Zhitomir; Shadow, 1865, 64 pp.

[5] I. Abrahams, *Hebrew Ethical Wills*. Philadelphia: Jewish Publication Society, 1926, pp. 101–116. Reprinted in 1976.

[6] I. Abrahams, Jewish Ethical Wills. *Jewish Quarterly Review*, 1891, Vol. 3, pp. 451–453.

INTRODUCTION 151

though it has no better claim to authenticity. However, continues Abrahams, it is a far finer work and deserves inclusion on its own merits.

> It was printed by Steinschneider and Edelman in the same volumes that contain Ibn Tibbon's Testament (see p. 53). In the Bodleian Ms. from which Steinschneider derived it, it is an introduction to the Testament mentioned above, and claims to be by Maimonides, . . . In 1852 Steinschneider was rather inclined to accept this ascription, but he afterwards withdrew his opinion (*HaMazkir*, ii, 8, iv, 107). For it turned out that the same text had been published anonymously under the title *Sefer HaMussar* in Cracow, in 1586. Moreover, L. Dukes discovered a Ms. of the text in the British Museum, entitled *Sha'are HaMussar el Hashalem Hassar Ish Romi*. This Ms. is written on the margin of fol. 137b, seg. of Harleian Ms. 5686. [pp. 101–102]

Abrahams hypothesizes that, although the manuscript is a fifteenth-century copy, it points to an older origin. In several places, the copyist must have had an old and faded manuscript before him, as he frequently was unable to read the original. It seems most probable, continues Abrahams, that the text is a product of the early thirteenth century and was thus written soon after Maimonides' death. The writer adopts several of the most prominent Maimonidean views, including the doctrines of free will and the mean or golden path. Abrahams concludes that the text is unmistakably not by Maimonides because the writer addresses his *children* in the plural, yet we know of only one child of Maimonides, his son Abraham.

The translation of the Hebrew title *Sha'are HaMussar* by Abrahams is "The Gates of Instruction." Alternate translations include "The Gates of Moral Instruction" or "The Portals of Discipline" or "The Gates of Exhortation."

In 1951, Simon Maurice Lehrman published English extracts of Maimonides' Last Will and Testament.[7] In 1955, Yehudah

---

[7] S. M. Lehrman, *The Jewish Design for Living*. London: Bachad Fellowship, 1951, pp. 329–332. Reprinted New York: Shengold, 1976.

Leib Maimon published a Hebrew version of the will[8] which he claims was reprinted from the 1909 Jerusalem edition of Shlomo Aharon Wertheimer's book *Zichron LaRishonim UleAcharonin*. Other early Hebrew versions include 1907 Warsaw and 1913 Pietrkow editions (see Dienstag's bibliography following this chapter).

In 1957, Jacob Minkin reprinted Israel Abrahams's English translation of Maimonides' Ethical Testament as an appendix to his (Minkin's) book *The World of Moses Maimonides*.[9] Minkin points out that scholars are divided on the authenticity of Maimonides testamentary letter to his son.

> Steinschneider, who first accepted the document as genuine, has afterwards recanted. Graetz found the instrument too diffuse and moralizing to measure up to the philosopher's known higher style of writing. What, however, set most critics against the authenticity of the Testament, is the fact that it is addressed to the writer's *children*, while Maimonides is known to have had only one child, his son Abraham, his other child, a daughter, having died in her infancy. [p. 421]

Nevertheless, continues Minkin, plausible as the arguments may seem, they are not in themselves sufficiently conclusive to dismiss the letter out of hand as spurious or inauthentic. Indeed, there is everything in the document to militate against such an assumption. The spirit of Maimonides as philosopher, theologian, and moral and ethical teacher, according to Minkin, is represented in almost every line and paragraph.

> His robust faith in God; his plea for justice, truth and righteousness; his exhortation to seek out the lowly and the downcast and not abash them by reason of one's gifts; his admonition not to become entangled in quarrels and arguments (*machlokot*) but practice forbearance in which is "true strength and real victory";

---

[8] Y. L. Maimon, *HaRam-Bamzal, Kovetz Torani-Mada'i*. Jerusalem: Mossad Harav Kook, 1955 (5715), pp. 41–45.

[9] J. Minkin, *The World of Moses Maimonides with Selections from His Writings*. New York and London: Yoseloff, 1957, pp. 421–427.

INTRODUCTION 153

his insistence upon the sanctity of one's word and verbal promise more binding than legal contracts or witnessed deeds, and, lastly, the philosophical reflections of the "Letter" on such matters as Free Will, the Golden Mean, etc.—how Maimonidean these things sound. [p. 421]

Minkin concludes that the "Letter" is indeed a human document of the highest value, containing all the elements of Maimonides' spiritual personality. Minkin also concludes that the "Letter" is addressed to Maimonides' "children" by which are meant his son Abraham and his offspring, for the religious and secular guidance of their lives.

In the Talmud[10] the plural term sons is often used to connote a single son or offspring in general. The Talmud[11] also states that he who raises a son in his home is as though he had begotten him. The same applies to one who teaches the Torah to the son of his neighbor.

The term "children" is often used in the sense of "disciples" or "learned men." For example, the Talmud[12] states that the disciples of the wise increase peace in the world, as it says, "And all thy children shall be taught of the Lord, and great shall be the peace of thy children."[13] Read not *thy children (banayich)* but *thy builders (bonayich)*, that is, learned men. See also the commentary of Rabbi Isaiah Pinto, known as *Harif*,[14] who states that *thy children* refers to the builders who impart knowledge and understanding in this world.

Finally, Maimonides himself, in the prefatory poem in his introduction to his *Commentary on the Mishnah*[15] uses the terms "children" and "sons" to connote "disciples" or "learned ones."

---

[10]*Baba Bathra* 143b.
[11]*Sanhedrin* 19b.
[12]*Berachot* 64a.
[13]Isaiah 54:13.
[14]I. Pinto, Commentary *Harif* in *Sefer Eyun Yaakov* by Jacob Habib on *Berachot* 64
[15]F. Rosner, *Moses Maimonides' Commentary on the Mishnah, Introduction to Seder Zeraim and Commentary on Tractate Berachot*. New York: Feldheim, 1975, pp. 37–38.

Hence, the use of the word *sons* in the *Last Will and Testament* cannot be used as evidence for or against the authenticity of this work as a Maimonidean writing.

In 1968, Leon Stitskin freely retranslated and edited into English Maimonides' *Last Will and Testament* in two parts,[16] which he entitled "Maimonides' Letter of Moral Instruction to his son Abraham." Nearly a decade later, Stitskin's two-part article was reprinted in his book *Letters of Maimonides*.[17] Stitskin does not even raise the possibility that the will is a forgery but assumes it to be authentic. Stitskin points out that in his *Last Will and Testament* to his son Abraham, Maimonides suggests that he would not have admonished his offspring to follow the established rules of conduct unless he had adequately prepared and trained him for their implementation in his childhood.

> Maimonides possessed an unequaled passion for the qualities of the human heart. Modesty and compassion were part of the generous qualities of his soul. All his severity was concentrated on himself; towards others he was of a most gentle amiability. His scorn he poured out only against false notions and feeble reasoning, but towards people he was forbearing and forgiving. The truths of Judaism, he held, could be exhibited and made convincing by their rational structure and also by the ethical behavior of its adherents. [p. 137]

According to Stitskin, in the first part of his last will to his son Abraham, Maimonides formulated a manual of intimate personal morality grounded in the metaphysical and psychological views expounded in his other works. The second part of the testament deals primarily with methodology, which, to Maimonides, was most crucial to any religio-philosophic enterprise.

In 1970, David Margalith reprinted the Hebrew version of

---

[16]L. D. Stitskin, Moses Maimonides. The Last Will and Testament of Maimonides. *Tradition*, Vol. 9 (Spring), 1968, pp. 80–90 and Vol. 10 (Winter), 1968, pp. 121–130.

[17]L. D. Stitskin, *Letters of Maimonides*. New York: Yeshiva University Press, 1977, pp. 137–158.

INTRODUCTION

Maimonides' Last Will and Testament[18] together with the title page of the 1802 book by Yagal entitled *Lekach Tov* (see above) that contains the will as an appendix. Margalith describes the two versions of the will and concludes, as do Steinschneider and Abrahams, that the *Last Will and Testament* of Maimonides is a spurious work but worthy of being studied. Margalith states that its style differs from the style of Maimonides' *Guide of the Perplexed* and other works "like the distance from East to West."

The *Last Will and Testament* continues to be reprinted in collections of Maimonides' letters and responsa[19] and a complete bibliography by Jacob Dienstag follows the new English translation. The latter is fully annotated and is based on the scholarly Hebrew version of Abrahams[20] already described. Words in brackets are my own additions to help clarify the meaning of the text.

---

[18]D. Margalith, *Derech Yisroel Birefuah*. Jerusalem: Academy of Medicine, 1970, pp. 197–204.

[19]*Iggrot Uteshuvot lehanesher hagadol Rabenu Moshe ben Maimon HaSefardi (Rambam)*. Jerusalem: Levin-Epstein, 1968 (5728), pp. 1–11.

[20]See Note 5.

THE GATES OF MORAL INSTRUCTION

I will bless the Lord who gave me counsel[1] and led me in the path of truth.[2] I will mention His benevolence according to all that He has bestowed upon me.[3] He has chastened me sore but has not given me over to death.[4] He held me by my right hand[5] and hid me in the shadow of His hand.[6] He delivered me from the burdens of the [turning] wheel of life and saved me from its vicissitudes. He refined me in the melting pot of time and cleansed me from the darkness of my youth.[7] He saved me[8] from backsliding and gave me tranquility from the conflict[9] of my impulses. He rebuked the serpent that enticed me and gave

---

[1] Psalm 16:7.
[2] Genesis 24:48.
[3] Isaiah 63:7.
[4] Psalm 118:18.
[5] Psalm 73:23. Steinschneider's version substitutes "in our days" (Hebrew: *beyomaymu*) for "my right hand" (Hebrew: *biyemini*).
[6] Isaiah 49:2.
[7] Abrahams adds the following explanatory footnote: cleansed him from the faults of youth.
[8] Literally: separated me.
[9] Literally: war. Steinschneider's version has "wars."

me sweetness[10] to taste. He raised me from the dust and sat me with princes.[11] The passage of days has taught me,[12] experience has made me wise, and time has chastened me. Until now, He has blessed me[13] and preserved me. He has granted me understanding greater than others and enabled me to distinguish between good and evil. He has made me aware that my end is in His hand but I do not know how long or how short-lived I am![14] Therefore, His love has inspired me[15] to admonish the children whom he graciously bestowed upon me, that they observe the way of the Lord. And I will teach them that which He taught me and bequeath to them the heritage that He bequeathed to me, before He calls me and His glory gathers me.[16]

Hearken to me, my children! "Blessed are you of the Lord who made heaven and earth;[17] with blessings of heaven above, blessings of the deep that couches beneath, blessings of the breast and of the womb."[18] Be strong and show yourselves men![19] Fear the Lord[20] the God of your father,[21] the God of Abraham, Isaac, and Jacob, and serve Him with a perfect heart,

---

[10] The British Museum text has "bitterness and sweetness." Abrahams states that one should here add the phrase "of contentment."

[11] 1 Samuel 2:8.

[12] Alternate translation: has impregnated me.

[13] Joshua 17:41. Abrahams cites the reference incorrectly as Joshua 17:4.

[14] Psalm 39:5. That is, the time of my death is unknown to me.

[15] Steinschneider's version has "will inspire me."

[16] Abrahams adds the following explanatory footnote: To Himself, or as E. takes it "to my fathers." The text (Isaiah 58:8) is applied to death in the Babylonian Talmud *Sotah* 9b (see also Kimchi's commentary on Isaiah *ad loc.*). Besides the references given, there are in this introduction several other biblical allusions which are not direct quotations, since the author sometimes paraphrases, sometimes alters for his rhymes, sometimes modifies by the introduction of post-biblical phraseology. But the result is a singularly fine specimen of the "mosaic" type of composition.

[17] Psalm 115:15.

[18] Genesis 49:25.

[19] 1 Kings 2:2. The actual quote is: "be strong and show yourself a man" in the singular. The British Museum manuscript omits this phrase.

[20] Psalm 34:10.

[21] The British Museum manuscript has "fathers."

from fear[22] and from love. For fear brings restraint[23] from sin, and love brings diligence[24] to meritorious deeds. Know that He brings all to judgment, for what is revealed and for what is hidden, for good and for evil.[25] He who performs good deeds[26] is rewarded in this world. Those who see him glorify him and those who know him[27] declare him blessed. And when he reaches a ripe old age[28] and he departs from his fellow men,[29] he rejoices in the worthiness of his work and finds comfort. And he is not greatly pained[30] by the [fear of] death because he is not worried about retribution. Rather, he anticipates the good reward, to see the good that is treasured up[31] for those who fear the Lord, and his house is established forever.

But if a person corrupts his way and pursues evil, the evil pursues him and overtakes him and corrupts his activities [even further]. Those that see him despise him[32] and mock him[33] [in his lifetime], and in his death "his flesh grieves for him and his soul mourns over him."[34] For he departs[35] into darkness and his name is covered with darkness.[36] And he shall lean upon his house and it shall not stand."[37]

---

[22]Steinschneider omits "from fear."
[23]Hebrew: *zehirut*.
[24]Hebrew: *zerizut*. Steinschneider reads in both cases *zerizut* whereas the British Museum manuscript reads in both cases *zehirut*.
[25]Ecclesiastes 12:14.
[26]Alternate translation: he who leads a good life.
[27]The British Museum manuscript omits "glorify him and those who know him."
[28]Literally: when the number of his days is full.
[29]Literally: from the children of men.
[30]Steinschneider has "worried."
[31]Literally: concealed.
[32]Literally: pervert him with their mouths.
[33]Literally: their lips will mock him.
[34]Job 14:22.
[35]Hebrew: *yelech*, literally: will go. The British Museum manuscript has *holech* meaning "goes" in the present tense.
[36]Ecclesiastes 6:4.
[37]Job 8:15. Abrahams points out that "in the previous verse, the house of

I beseech you to recognize the superiority of light over darkness.[38] Despise death and evil and choose life and the good,[39] for free choice is given to you.[40] Habituate yourself to righteous conduct[41] because the nature of man is related to habit, and habit becomes established in his nature.

Know that perfection of the body precedes perfection of the soul and the former is like a key that unlocks [the gates of] a palace.[42] Therefore, the main intent behind my moral message about the perfection of the body and the purification[43] of the soul is to open the gates of heaven for you. Conduct yourselves with seriousness and with honor.[44] Avoid the company of the wanton and [avoid] sitting in the streets and playing with the young for the fruit that emanates therefrom is evil. Be found always among the great[45] and the learned[46] but [act] with humility and with submissiveness and [occupy] the lower seats.[47] Incline the ears of[48] your head and open the ears of your heart to hear and to understand[49] their words and what they denounce and what they praise. Weigh[50] their opinions carefully[51] and thus you will become wise. Guard your mouth

---

the wicked is likened to a spider's web for frailty and that there are throughout this part of the Testament reminiscences of the Choice of Pearls."

[38] Ecclesiastes 2:13.
[39] Deuteronomy 30:19.
[40] *Abot* 3:15.
[41] Literally: good characteristics.
[42] Hebrew: *teraklin*, literally: reception room, salon, parlor, or inner chamber.
[43] Alternate translation: perfection.
[44] Abrahams translates: gravity and decency.
[45] Job 15:10.
[46] The British Museum manuscript has "honorable."
[47] Abrahams points out that in olden times, the disciple sat on the ground. See *Abot* 1:4 and *Megillah* 21a. See also Matthew 23:6.
[48] Steinschneider omits "the ears of."
[49] Steinschneider substitutes "to listen."
[50] Following a different punctuation, Steinschneider has "weigh what they denounce and what they praise."
[51] Literally: little by little.

and your tongue from entreating them excessively.[52] Measure your words with judgment[53] for the more your words, the more your errors.[54] Do not be supercilious or conceited before them, but do not be ashamed to ask about that which is unclear to you, but [do so] at the proper time[55] and in appropriate language. Ponder and weigh the matter before you utter it[56] because you cannot withdraw it [afterwards].

Love wisdom, seek her as silver and search for her as for hidden treasures.[57] Gather in the homes of the wise, those who learn[58] and those who teach. Thereto should be your excursions and rejoice there in listening to the sciences[59] and moral instructions and novel interpretations and analytical reasoning[60] of the students. Emulate[61] those with knowledge[62] and despise the boorish in your heart. When you ask or answer a question, do not [speak] hastily and do not [speak] in obscurity and do not shout and do not speak with stammering lips.[63] Speak using choice language and purity[64] of language with a calm voice[65] and directly to the point,[66] like one who seeks to learn and discover the truth, not as one who seeks to win an argument. Stay there[67] willingly[68] and try[69] to extract benefit

---

[52] Literally: from entreating matters before them.
[53] Alternate translation: Condense your words into one sentence.
[54] Steinschneider substitutes "claims."
[55] The British Museum manuscript adds "and with wisdom."
[56] Literally: before you let it out of your mouths.
[57] Proverbs 2:4.
[58] The British Museum manuscript omits "those who learn."
[59] Alternate translation: wisdoms.
[60] Hebrew: *pilpulim*. Abrahams translates "ingenious arguments." See *Nedarim* 38a.
[61] Literally: be jealous of.
[62] The British Museum manuscripts substitutes "the students."
[63] Isaiah 28:11.
[64] The British Museum manuscript substitutes "weightiness."
[65] The British Museum manuscript omits "with a calm voice."
[66] Literally: with contemplation of the matters.
[67] In the house of study.
[68] Steinschneider substitutes "with your will."
[69] Literally: consider, reflect.

therefrom; then study will be pleasant and easy for you. But if you let your heart wander[70] here and there, you lose the main value of your attendance for you learn nothing[71] and the confinement weighs heavily on you and afflicts your body.[72] When you depart [the house of study], realize what you are taking home, engrave it in your brain, and bind it to your heart.

Learn in your youth when you eat what others prepare, when your mind[73] is still free and before it becomes filled with thoughts and [before] the power of memory weakens. For the time will come when you will want to learn but will be unable to do so. And even that which you are able to acquire will require much effort with little benefit because the mind lags behind the mouth,[74] and even that [knowledge] which you acquire will not be sustained but forgotten.

Behold, my moral instruction is committed into your hand,[75] there is great benefit therein when you study it to strengthen the faith,[76] to settle the mind, and to dispel confusion. When you find a deep verse or a perplexing saying in the Torah or Prophets or books of the Sages that you do not understand and cannot comprehend its hidden meaning, and it appears as if it contradicts the cornerstones of the Torah or represents vain words, do not budge from your faith and do not let your mind be confounded. Stand fast in your strength and attribute that deficiency [in understanding] to yourselves, "for it is no vain thing"[77] but [the deficiency stems] from you.[78] Place it in a

---

[70] Literally: send your hearts.

[71] Literally: you will not learn.

[72] Alternate version: and it weighs heavily on you like an affliction confined in the body.

[73] Literally: heart.

[74] Literally: the heart cannot chase the mouth.

[75] The British Museum manuscript has "behold, there is committed to your hand the moral instruction . . ."

[76] Alternate version as given by Steinschneider: "to confirm the truth."

[77] Deuteronomy 32:47. See also the Jerusalem Talmud *Peah* 1:1.

[78] Steinschneider omits the words "but from" so that the verse corresponds exactly to the biblical phrase in Deuteronomy 32:47. Abrahams points out that Maimonides, in his *Guide of the Perplexed*, Part 3, chapter 26, cites this use of the test in Deuteronomy 32:47: "The giving of these commandments

corner[79] and do not detest your entire faith because of your lack of understanding of a [single] matter of wisdom.[80] "God understands the way thereof and He knows its place."[81]

Love truth and righteousness[82] and cleave to them for you will succeed in them and that success will endure[83] as if it were built on the rock foundation of flint.[84] Hate falsehood and injustice and do not covet their savory delicacies, for the latter [behavior] is like building[85] on sand[86] and about those [who so behave] Scripture states: "say unto those who daub a wall with white plaster, that it shall fall."[87]

Therefore, let truth and righteousness[88] be more pleasant to you, even if it seems that you lose from them,[89] than falsehood and injustice, even if it seems that you profit from them.[90] So, too, did the Sage say in his moral instruction: "Buy the truth, and sell it not."[91] Know that truth and righteousness are adornments of the soul and they give strength, confidence, and permanence to the body. I have not found a remedy for weakness of the heart[92] like a combination of truth and

---

[whose object is not clear] is not a vain thing and without useful purpose, and if it appears so to you in any commandment, it is owing to the deficiency in your comprehension."

[79] Abrahams cites the Talmud (*Kiddushin* 66a) where this phrase is used. Here, he continues, the sense is: "set it apart for further thought."

[80] Abrahams translates: "because you are incompetent to solve a single problem of philosophy." The British Museum manuscript has: "that matter or a single [matter of] wisdom."

[81] Job 28:23.

[82] Alternate translation: truth and justice.

[83] Steinschneider omits "will endure."

[84] Deuteronomy 8:15. That is, built on a sure rock.

[85] The British Museum manuscript has "built."

[86] Abrahams refers the reader to *Abot* de Rabbi Nathan 1:24, to Matthew 7:24–27 and to I. Abrahams, *Studies in Pharisaism*, p. 92.

[87] Ezekiel 13:11.

[88] Alternate translation: truth and justice.

[89] Steinschneider substitutes "it."

[90] Steinschneider substitutes "it."

[91] Proverbs 23:23.

[92] Abrahams states that the sense of this phrase here is "timidity." See Deuteronomy 20:8.

righteousness. Nor did I feel secure in the company of friends or in [the deep canyons of] Ashterot Karnayim, or [protected by the] javelin or coat of mail, as [I did wearing] the helmet of truth and the shield or righteousness.[93]

And it shall come to pass on the day when I will bequeath to you that which the Creator has graciously bestowed upon me,[94] I will bequeath to you the faithfulness through which the Creator enabled me to possess all this wealth, for with my staff I crossed over[95] to gain the daily bread and its drink offering,[96] and behold, the Lord has blessed me until now. Faithfulness gave me admission to places where my relatives could not admit me and caused me to possess that which my fathers did not leave me as an inheritance. It made me rule over greater and better men than I and it gave me prosperity and benefited me and others besides me.

Therefore, be careful therein, even with one of whom the Torah does not enjoin to seek his peace.[97] Stand by[98] your words. Let not a legal deed or witnesses or possessions be stronger in your eyes than your verbal promise, whether in public or in private. Reject and disdain deep reservations, cunning subterfuges, tricky pretexts, sharp practices, and flaws and evasions.[99] Woe unto him who builds his house upon them, for [he who gets riches and not by right] shall leave them in the midst of his days and at his end he shall be impious.[100] Live by

---

[93]The British Museum manuscript is defective here. Abrahams translates according to Genesis 26:26 as interpreted by the Targum. He also points out that Ashterot Karnayim, situated east of the Jordan in a deep dale between two hills, was a completely sheltered spot. See *Sukkah* 2a.

[94]Steinschneider substitutes: "that which the Creator has caused me to inherit."

[95]Allusion to Genesis 32:11.

[96]Allusion to Numbers 15:24, 28:7, 28:9, 28:15, 28:24, and more.

[97]Here Abrahams adds in a footnote that "the Talmud has a beautiful term for those aspects of morality which are not susceptible of legal definition: They are described as "matters given over to man's heart" (see for example, *Baba Metzia* 58b)."

[98]The British Museum manuscript adds: "and fulfill."

[99]Repudiate fraudulent, sly, and underhanded practices.

[100]Jeremiah 17:11 In a footnote Abrahams adds here that "the terms used

purity, integrity, and innocence.[101] Do not touch that which is not yours, be it a small or a great matter. Do not taste the least from that which is not clearly and decidedly yours. Flee from doubtful possessions and treat them as the possessions of others.[102] Know that the tasting[103] of doubtful things leads to indifference[104] about [tasting] the certain, the little to the much, the inadvertent to the designed,[105] until one becomes a [hardened and confirmed] cheat, liar, thief, and robber from whom people flee.[106] The one who buys from him will not rejoice and the one who sells to him will not mourn.[107] He will be ashamed in his life and confounded in his death. I have seen all this and put it to my heart. He who conceives chaff brings forth stubble,[108] but he who sows in righteousness reaps in kindness.[109] Ennoble yourself with your moral values and be satisfied with your faithfulness because there is no nobility like that of morality and there is no inheritance like faithfulness.[110]

Bring near those that are far off. Bow to the lowly.[111] Cause your countenance to shine upon the humble. Have compassion upon the destitute and the oppressed. Let them share in your

---

by the author in explanation refer literally to the commodities about which the duty of tithing is doubtful or certain."

[101] The British Museum manuscript substitutes "be pure, upright, and innocent."

[102] Alternate translation: establish them firmly in the possession of those they belong to.

[103] The British Museum manuscript substitutes "touching."

[104] Alternate translation: "weariness."

[105] Literally: "the hidden to the revealed."

[106] Steinschneider substitutes: "flee from such a person."

[107] Allusion to Ezekiel 7:12.

[108] Allusion to Isaiah 33:11.

[109] Allusion to Hosea 10:12. Abrahams points out in a footnote that "the quotations are slightly modified by the author to suit the structure of his sentence."

[110] Abrahams, referring to a quotation in Ben Jehudah's *Millon*, 2025a, translates slightly differently: "let your moral life be your pride of lineage, and your loyalty to truth your sufficient wealth, for there is no pedigree as noble as virtue, no heritage equal to honor."

[111] Literally: little ones.

joy and have them participate[112] in your festivals according to the good hand of the Lord upon you.[113] Be careful not to shame them in that their faces blush by reason of your gifts. Do not cease doing good to whomever you can and beware of doing evil[114] to anyone.

Despise idleness and abhor ease for these are causes of the destruction of the body, of want, of penury, of perversity, of crookedness of the mouth, and perverseness of the lips. These [evils] are the ladder to Satan and his servants, and these constitute the pernicious fruits of sloth whereas in all labor there is profit.[115]

Do not make your souls abominable[116] by quarrelsomeness that destroys the body, the soul, and the property,[117] and what else remains? I have seen the white become black, the low brought even lower, families torn asunder, princes deposed from their greatness, great cities laid in ruins, assemblies dispersed, pious men destroyed, men of faith lost, and honorable men held in low esteem and disparaged—all because of quarrelsomeness. Prophets have prophesied, wise men have said wise things, and philosophers have searched—all have dwelt and enlarged upon the evils of quarrelsomeness but they have not exhausted the subject.[118] Therefore, hate it and flee from it. Distance yourself from all its friends, supporters, and admirers. Even if your own flesh and blood[119] are among the lovers of strife, be like a stranger to them, and distance your

---

[112] Literally: count them.
[113] Allusion to Ezra 8:18.
[114] Steinschneider omits "of doing evil."
[115] Proverbs 14:23.
[116] Leviticus 11:43.
[117] Literally: money.
[118] Literally: did not reach its end. Abrahams adds in a footnote that "the evils of contention and faction are a fertile theme of Jewish moralists of all epochs. Our author writes with a heat patently due to personal experience. If the author be indeed Maimonides, his denunciation is prophetic of what occurred after his death, and in connection with his philosophical writings. But the ascription of the Testament to Maimonides is highly improbable."
[119] Allusion to Leviticus 18:6.

relationship,[120] lest you be consumed in all their sins.[121] Glory in forbearance because that is the real strength and the true victory; for if you seek revenge, perhaps you may not attain it and your heart will become sick by hope deferred[122] and you may add shame[123] to your disgrace like one who rolls a stone[124] that returns unto him.[125] And even if you attain [the revenge you sought], behold, you have sinned against the Lord[126] and know that your sin will find you out.[127] [It will cause] hatred, a vindictive heart, confusion of the mind, troubled sleep, interruption of work,[128] and exposure of faults and failings.[129] It also gives rise to degeneration of appearance and speech, destruction of the soul, a devouring jealousy, the disturbance of family peace,[130] and, in the end, remorse.

Therefore, recognize the value of forbearance.[131] Sanctify yourselves and you will be holy[132] in the eyes of your enemies. Those who injured you will feel remorse, and your soul will be great in their eyes. They will repent and will better their heart[133] if they are indeed men of heart. But if they are base people[134] they will be pained and vexed that you are not as despicable as they are in doing what they do, and you will reign over them with the crown of morality. Conduct yourselves with

---

[120]That is, ignore or remove your relationship.
[121]The British Museum manuscript has "your sin." The allusion is to Numbers 16:26 concerning the story of Korach.
[122]Allusion to Proverbs 13:12.
[123]The British Museum manuscript omits the word "shame."
[124]Alternate version: "because he who rolls a stone."
[125]Allusion to Proverbs 26:27.
[126]Deuteronomy 9:16 and Jeremiah 40:3 and 44:23.
[127]Numbers 32:23.
[128]Steinschneider has "confusion of work."
[129]Literally: blemishes.
[130]Steinschneider adds "to accuse others of committing sins and inducing others to sin."
[131]The British Museum manuscript substitutes "the intellect."
[132]Allusion to Leviticus 11:44 and 20:7.
[133]The British Museum manuscript substitutes "will better themselves."
[134]Literally: people of Beliyal. Allusion to 1 Kings 21:13.

humility for it is the ladder to ascend to the topmost heights;[135] if you have this[136] quality of humility, forbearance is not necessary. Know that there is no ornament like humility. Behold[137] the Master of the prophets was not so distinguished [in Scripture] for any of his good[138] qualities as for that of humility.[139] Keep a muzzle upon your mouth and a bridle upon your tongue.[140] Know that God bestowed the faculty of speech upon man because He loved him above all other creatures; thereby he can lust for understanding. And [through the gift of speech] it is good to give thanks to God[141] and to extol Him and declare His wonders, and to meditate in the Torah, to learn and to teach, and to promote peace between man and his fellow man.[142] Therefore, it is improper to convert good to evil[143] and to speak obscenity, falsehood, and slander[144] because it is an iniquity [to be punished by judges].[145]

Subject matter to mind,[146] that is to say the body to the soul, for this subjection is your freedom in this world and in the hereafter. Therefore, [as to the body], "further not its evil device"[147] for ministering to its cravings increases its demand and it[148] will never be satisfied until it yearns for that which it cannot attain, and ultimately the divine element perishes with it. But if the [rational] mind[149] rules and the body is subservient

---

[135]The British Museum manuscript substitutes "the ladder whose steps you can climb to the heights" (of virtue and morality).

[136]Literally: with this.

[137]The British Museum manuscript substitutes: "Moses who is called."

[138]Steinschneider omits the word "good."

[139]Numbers 12:3.

[140]Psalm 39:1.

[141]Psalm 92:2.

[142]Steinschneider omits from "and to meditate . . ." until here.

[143]Allusion to Leviticus 27:10.

[144]The British Museum manuscript adds here "and words of nonsense."

[145]Allusion to Job 31:11.

[146]Alternate translation: subject the material (or physical) substance to the spiritual.

[147]Psalm 140:9.

[148]Abrahams suggests that "it" might be rendered "he" and the pronouns thus refer to man, or the physical part of man.

[149]That is, the spiritual part of man.

and humbled, man will seek only that which is necessary[150] and he will be satisfied with little and disdain superfluities;[151] he will be contented with life and comforted in death.

Eat that you may live and ban that which is superfluous. Do not believe that abundance of food and drink strengthens[152] the body and sharpens[153] the mind, as a sack that is filled by what is put therein; it is just the opposite. If you eat [only a] little, the stomach has the strength to receive it[154] and the natural [body] heat to digest it.[155] Thus will a man grow in physical health and his mind will be calm and settled.[156] But if he eats more than enough the stomach cannot receive it and the natural body heat cannot digest it; it will come out before him.[157] "It is an abomination, it shall not be accepted."[158] His body will become emaciated and his intellect will be dulled and his purse will become emptied. Be careful that you not eat to the point where you cannot digest because [overeating] destroys the body and the purse[159] for it is the cause of most maladies. Exercise before you eat[160] and rest after you have eaten.[161] Do not eat ravenously like people afflicted with bulimia.[162] Do not fill your mouth like a glutton with large pieces, one upon the other.[163]

---

[150]Steinschneider substitutes: "if his evil device is humbled, he will seek only that which is necessary."

[151]Excesses, or luxuries.

[152]Literally: enlarges.

[153]Literally: increases.

[154]That is, absorb, digest, and assimilate the food.

[155]The British Museum manuscript substitutes: "to tolerate it."

[156]Abrahams translates: "a man's vigor and health increase and his mind becomes clear and calm."

[157]? Emesis or diarrhea.

[158]Leviticus 19:7.

[159]This sentence is not translated by Abrahams.

[160]See Chapter 4 of Maimonides' *Hilchot De'ot* in his *Mishneh Torah*, where he discusses exercises in relation to meals.

[161]The British Museum manuscript omits this clause.

[162]Abrahams cites the Talmud (*Yoma* 8:6) where this term is used. It is a word derived from the Greek and refers to a ravenous appetite.

[163]Abrahams translates: "do not fill your mouth gulp after gulp without breathing space."

Hate injurious food as a man would hate his foe who seeks to kill him.[164] Do not eat in public places[165] and do not nibble[166] incessantly[167] like rats, but at fixed hours and in your homes.[168] Avoid feasting often with young men. Know that at public dinners the behavior of a man becomes known, whether good or bad. Many times I returned to my house hungry and thirsty because I was afraid after I saw the disgraceful conduct of others. Beware of wine, which destroys the mighty and disgraces the honored. How excellent[169] in my eyes is the injunction of Jonadab to his sons.[170] But I will not give a similar injunction because I did not accustom you [to complete abstinence from wine] from your earliest years.[171] Rather, break its strength with water and drink it by way of nourishment and not by way of [mere] enjoyment.[172] Consider,[173] not in vain was the shame of the righteous Noah recorded [in Scripture];[174] but [it was recorded] to serve as a moral teaching.

Know that expenditure is divided into four categories: profit, loss, aversion, honor. Profit is [involvement in] acts of loving kindness, the interest of which you enjoy [in this world] while the capital remains [as an endowment in the world to come].[175] Loss is gambling by which man loses his money, his dignity, and

---

[164]Steinschneider has: "his neighbor who hates him and seeks to kill him."
[165]Literally: on the roads.
[166]Literally: eat.
[167]Steinschneider omits the word *incessantly*.
[168]Abrahams cites the Talmud (*Kiddushin* 40b) in support of this position. Elsewhere (*Pesachim* 49a) the Talmud speaks against dining out.
[169]Literally: good.
[170]See Jeremiah 35:6–10. The sons of Jonadab, the son of Rechab, were commanded by their father to abstain from wine. Abrahams points out that this sentiment is contrary to that expressed by Maimonides in his *Eight Chapters*.
[171]Literally: from the beginning of your creation.
[172]Literally: luxury.
[173]Literally: observe or see. The British Museum manuscript substitutes: "Know."
[174]Genesis 9:21.
[175]*Mishnah Peah* 1:1.

his time. Even if he wins[176] "he weaves a spider's web";[177] "it is a trespass, he is certainly guilty."[178] Aversion is the [extravagant expenditure] on food.[179] Honor is the expenditure on wearing-apparel for his skin;[180] therefore, one should dress according to one's means.[181] But eat less than you can afford, just sufficient to sustain your lives. Despise gambling and distance yourself from gamblers. Sow in righteousness[182] beyond your means and reap according to kindness.[183]

Live happily with your partner, the wife of your young manhood,[184] but do not touch the one that is not yours,[185] "for she has caused the downfall of many; yea—a mighty host are all her slain."[186] Imagine as if you lived in Noah's ark, and be comforted. Even with your [wife, conduct yourself] with order and judgment[187] to raise offspring and to propagate the human race. When the burning fire [of sexual desire] overtakes you, extinguish it. The wise combats it and satisfies it only when necessary and derives benefit therefrom.[188] Allow it to pursue you but you should not pursue it. Honor your wives for they are your honor. Do not withhold moral instruction from them but let them not rule over you. Their honor is to remain within

---

[176] Literally: if he profits.
[177] Isaiah 59:5.
[178] Leviticus 5:19.
[179] Literally: that which is eaten.
[180] Exodus 22:26.
[181] Here Abrahams refers the reader to the Talmud, *Chullin* 84b, where Rabbi Yochanan said that if a person inherits a fortune from his parents, he can wear linen garments, especially Roman linen, which Rashi interprets to be very expensive.
[182] Hosea 10:12.
[183] Hosea 10:12.
[184] Abrahams points out in a footnote that this combination of the society of friends and the love of wife, as conditions of a happy life, is directly derived from Maimonides' *Guide of the Perplexed*, Part 3, Chapter 49.
[185] Abrahams translates: "Remember the warnings of Scripture against unchastity."
[186] Proverbs: 7:26.
[187] That is, not promiscuously.
[188] Abrahams translates as follows: "Never excite desire, and when in the course of nature it comes upon you, satisfy it in the manner ordained by moral rule, to raise up offspring, and perpetuate the human race."

the palace,[189] the less visible, the less damaging.[190] Do not reveal to them all the secrets placed in your keeping.[191] Serve those who love you and your relatives[192] with your person and your substance[193] according to the good hand of the Lord upon you.[194] But be extremely careful lest you serve them with your soul, because that is the divine portion.[195]

---

[189] Psalm 45:14, often used by moralists to typify the home as the woman's sphere.

[190] Abrahams does not translate the latter phrase. An alternate translation is: "the less they are exposed, the less they are injured."

[191] Literally: mysteries of your heart. Abrahams cited Micah 7:8 here.

[192] Alternate translation: those near unto you.

[193] Literally: your body and your might.

[194] Ezra 7:9 and 8:18 and Nehemiah 2:8.

[195] In his final footnote, Abrahams states: "a fine caution, finely expressed. Ardent devotion to the cause of one's family and friends may tempt one to sacrifice ideals. See the Sifra on Leviticus 19:3 and the Talmud, *Baba Metzia* 32a. Closely parallel to some of the sentiments in the latter sections of this testament are the views of Maimonides as expressed in the *Guide*, chapters 8, 38, and 48 of part 3, and in the passages cited there by Maimonides in cross-reference to his other works."

BIBLIOGRAPHY

by Jacob I. Dienstag

א. צוואה המיוחסת להרמב"ם — מקור ותרגום *

רע"ז לערך 1517

1] תשובות שאלות ואגרות המאור הגדול הנר המערבי מרנא ורבנא רבינו משה המימוני זצ"ל שבאו אליו ממזרח וממערב מצפון ומים מחכמי צרפת וספרד ותימן ובבל. קושטנטינא רע"ז לערך 24 דאף. או"ר.

דף ב, א-ב (ספירת עמודים ראשונה).

שנת הדפוס ע"פ א. יערי, הדפוס העברי בקושטא (תשכ"ז), מספר 87.

ש"ד 1544

2] אגרות להמאור הגדול... רבינו משה המימוני זצ"ל, שבאו אליו... מחכמי צרפת, וספרד, ותימן, ובבל, ודברי מוסר וצוואה שצוה... לבנו החכם רבי אברהם ז"ל ושאלות ששאל מהרב... ותשובותיו עליהן. ויניציאה: בבית וואני די פארי ואחיו, ש"ד 1544. צ"ה דף. 8°.

דף ב,א-ה,ב:

ש"ה 1545

3] אגרות להמאור הגדול... רבינו משה המימוני ותשובותיו... ויניציאה: קורניליו אדילקינד, ש"ה 1545. צ"ה דף.

דף ב,א-ה,ב: צוואה.

שמ"ו 1586

4] דברי מוסר חכמים. בסוף **אגרת התשובה** לר' יונה גירונדי, קראקא, שמ"ו. 8°. ללא מספור עמודים.

נדפס פה בהעלם שם המחבר. והוא הנוסח החדש של הצוואה ששטיינשניידר

הוציא ע"פ כתב יד אוקספורד בלי לדעת אדות דפוס קראקא, ולכן חזר בו מהשערתו
שהרמב"ם הוא מחבר הצוואה. ראה להלן: תרי"ב 1852.

שפ"ט 1629

5] In: Johann Buxtorf, *Institutio Epistolaris Hebraica, Sive de conscribendis epistolis Hebraicis liber*, Basileae: Sumptibus Ludovici Regis, 1629, pp. 437-443. בעברית.

ראשי תיבות: חמ"ד, חסר מקום דפוס; חש"מ, חסר שם מדפיס; חש"ד, חסר שנת דפוס; חמוש"ד, חסר מקום ושנת דפוס.

תכ"ה 1665

6] אגרות להמאור הגדול... רבינו משה המיימוני זצ"ל... הובא אל הדפוס פעם שלישית על יד... כמהר"ר משה חיים צלח נר"ו מתושבי ירושלים... ויניציאה: דפוס וינדראמינה, [תכ"ה 1665]. [56] דף. 16°.
ללא מספור עמודים.

תע"ב 1712

7] אגרות ושאלות ותשובות להמאור הגדול... רבינו משה המיימוני זצ"ל... אמשטרדם: בדפוס שלמה בן יוסף פרופס. [תע"ב 1712]. 8°. (1), נח דף. דף א,א-ג,א: אגרת לר' אברהם בנו.

תפ"ו 1726

8] אגרת תשובת רמב"ם ז"ל... וגם העתקנו פה כל הכתבים של הס' נובלות החכמה... פראג: המחוקקים נכדי ר' משה כ"ץ [תפ"ו 1726]. א' מרובע. דף א,ב-ג,א: אגרת לר' אברהם בנו.

תקכ"ד 1764

9] כתב מאת רבינו רמב"ם ז"ל ליד בנו הנחמד לו הר"ר אברהם ז"ל. **בכתבי קדש**... להראות... יקר מליצת... רבינו משה מיימוני, והמדקדק... ר' דוד קמחי ורבינו נחמן ורבינו בחיי, ודברי... ר' שמואל אבן תבון וזולתם... ברלין: איציג שפייער, תקכ"ד 1764. 8°. ללא מספור עמודים.

תקל"ב 1772

10] כתב מאת ר' משה ב"מ ליד בנו הנחמד לו הר"ר אברהם ז"ל. **בכתבי קדש** להרמב"ם... זאלקווא: דוד ב"ר מנחם מן וגיסו חיים דוד ב"ר אהרן הלוי סגל. [תקל"ב 1772], קרוב לסוף. ללא מספור עמודים.

תקנ"ה 1795

11] אגרת ושאלות ותשובות להמאור הגדול... רבינו משה המיימוני... וצוואה שצוה הרב... לבנו החכם... הוראדנא (חש"מ). תקנ"ה 1795(?). 8°. בראשו. ללא מספור עמודים וכותרת. אותיות רש"י.

תקנ"ז 1797

12] אגרת מהרמב"ם ז"ל לבנו החכם ר' אברהם זצ"ל. באגרת תשובת רמב"ם ז"ל... בדין: יאזעף קארל ניימאנן, תקנ"ז 1797, דף א,ב-ב,ב.

תקס"ז 1807

13] כתב מאת רבינו מב"מ ליד בנו הנחמד לו הר"ר אברהם ז"ל. כתבי קדש להרמב"ם. [ווילנא], חש"מ, תקס"ז. ללא מספור עמודים. 12°.

תרי"ב 1852

14] מוסר נאה מאד מהרמב"ם ז"ל להרב החכם ר' אברהם בנו ז"ל. בצוואת ר' יהודה אבן תבון, וצוואת הרמב"ם, ומשלי חכמים. הוציאם לאור ראשונה... מאת אוצרות כ"י אוקספורד... משה שטיינשניידער. בערלין תר"ב [צל: תרי"ב], עמ' 16-20. שער לועזי:

Ermahnunungsschreiben des Jehuda Ibn Tibbon... des Moses Maimonides an seinen Sohn Abraham und Sprueche der Weisen... aus Bodlejanischen Handschriften zum erstenmal herausgegeben, mit einer deutschen Charkteristik und biographischen Skizze begleitet von M. Steinschneider. Berlin: A. Asher, 1852.

נוסחאה אחרת לגמרי ואין בה הבקורת על חכמי צרפת והשבחים על ר' אברהם ן' עזרא הנמצאים בהוצאות הקודמות. שטיינשניידר נוטה להאמין שהרמב"ם הוא מחברה, אבל אח"כ נודע לו שנוסחאה זו נדפסה באגרת התשובה לרבינו יונה גירונדי (קראקא, שמ"ו) כספר אנונימי (ראה המזכיר, 2, עמ' 8), תחת השם "ספר המוסר". עיין ישראל אברהם, צוואות גאוני ישראל, חלק א', פילדלפיא, תרפ"ז, עמ' 102.

15] מוסר נאה מאד מאד. מהרמב"ם ז"ל להרב החכם ר' אברהם בנו ז"ל. בדרך טובים... נעתקו ראשונה מכתבי יד בבית אוצר הספרים אשר בעיר אקספרד ויצאו לאור הדפוס עם העתקה בלשון אנגלי [מאת מ. ברעסלוי]. לונדון, תרי"ב, עמ' 16-19. זהה להוצאת שטיינשניידר הנ"ל. תרגום אנגלי:

The Last Will of Rabbi Moses Maimonides addressed to his son Rabbi Abraham. In: *The Path of Good Men*. Edited from manuscripts in the Bodleian Library, Oxford, accompanied by an English translation [by M.H. Bresslau], London, 1852, pp. 25-33.

תרי"ז 1857

16] פרק ממאמרי הרמב"ם ז"ל לאחד מחבריו ז"ל. במחקרו של א. גייגר, אוצר נחמד, ב' (תרי"ז/1857), 101-100 [= קבוצת מאמרים מאת גייגר, ורשה, תר"ע, עמ' 129-130]. קטע. ראה על זה: י. זנה, תרביץ, 10 (תרצ"ט), 148.

17] אגרת תשובת רמב"ם ז"ל... 1857, D.H. Schrenzel :Lemberg. ללא מספור עמודים. בראשו: אגרת הרמב"ם לבנו ר' אברהם לפי הנוסח שלפני הוצאת שטיינשניידער וועדעלמאן הנ"ל.

תרי"ח 1858

18] לקח טוב להרב אברהם יג"ל... צוואת הרמב"ם ז"ל... [קניגסבערג: טוביה הכהן אפרתי ויוסף בעקקער, תרי"ח 1858]. 16°.

עמ' 23-28: מוסר נאה מאד מאד מהרמב"ם ז"ל. זהה להוצאת שטיינשניידער הנ"ל (תרי"ב). ראה בקרתו החריפה בהמזכיר, ב' (1859), עמ' 7-8.

תרי"ט 1859

19] אגרת תשובת רמב"ם ז"ל... קניגסבורג: אלבערט ראסבאך, [תרי"ט], 12^0. 132 עמ'.
דף ב,א-ד,א: אגרת מהרמב"ם ז"ל לבנו החכם הרב ר' אברהם ז"ל.
לפי הנוסח של ההוצאות לפני שטיינשניידר הנ"ל (1852).

20] מוסר נאה מאד מהרמב"ם ז"ל. בקובץ **תשובות הרמב"ם ואגרותיו**, הוצאת אברהם ליכטענבערג, לפסיא: בדפוס ש"ל שנויס, תרי"ט/1859, חלק ב', דף לח,א-מ,ב.
הנוסח הרגיל שלפני הוצאת שטיינשניידר. צלומים מזה ראה להלן. (תשכ"ז-תשכ"ט).

תרכ"ד 1864

21] ספר נועם המוסר דאס איז איין הייליגער מוסר מרבינו הגדול הרמב"ם ז"ל וואס ער האט גישריבין צו זיין זון רבינו ר' אברהם ז"ל און ווייל דער ספר איז איין תועלת פאר דיא לייט וואס ווילין וויסין די וועג פון הש"י"ת און גילוסטין צוא דיא הייליגע רייד דארום האבין מיר מעתיק גיווען אויף עברי דייטש בכדי עס זאלין פאר שטיין גרויס און קליין. גם האבין מיר מוסיף גיווען נאך זאכין פון הייליגע ספרים דהיינו (ברכי נפשי) פון (ספר חובת הלבבות) און התעוררות התשובה און איין אלף בית על דרך המוסר און (דברי כבושין) פון (ספר הישר לרבינו תם ז"ל זכותו יגן עלינו). ווילנא, בדפוס של ר' אברהם יצחק דווארזעץ, 1864. 56 עמ'. 12^0.

רשיון הצנזורה ניתן ביום 22 ביוני 1864 בווילנא. — כולל: צוואת הרמב"ם לבנו; תוכחה לרבינו בחיי (שניהם עברית ואידיש זו למטה מזו); התעוררות צו תשובה ותקוני תשובה (שניהם באידיש בלבד) אדם להבל דמה נשמו משותף באדמה (עברית ואידיש); אדם יסודו מאופיר יקר (באידיש בלבד). — לפי כל הסמנים של [א"מ] דיק הוא.

הצוואה נגמרה בדף יב,א. הנוסח זהה להוצאת שטיינשניידר (1852).
ראה: א. יערי, מספרי אייזיק מאיר דיק שבירושלים", **קרית ספר**, 32 (1957), עמ' 229, מספר 160.

תרכ"ה 1865

22] מוסר נאה מאד מהרמב"ם ז"ל. **במוסר אב**. שני מכתבים... משני אבות העולם שכתבו לבניהם. האחד... הרמב"ם לבנו ר' אברהם, והשני... ר' יהודה אבן תבון לבנו ר' שמואל... הגהתי... והוספתי... מאמרי חכמה... משלי ושל [ר' מענדיל (לעוויו) מסטנאב מספר חשבון הנפש]... אני אליעזר צבי הכהן צוויפעל. זיטאמיר: בדפוס שאדאוו, תרכ"ה 1865, עמ' 34-42. 64^0.
הנוסח החדש.

תרל"ג 1873

23] The Last Will of Rabbi Moses Maimonides, Addressed to His Son Abraham. *New Era*, 3 (1873) pp. 446-447. From *The Path of Good Men*, translated by M.H. Bresslau. London, 1852.

תרל"ז 1877

24] מוסר נאה מאד מהרמב"ם ז"ל לבנו הרב החכם ר' אברהם ז"ל. **בלקח טוב** להרב אברהם יגל עם צוואת הרמב"ם... לבנו... אברהם... ווילנא: דפוס קאצינעלינבויגען,

תרל"ז 1877, עמ' 25-31. ‎12^0.
ראה הערה בסוף ההוצאה משנת תרי"ח.

25] אגרת מהרמב"ם ז"ל לבנו החכם ר' אברהם זצ"ל. באגרות ושאלות ותשובות להמאור... רבינו משה המיימוני... ובסופו נלוה גם תולדות הרמב"ם ז"ל נדפס ראשונה באמשטרדם בשנת תע"ב, וכעת נדפס שנית בהוספת מכתבים רבים מכת"י. ווארשא: יצחק גאלדמאן תרל"ח 1877, עמ' 8.
הנוסח הישן.

תרמ"ד 1884

26] לקח טוב להרב אברהם יגל... העתקנו אותו לעברית אשכנזית (שזארגאן)... והוספנו... צוואת הרמב"ם. ווילנא: דפוס מ"ץ, תרמ"ד 1884, עמ' 55-60. ‎12^0.
בעברית ויודי ושער ביודית.
צלום מזה, להלן (תרפ"ט).

תרמ"ה 1885

27] דעם רמב"ם'ס צוואה. דא ווערט באשריבין דיא לעבענס-גישיכטע פון דעם גרויסין היילינגען מאן... רבינו משה בן מימון... זייער שיינע אינטערעסאנטע ספורים (ערצייילונגען). אויך די היילינגע צוואה וואס ער האט גישריבין פיר זיינע קינדער. ווילנא: אליעזר ליפמאן מ"ץ, תרמ"ה 1885. 32 עמ'. עמ' (3)-16: תולדות הרמב"ם: 17-32: צוואת הרמב"ם. תורגם מס' לקח טוב, ע"י ר' בן ציון אלפס — ראה: א"ר מלאכי, בלעקסיקאן פון דער נייער יידישער ליטעראטור, באנד 1, ז' 119. דפוסי צלום (בלי השער, נלוו לספר **רפואת הנפש ורפואת הגוף** מאת הרמב"ם בתרגום ר' יהודה רוזנברג תשכ"ח ובסוף רשימה זו: חסרי שנות הדפוס).

תרנ"א 1891

28] Abrahams, Israel, 1858-1925.
Jewish Ethical Wills. JQR, 3 (1891), pp. 451-453. Extract. See complete text in his *Hebrew Ethical Wills* (1926).

תרנ"ה 1895

29] דעם רמב"ם'ס צוואה... אויך די היילינגע צוואה... ווילנא: אליעזר ליפמאן מ"ץ, תרנ"ה 1895, 32 עמ'. ‎12^0.
זהה לדפוס תרמ"ה 1885 (למעלה).
תורגם מס' לקח טוב.

תרס"ז 1907

30] דעם רמב"ם'ס צוואה... דיא לעבענס געשיכטע פון משה בן מיימון. ווילנא, 1907. ע"פ הקטלוג של הספריה הציבורית בניו יורק, כרך 3, עמ' 12108: נעלם ולא נמצא. לי נראה שזו היא דפוס חדש של הוצאת תרמ"ה בתרגום ר' בן-ציון אלפס.

תרס"ט 1909

31] ספר הצווי לרבוי משה ב"ר מיימון. **בזכרון לראשונים ולאחרונים**, מוציא לאור תורתן של ראשונים... וגם לאחרונים... מאתי שלמה אהרן ווערטהיימער. ספר א. ירושלים: האחים סלומון, תרס"ט 1909, דף א'-ד'.
כולל הנוסח החדש והישן בלוית הערות מאת המהדיר ובהוספת סעיף של מאמרי חז"ל (מס' סוטה ונזיר).

בהקדמת המו"ל נאמר: "ספר הצווי לרבנו משה ב"ר מיימון ז"ל, אשר צוה סמוך
לפטירתו לבנו הרב ר' אברהם בשם זה מצאתי הספר הזה בכת"י ישן פה ירושלם
עה"ק ת"ו, ואם אמנם כבר נדפס הוא בתוך אגרות הרמב"ם בלי נקיבת שם מיוחד
עליו, אך שם הוא מלא שבושים וטעיות המשחיתות לרוב גם את הכוונה, אבל בספר
כת"י זה הוא שלם ומוגה ומתוקן וטוב ויפה נקי מכל שבוש, וגם נוסף בו בסוף
מאמר שלם שלא בא בדפוס עד כה — — — — בכמה מקומות העירותי על
השינויים בכת"י אבל במקום שהטעות ברור ונעלה מעל כל ספק לא הטרחתי את
עצמי וגם את הקוראים וחדלתי מלציין עליו, וסמכתי על הקורא המבין כי יבין דבר
לאשורו". ראה גם הערתו על־דבר בעלותו של הרמב"ם כמחבר האגרת.

תרע"ג 1913

[32] רפואת הנפש ורפואת הגוף מאת הרמב"ם אויף לשון קודש און אויף עברי
טייטש... הלכות דעות [איבערזעטצט פון] ר' יודל ראזענבערג... חלק שני. ווארשא:
אהרן צייילינגאלד, תרע"ג/1913. עמ' 29־30: די צוואה פון רמב"ם צו זיינע קינדער.
קיצור בי"ג סעיפים. נעתק כמו כן ע"י מ. מייער (1935) ומ"מ מאנזאהן (1937).

[33] מוסר נאה מאד מאד מהרמב"ם ז"ל לבנו הרב החכם ר' אברהם ז"ל. בס' **לקח
טוב** להר' אברהם יגל... נדפס מחדש ע"י ר' נח ווינטראב. פיעטרקוב: בדפוס של ר'
חנוך העניך פאלמאן, תרע"ג 1913, עמ' 13־16.
לא בשלמותה.

תרפ"א 1921

[34] די צוואה פון דעם רמב"ם צו זיין זוהן ר' אברהם. דעם רמב"ם'ס לעבענס־
בעשרייבונג. זיין לעבען, זיינע ספרים און זיין ווירקונג אויף דער אידישער נאציאן. פון
י.ח. זאגאראדסקי. ניו יארק: היברו פאבלישינג קא., 1921, עמ' 25־32.
תורגם מן הנוסח החדש.

תרפ"ז 1926

[35] שערי המוסר (המיוחס להרמב"ם). בצוואות גאוני ישראל. לקטו נערכו הוגהו ונעתקו
על ידי ישראל בן ברוך בר אברהם, חלק א. פילאדלפיא: החברה היהודית להוצאת
ספרים אשר באמריקה, תרפ"ז, עמ' 101־116.
בלווית תרגום אנגלי המבוא, עמוד מול עמוד (עמ' 101־116). ע"פ הוצאת
שטיינשניידר (תרי"ב). שער לועזי:

Hebrew Ethical Wills. Selected and edited by Israel Abrahams. Part I,
Philadelphia: Jewish Publication Society of America, 1926. Pp. 101-116: The
Gate of Instruction attributed to Maimonides.

תרפ"ז 1927

[36] אגרת המוסר לרבי אברהם בנו. בתוך: אגרות ותשובות לרבינו משה בן מימון
הספרדי [הרמב"ם], ורשה: "טרקלין", תרפ"ז 1927. ספירת עמודים חמישית: עמ' א־
יא.
הוצאה זו מכילה הנוסח החדש של שטיינשניידר (עמ' א־ו) והנוסח הישן (עמ' ו־
יא).
דפוסים סטראוטיפיים של מהדורה זו, ראה להלן מספר 43, 50, 55, 60.

[37] מכתב לבנו אברהם, והוא מעין צוואה ומוסר נאה מאד. בתוך: מבואו של הרב
ישעיהו גלאזער ל**משנה תורה** לרמב"ם, כרך א' בלווית תרגום אנגלי. ניו יארק:
הוצאת מיימון פובלישינג קא., תרפ"ז 1927, עמ' כא-כו.
קיצור של הנוסח החדש הנ"ל (עמ' כא-כה) בלווית קטע של הנוסח הישן המכיל,
כמו כן דברי שבח על ר' אברהם אבן עזרא.

תרפ"ט 1929

[38] לקח טוב להרב אברהם יגל... העתקנו אותו לעברית אשכנזית (שזארגאן)...
והוספנו. צוואת הרמב"ם... ווילנא: דפוס מ"ץ, תרפ"ט, עמ' 55-60. 12°. זהה להוצאת
תרמ"ד (למעלה).

תרצ"ה 1935

[39] ברבנו משה בן מיימון. חייו, ספריו, פעולותיו ודעותיו. קובץ תורני-מדעי. ערוך
ומסודר... בעריכת הרב יהודה ליב הכהן פישמן. ירושלים: המרכז העולמי של
המזרחי, תרצ"ה 1935, עמ' קיט-קכג [= חיי הרמב"ם, ספריו ופעולותיו... מאת הרב
יהודה ליב הכהן פישמן. ירושלים, תרצ"ה, עמ' קיג-קיז].
הנוסח החדש

[40] קאפלאן, פסח, הי"ד, 1870-1943.
רמב"ם אין יידיש. געקליבענע שריפטן. איבערזעצט... ביאליסטאק: "אונזער
פרעסע", 1935. 159 עמ'.
עמ' 88-94: רמב"ם'ס בריף צו זיין זון אברהם.
תרגום של נוסח הישן בהוספת קטע מהנוסח החדש: נדפס שוב **בדוקא** כרך ה',
חוברות 18-19 (תשי"ד), עמ' 118-121.

[41] מייער, מאריס משה, 1870-1944.
דער רמב"ם מיימאנידעס. **די צייט** (לונדון), 5. מכיל צוואה מקוצרת בי"ג סעיפים:
לקוח **מספר רפואת הנפש ורפואת הגוף** מאת הרמב"ם בתרגום יודי מאת ר' יהודה
רוזנברג (תרע"ג).

תרצ"ז 1937

[42] צוואת הרמב"ם ז"ל. גוטע הנהגות פון דעם רמב"ם צו זיינע קינדערן ב"דעם
רמב"ם'ס היסטארי און זיין פארצאג צו זיינע קינדער". איבערזעצונג פון מנחם מענדל
מאנזאהן. ברוקלין, נ.י.: מאינעשטער פאבלישינג קא. (ק. 1937. [2] עמ'.
מקוצר; מיוסד על נוסח של ר' יהודה רוזנברג (תרע"ג 1913). נלוה אליו תרגום
אנגלי:

Last Will and Testament of the Rambam; valuable instructions of the
Rambam to his children. Translated by Mendel Monsohn. In his *History of
the Rambam.* New York, 1937. [2] p.

תש"ה 1945

[43] אגרת המוסר לרבי אברהם בנו. בתוך: **קובץ מאמרי הרמב"ם-תשובות לרבינו
משה בן מימון הספרדי ז"ל**... ניו-יורק: הוצאת "ישרון", תש"ה, 1945, ספירת עמודים
חמישית: עמ' א-יא.
ד"צ מוגדל של מהד' ורשה תרפ"ז בשינוי שם על שער הספר.

44] * צוואת הרמב"ם ז"ל. נלוה ל**קיצור חובות הלבבות** מאת רבינו מנחם בן הקדוש ר' אהרן בן זרח... יוצאים לאור על ידי הרב שמעון הלפרין. ירושלים תש"ה 1945. ח' עמ'. 16⁰.

תש"ח 1948

45] **שערי המוסר** (המיוחס להרמב"ם). בצוואות גאוני ישראל, לקטו נערכו הוגהו ונעתקו על ידי ישראל בן ברוך אברהם, חלק א, פילאדלפיא: החברה היהודית להוצאת ספרים אשר באמריקא, תש"ח, עמ' 101־116. בלוית תרגום אנגלי ומבוא עמוד מול עמוד (101־116). ד"צ הוצאת 1926. שער לועזי:

Hebrew Ethical Wills. Selected and edited by Israel Abrahams. Part I, Philadelphia: Jewish Publication Society of America, 1948. 8⁰. Pp. 101-116: The Gate of Instruction attributed to Maimonides. Reproduction of the 1926 edition.

תשי"א 1951

46] Last Will and Testament. In Simon Maurice Lehrman, *The Jewish Design for Living*. London: Bachad Fellowship, 1951, pp. 329-332.

תשי"ב 1952

47] מאגרת המוסר לרבינו אברהם בנו. בס' **נעים זמירות ישראל** מאת יצחק גרשטנקורן, ספר ב' חלק ב', בני ברק (דפוס דוב גוטרמן, תל־אביב), תשי"ב, עמ' תב־תה.
לפי נוסח של שטיינשניידר בשנת תרי"ב.

תשי"ד 1954

48] דעם רמב"ם'ס בריוו צו זיין זון אברהם. **דוקא**, באנד 5, נומער 18־19 (טבת־סיון תשי"ד/יאנואר־יוני 1954), 118־121: נומער 20 (תמוז־אלול תשי"ד), 256־259.
נעתק מתרגומו של פסח קאפלאן, הי"ד (ראה למעלה: 1935).

49] אגרת המוסר לרבי אברהם בנו. ב**מבחר המחשבה והמוסר ביהדות מתקופת רב סעדיה גאון עד ימינו**. מאת י. צבי זהבי. תל־אביב: אברהם ציוני, תשי"ד, עמ' נח־סג (לפי נוסחאו של שטיינשניידר, בשנת תרי"ב) בלוית קטע מן הנוסח הישן (עמ' סב־סג).

50] אגרת המוסר לרבי אברהם בנו. בתוך: אגרות ותשובות להנשר הגדול רבינו משה בן מימון הספרדי [הרמב"ם], ירושלים: לוין־אפשטיין, תשי"ד, ספירת עמודים חמישית: עמ' א־יא.
ד"ס של הוצאת ורשה תרפ"ז. שנת הוצאה נרשמה כאן עפ"י "קרית ספר", 33 (תשי"ח), עמ' 144.

תשט"ו 1955

51] מוסר אב. במאמרו של הרב יהודה ליב הכהן מימון על הרמב"ם. **סיני**, כרך לו, חוברת ד' (טבת תשט"ו), רלה־רלט [־**הר"מ במז"ל**: **קובץ תורני־מדעי** ערוך ומסודר למלאות שבע מאות וחמשים שנה לפטירת הרמב"ם ז"ל בעריכת הרב יהודה ליב הכהן מימון. ירושלים: מוסד הרב קוק, תשט"ו, עמ' מא־מה; **הרמב"ם. תורתו ואישיותו**... בעריכת שמעון פדרבוש. ניו־יורק: מחלקת התרבות של הקונגרס היהודי

העולמי, המחלקה לחינוך ותרבות תורניים של הסוכנות היהודית, תשט"ז, עמ' 30-35;
מדי חדש בחדשו, מחזור א', ירושלים: מוסד הרב קוק, תשט"ו, עמ' 260-264].
ב' נוסחאות בהשמטות; חסרות דברי שבח על אבן עזרא ובקורת על חכמי אשכנז.

תשט"ז 1956

52] אגרת והיא צוואה.
בספר המעלות, ערוך ומסודר בידי אליעזר שטיינמן. תל-אביב: יהושע צ'צ'יק, תשט"ז, עמ' 53-59.
הנוסח החדש עם הקדמת העורך. "בין שהאגרת נכתבה על ידי הרמב"ם עצמו... חותם הרמב"ם עליה, היא יצאה מבית היוצר שלו...".

תשי"ז 1957

53] Maimonides' Ethical Testament. In: Jacob S. Minkin, *The World of Moses Maimonides with Selections from His Writings*. New York: Yoseloff, (c. 1957), pp. 421-427. English translation by Israel Abrahams (see 1926 and 1948).

תש"ך 1960

54] **ברבנו משה בן מיימון** מאת הרב יהודה ליב הכהן מימון. ירושלים: מוסד הרב קוק, תש"ך, עמ' קעח-קפא.
הנוסח החדש בלי כותרת.

תשכ"א 1961

55] אגרת המוסר לרבי אברהם בנו. בתוך: **אגרות ותשובות להנשר הגדול רבינו משה בן מימון הספרדי** [הרמב"ם]. ירושלים: לוין-אפשטין, תשכ"א, ספירת עמודים חמישית: עמ' א-יא.
ד"ס של הוצאת ורשה תרפ"ז.

תשכ"ה 1965

56] מוסר נאה מאד מהרמב"ם ז"ל לבנו הרב החכם ר' אברהם ז"ל. **בלקח טוב** להרב... אברהם יג"ל. מחובר... צוואת הרמב"ם לבנו... אברהם... ישראל, תשכ"ה, עמ' 25-31.
ד"צ מהוצאת תשל"ז. ראה הערה להוצאת הס' לקח טוב משנת תרי"ח. (ע"פ **קרית ספר** 42 (תשכ"ז), עמ' 11).

תשכ"ו 1966

57] אגרת המוסר. בתוך: **אגרות אקטואליות של רבינו משה בן מיימון הספרדי**, תורגם ועובד ע"י מ. בר-יוסף. בני-ברק: מכון למדעי היהדות = מכון מרדכי להוצאת ספרי יהדות, תשכ"ו 4°. חלק ב'. 11 עמ' (ספירת עמודים ששית) בלוית "נספח לאגרת הצוואה בקטע חכמי הדן בחכמי צרפת" ו"נספח לצוואתו של רבינו אל בנו הדן בקטע המתיחס לפחיתותם התרבותי והחברתי של ילידי ארצות אשר נזכרו על ידי רבינו". [2] עמ'. "מיועד לקוראי ימינו". משוכפל.
התרגום הוא מהנוסח החדש (עמ' 1-8) בלוית קטע מהנוסחא הישן אדות מצות שבת, אבן עזרא וחכמי צרפת (עמ' 8-11).

תשכ"ז 1967

58] מוסר נאה מאד מהרמב"ם ז"ל. **באגרות הרמב"ם.** ירושלים (חש"מ), תשכ"ז, דף לח, א-מ, ב.
דפוס צלום מקובץ תשובות הרמב"ם ואגרותיו, חלק ב', לפסיא תרי"ט (ראה למעלה).

59] מוסר נאה מאד מהרמב"ם ז"ל לבנו הרב החכם ר' אברהם ז"ל. ב"חבורים רפואיים שיוחסו לרמב"ם ולרמב"ן" מאת דוד מרגלית. **קורות**, 4, חוברת ג-ד (סיון תשכ"ז/1967), 208-217 [=דרך ישראל ברפואה. ירושלים: הוצאת האקדמיה לרפואה, תש"ל, עמ' 197-204].
הנוסח החדש.

תשכ"ח 1968

60] אגרת המוסר לרבי אברהם בנו. בתוך: **אגרות ותשובות להנשר הגדול רבינו משה בן מימון הספרדי [הרמב"ם]**. ירושלים: לוין-אפשטיין, תשכ"ח, ספירת עמודים חמישית: עמ' א-יא.
ד"ס של הוצאת ורשה, תרפ"ז.

61] די צוואה פון רמב"ם צו זיינע קינדער. ב"דער רמב"ם: זיין לעבענס בעשרייבונג, זיינע ספרים און זיין ווירקונג אויף דעם אידישען נאציאן" איבערזעצט פון... יודל ראזענבערג. ניו יורק: הוצאת תפארת יעקב פאבלישינג הובא לבית הדפוס אחים גרויס, תשכ"ח, עמ' 29-30.
צלום מדפוס ווארשא, תרע"ג.

62] Stitskin, Leon D., 1910-1978.
The Methodology of Maimonides. The Last Will and Testament of Maimonides. *Tradition*, IX, no. 4 (Spring, 1968), pp. 80-90; X, no. 2 (Winter 1968), pp. 121-129 [-Letters of Maimonides. Trans. by Leon D. Stitskin. New York: Yeshiva Univ. Press, 1977, pp. 137-158]. Translation of both versions.

תשכ"ט 1969

63] מוסר נאה מאד מהרמב"ם ז"ל. ב**קובץ תשובות הרמב"ם ואגרותיו**. חלק ב, 1969, Farnborough: Gregg, דף לח, א-מ,ב.
ד"צ של הוצאת לפסיא, תרי"ט.

תש"ל 1970

64] איגרת המוסר אשר שלח הרמב"ם לבנו רבי אברהם. ב**רבינו משה בן מימון: אגרות ותולדות חייו**. בעריכת מרדכי בר-יוסף. (תל אביב: מכון מרדכי להוצאת ספרי יהדות, תש"ל), עמ' 129-138.
"בעברית המדוברת בימינו", בלוית תוכן העניינים בראשי פרקים והערות.
התרגום הוא מן הנוסח החדש (עמ' 131-136 בלוית קטע מהנוסח הישן אודות מצוות שבת, אבן עזרא וחכמי צרפת (עמ' 136-138).

65] מוסר נאה מאד מהרמב"ם ז"ל להרב החכם ר' אברהם בנו ז"ל. ב**דרך טובים**... נעתקו ראשונה מכתבי יד בבית אוצר הספרים אשר בעיר אקספרד ויצאו לאור הדפוס עם העתקה בלשון אנגלי [מאת מ. ברעסלוי]. על ידי צבי הירש עדעלמאן... ירושלים: "קדם", תש"ל, עמ' 16-19.

The Last Will of Rabbi Moses Maimonides addressed to his son Rabbi Abraham. In: *The Path of Good Men*. Edited from manuscripts in the Bodleian Library, Oxford, accompanied by an English translation [by M.H. Breslau], by Hirsch Edelman. Jerusalem: "Kedem," 1970, pp. 25-33.

דפוס צלום של הוצאת לונדון, תרי"ב 1852.

66] מוסר נאה מאד מהרמב"ם ז"ל לבנו הרב החכם ר' אברהם ז"ל. **בדרך ישראל ברפואה** מאת דוד מרגלית. ירושלים: הוצאת האקדמיה לרפואה, תש"ל, עמ' 197־204 [=**קורות 4, חוברת ג־ד** (סיון תשכ"ז/1967), 208־217].
הנוסח החדש.

תשל"א 1971

67] בתוך: **מבחר ספרות המוסר**; פרקים נבחרים בצירוף ציונים, ביאורים ומבואות מאת ישעיהו תשבי בשיתוף עם יוסף דן. ירושלים־תל־אביב: הוצאת מ. ניומן, תשל"א, עמ' 347־352.
לקוטים משתי הנוסחאות עם הערות על פי הוצאת ישראל אברהם (1926), **וקובץ תשובות הרמב"ם ואגרותיו** (תרי"ט).

68] אגרת המוסר לרבנו הרמב"ם. בתוך: **דרך ארץ ונימוסים** להרב ברוך ישר. ירושלים, תשל"א, עמ' ס־סז.
לפי הנוסח החדש בלוית הערות.

תשל"ד 1974

69] מוסר נאה מאד מהרמב"ם ז"ל לבנו הרב החכם ר' אברהם ז"ל. **בלקח טוב** להרב... אברהם יג"ל... מחובר... צוואת הרמב"ם לבנו... אברהם... ברוקלין: דפוס אחים גרויס; הוצאת בית הספר, תשל"ד, עמ' 25־31.
ד"צ מהוצאת תרל"ז. ראה הערה להוצאת הס' לקח טוב משנת תרי"ח.

תשל"ו 1976

70] Last Will and Testament. In: Simon Maurice Lehrman, *The Jewish Design for Living*. New York: Shengold, 1976, pp. 329-332.

71] שערי המוסר (המיוחס להרמב"ם). **בצוואות גאוני ישראל**. לקטו נערכו הוגהו ונעתקו על ידי ישראל בן ברוך בר אברהם, חלק א. פילאדלפיא: החברה היהודית להוצאת ספרים אשר באמריקא, תשל"ו 1976, עמ' 101־116.
בלוית תרגום אנגלי ומבוא, עמוד מול עמוד (101־116). צלום דפוס תרפ"ו 1926.

The Gate of Instruction Attributed to Maimonides. In: *Hebrew Ethical Wills*. Selected and edited by Israel Abrahams, Part I, New Foreword by Judah Goldin. Philadelphia: Jewish Publication Society of America, 1976, pp. 101-116.

דפוס צלום של הוצאת תרפ"ז 1926. 12°.

1977

72] Letter of Moral Instruction to his Son Abraham: The Last Will and Testament. In: Leon D. Stitskin, *Letters of Maimonides*. Translated and edited with introductions and notes. New York: Yeshiva Univ. Press, 1977, pp. 137-158.

1987
73] Maimonides' Ethical Testament. In: Jacob S. Minkin, *The Teachings of Maimonides*. Northvale, NJ: Jason Aronson, 1987, pp. 421-427. Reprinted from 1957 edition under the title *The World of Moses Maimonides*.

1991
74] Sha'are Hamusar (Last Will and Testament). In: *Six Treatises Attributed to Maimonides*. Translated and annotated from the Hebrew editions by Fred Rosner. With bibliographies by Jacob I. Dienstag. Northvale, NJ: Jason Aronson, 1991.

חסר מקום ושנת דפוס

75] מוסר נאה מאד... מהרמב"ם ז"ל לבנו הרב החכם ר' אברהם ז"ל. בסוף ספר **לקח טוב** להרב... אברהם יג"ל... חמוש"ד, עמ' 25־31. °12. ד"צ מהוצאת ווילנא תרל"ז.

76] אגרת מהרמב"ם ז"ל לבנו החכם ר' אברהם זצ"ל. **באגרות ושאלות ותשובות להמאור**... רבינו משה המיימוני. ווארשא: יצחק היינערמאן, חש"ד, עמ' 5־3. ד"ס ורשה תרל"ח.

77] **בשלשה ספרים נפתחים**. ירושלים: הוצאת תל תלפיות, חש"ד, עמ' לה־מ. °16.

78] [דעם רמב"ם'ס צוואה. דא ווערט באשריבין דיא לעבענס־גישיכטע פון דעם גרויסן הייליגען מאן... רבינו משה בן מימון... זייער שיינע אינטערעסאנטע סיפורים (ערציילונגען). אויך די הייליגע צוואה וואס ער האט גישריבין פיר זיינע קינדער]. ברוקלין נ.י.: שלמה יוסף מייזליץ, חש"ד, עמ' 17־32 (בהשמטת השער). ד"צ ווילנא תרמ"ח. נלוה לספר רפואת הגוף ורפואת הנפש מאת הרמב"ם... [איבערזעצט פון] יודל ראזענבערג, ברוקלין: שלמה יוסף מייזליץ, חש"ד. °12.

79] דעם רמב"ם'ס צוואה... אויך די הייליגע צוואה... חמוש"ד, עמ' 17־32 (בהשמטת השער). ד"צ ווילנא תרמ"ה. נלוה לספר **רפואת הנפש ורפואת הגוף** מאת הרמב"ם... [איבעזעצט פון] יודל ראזענבערג. חמוש"ד. יצא לאור ע"י ישראל משה געליס. °12.

80] די צוואה פון דעם רמב"ם צו זיין זוהן ר' אברהם. **דעם רמב"ם'ס לעבענס־בעשרייבונג. זיין לעבען, זיינע ספרים און זיין ווירקונג אויף דער אידישער נאציאן**. פון י.ח. זאגאראדסקי חמוש"ד, עמ' 25־32. זהה להוצאת 1921.

81] די צוואה פון רמב"ם צו זיינע קינדער. בס' **רפואת הנפש ורפואת הגוף** מאת הרמב"ם [איבערזעצט פון] יודל ראזענבערג; ברוקלין, נ.י.: שלמה יוסף מייזליץ, חש"ד, עמ' 29־30. °12. תרגום מקוצר בשלושה עשר סעיפים: ד"צ מהוצאת ווארשא, תרע"ג.

82] די צוואה פון רמב"ם צו זיינע קינדער. בס' רפואת הנפש ורפואת הגוף מאת הרמב"ם. [איבערזעצט פון] יודל ראזענבערג. חמוש"ד, עמ' 29־30. °12. י"ל ע"י ישראל משה געליס, ד"צ מהוצאת ווארשא, תרע"ג.

BIBLIOGRAPHY

[83] די צוואה פון רמב"ם צו זיינע קינדער.
בס' **רפואת הנפש ורפואת הגוף** מאת הרמב"ם איבעזעצט פון יודל ראזענבערג; •
ווארשא: צייילינגאלג, חש"ד, עמ' 29-30.
זהה להוצאת ווארשא תרע"ג.

[84] מאנזאהן, מנחם מענדל
דעם רמב"ם'ס היסטארי און זיין פארזאג צו זיינע קינדער, חמוש"ד [ניו-יורק],
מקוצר; מיוסד על נוסח של ר' יהודה רוזנברג (תרע"ג). זהה להוצאת 1937. נלוה
אליו תרגום אנגלי:
The History of the Rambam and valuable instructions to his children.

ב. על צוואת הרמב"ם בספרות ימי הביניים
ר' אפרים בן ר' גרשון. ראה מספר 144 (להלן).

[85] בכרך, ר' יאיר חיים ב"ר משה שמשון, 1638-1702.
הקדמה לספרו "יאיר נתיב". **בכורים**, א' ווין, תרכ"ד, עמ' 20. י"ל על פי כתב יד
המחבר ע"י א. יעללינעק; נדפס שוב ע"י הרב י"ל מימון, **סיני**, 40 (תשי"ז), רה [=
מדי חדש בחדשו, מחזור ג', ירושלים: מוסד הרב קוק, תשי"ז, עמ' 143].

[86] בשיצי, אליהו בן משה, הקראי, 1420-1490 בערך.
ספר המצות הנקרא אדרת אליהו. ענין קדוש החדש, סוף פרק ו'. [קושטנטינא,
רצ"ב לערך]; גוזלוו: יעקב פינקעלמאן, תקצ"ה/1835, אודססא:ל. ניטצשע,
תרל"א/1870.
מצטט את הבקורת על חכמי צרפת בשם "התלמודיים הבאים מאשכנז שאוכלים
השלשא עם השומים".

[87] כספי, ר' יוסף ן', 1297-1340.
טירת כסף (נלוה לספרו **משנה כסף**). פרעבורג, תרס"ה, דף קלח.

[88] לוריא, ר' שלמה (מהרש"ל), 1510-1574.
הקדמות לספרו **ים שלמה**, מסכתות בבא קמא וחולין.
בקורת על הקטע בצוואה המיוחסת להרמב"ם שבה גינה הרב את חכמי צרפת
בו בזמן ששיבח את הראב"ע "אשר לא היה בעל תלמודא". סכום מאת ח. טשרנוביץ
(רב צעיר), **תולדות הפוסקים**, חלק ג', ניו יורק, תשי"ח, עמ' 78-79, 83.

[89] קארו, ר' יצחק, המאה הט"ו-ט"ז
תולדות יצחק, סוף פרשת תרומה. קושטנטינא, רע"ח; ריווא דטרינטו, שי"ח;
מנטובה, שי"ח; קראקא, שנ"ג; אמסטרדם, תס"ח; ורשה, תרל"ז.

ג. מאמרים ומחקרים על הצוואה

[90] אברהם, ישראל, 1859-1925.
שערי המוסר (המיוחס להרמב"ם). בצואות **גאוני ישראל**. חלק א', פילאדלפיא:
החברה היהודית להוצאת ספרים אשר באמריקא, תרפ"ז, עמ' 101-103.
"יש שתי צוואות המיוחסות לרבי משה בן מיימון... האחת, הנודעת עפ"י רוב

כצוואת הרמב"ם... ונדפסה פעמים רבות למיום הופעתה הראשונה בויניציה בשנת ש"ד. הצוואה הזאת יש לה חשיבות פולמית יותר ממוסרית. יען כי כל עיקרה לא בא אלא להלשין באופן גס ומעליב על חכמי ישראל בצרפת... חשבתי לטוב ונכון להשמיטה מן הכרך שלפנינו. והנה צוואת הרמב"ם שנתי פה איננה בחזקת מקוריות יותר גדולה, אבל לכל הפחות היא חבור יותר יפה ומעולה מן הראשונה, וראויה היא למקום פה בשביל מעלותיה העצמיות, שטיינשניידר ועדלמאן הדפיסו אותה בספריהם המכילים הצואה של אבן תבון..." ונעלם משטיינשניידר שאותו הנוסח עצמו נדפס בהעלם שם המחבר בסוף **איגרת התשובה** לרבינו יונה גירונדי בקראקא בשנת שמ"ו (עיין במדור הראשון של רשימה זו).

[91] אוריון, מאיר, 1910-1979.
הצוואה. **הצופה**, כ' טבת תשט"ו, עמ' 4,6.
השוואה בין אישיות של הרמב"ם ושל אריסטו ע"פ הצוואות שלהם.

[92] בכר, בנימין זאב, 1850-1913.
הרמב"ם פרשן המקרא. מתורגם מגרמנית ע"י א.ז. רבינוביץ. תל-אביב (דפוס "אחדות"), תרצ"ב, עמ' 24.
"זיופו ניכר מתוכו".

[93] גידמן, משה, 1835-1918.
התורה והחיים בארצות המערב בימי הבינים... העתקת א"ש פרידברג, חלק א'. וארשא: האחים שולדברג, תרנ"ז/1896, עמ' 55.
שהצוואה הראשונה לא יצאה מעטו של הרמב"ם.

[94] גינצבורג, לוי, 1873-1953.
מצוטט בספרו של ש. גולדמן, **היהודי והעולם**, תל-אביב: "דביר", ת"ש, עמ' 236, הערה 4.
מטיל ספק בעצם העובדא שהרמב"ם הכיר את חיבורי הראב"ע. לדעתו האגרת או צוואה מזויפת. ראה גם כן במדור הלועזי.

[95] ורטהימר, שלמה אהרן, 1866-1935.
זכרון לראשונים ולאחרונים, ספר א'. ירושלים: האחים סלומון, תרס"ט/1909, עמ' א, בהערה.
מקיים את הצוואה להרמב"ם.

[96] זק"ש, שניאור, 1815-1892.
תוספות לשני המאמרים הנ"ל. **היונה**, תרי"א (דפוס צילום: ירושלים: הוצאת תשבי, תש"ל), 88.
הוא כן מיחס את הצוואה להרמב"ם.

[97] זק"ש, שניאור, 1815-1892.
בשירי השירים אשר לשלמה ו' גבירול, פאריס, 1868, עמ' כ"ט.
חזר בו ממה שכתב ביונה הנ"ל. שהאיגרת היא מזויפת ושהרמב"ם לא הכיר את ספרי אבן עזרא.

[98] חבצלת, מאיר, 1927-
על זהוי "צוואת הרמב"ם" ועל יחסו לחכמי צרפת. **בצרון**, 68 (תשלח), 241-243.
מאשר הימנות הצוואה שהיא מהרמב"ם.

99] כהנא, דוד, 1838־1915.
המכתב שכתב הרמב"ם לבנו אודות הראב"ע, אם מזויף הוא או לא? **ברבי אברהם אבן עזרא**, כרך ב', חלק ב'. ורשה: האחים שולדברג, תרנ"ד/1894, עמ' 82־86.
נגד ש"י רפופורט (ראה להלן) שכתב שהצוואה היא מזויפת. מאשר דברי הרמב"ם מה שכתב בה על הראב"ע ועל חכמי צרפת.

100] לוצאטו, שמואל דוד, 1800־1865.
[אגרת לר' יום טוב ליפמן צונץ], **אוצר נחמד**, ב' (תרי"ז), 12. הערה על ספרו של צונץ, "צור געשיכטע", עמ' 200, שבו הוא מזכיר את יחסו השלילי של הרמב"ם נגד חכמי צרפת על יסוד צוואת הרמב"ם. עיין ש"י רפופורט **בישרון** ג' (תרי"ז) ותשובת שד"ל **בהמגיד** ב' (י"ד שבט תרי"ח), 14־15. ראה להלן.

101] לוצאטו, שמואל דוד, 1800־1865.
על אגרת אחת להרמב"ם שנחשבה מזוייפת. **המגיד**, 2, גליון 4 (י"ד שבט, תרי"ח), 14־15 [= **פניני שד"ל**, פרזעמישל, תרמ"ח, עמ' 441־444].
תשובה לדבריו בקורת של ש"י רפופורט **בישרון** ב' (תרי"ז), 55 על אגרת שד"ל לצונץ **באוצר נחמד**, ב' (תרי"ז), 12, אודות יחסו של הרמב"ם לחכמי צרפת על פי מה שכתב **בצוואה** המיוחס לו. לוצאטו מסכים עכשיו עם שי"ר שהיא מזוייפת.

לוריא, ר' שלמה בן יחיאל (מהרש"ל), 1510?־1574.
ראה במדור **צוואת הרמב"ם בספרות ימי הביניים**, מספר 88.

102] נאכט, יעקב, 1873־1959.
אכילת דגים בשבת. **סיני**, י"א (תש"ב־תש"ג), קמט־קן.
אודות הדברים החריפים נגד חכמי צרפת: "והנה כל מי שבקי קצת בדרכי המוסר של הרמב"ם קשה לו להאמין שהדברים האלה יצאו מפה קודש זה...".

103] סיד, ר' יהודה ב"ר מנוח, ? — 1815.
נר מצוה, חלק ב', שאלוניקי: בדפוס סעדיה הלוי אשכנזי תקע"א 1811, חלק כללי הפוסקים, כלל קמ"א; קצור בקונטרטס **אור הנר**, בסוף כללי הפוסקים, שם.
"...וכתב מהרש"ל בהקדמת **ים של שלמה** דמ"ש **באגרות [צוואת]** הרמב"ם נגד חכמי צרפת על הרוב אינן דברי הרמב"ם...".

104] עמדן, ר' יעקב ישראל, 1697־1776.
מטפחת ספרים, לבוב, תר"ל, עמ' 71.
שהצוואה היא מזוייפת. מצוטט ע"י אברהם ביק. ראה הערך הבא.

105] עמדן, ר' יעקב ישראל, 1697־1776.
הערות יעב"ץ לאגרות הרמב"ם. **סיני**, כרך פה, חוברת א־ב (ניסן־אייר תשל"ט), מח־נד.
הערות לאגרות הרמב"ם, דפוס אמשטרדם, תע"ב: בעיקר על **צוואת** הרמב"ם, שהיא לפי דעתו מזוייפת. יצא לאור ע"י אברהם ביק.

106] קמפף, שאול יצחק, 1818־1892.
שיר תלונה להראב"ע.

S. I. Kaempf, *Nichtandalusische Poesie andalusischer Dichter aus dem 11, 12, und 13 Jahrhundert. Ein Beitrag z. Geschichte d. Poesie des Mittelalters.* Prag; Carl Bellmann's Verlag, 1858, pp. 220-221.

מסכים עם ש"י רפופורט (ראה להלן) שצוואת הרמב"ם (שבה מסופר על האבן עזרא), מזויפת.

107] רפופורט, שלמה יהודה (שי"ר), 1790־1867.
מכתב ד'. **ישרון**, ג' (תרי"ז), 46־55.
שצוואת הרמב"ם מזויפת. עיין נגדו: ד. כהנא (למעלה).

108] שור, יהושע השל, 1818־1895.
דבר בעתו. **החלוץ**, ה' (תר"ך), 45.
שצוואת הרמב"ם מזויפת.

109] שטיינמן, אליעזר, 1892־1970.
ספר המעלות. תל־אביב: יהושע צ'צ'יק, תשט"ז, עמ' 56.
"בין שהאגרת נכתבה בידי הרמב"ם עצמו...חותם הרמב"ם עליה, היא יצאה מבית היוצר שלו...".

110] שלום, גרשם, 1897־1982.
מחוקר למקובל (אגדת המקובלים על הרמב"ם). **תרביץ**, שנה ו', ספר ג' (ניסן תרצ"ה), 335 [—**ספר הרמב"ם של התרביץ**, ירושלים: חברה להוצאת ספרים על יד האוניברסיטה העברית, תרצ"ה, עמ' 91; **מקראה בחקר הרמב"ם**. יוצאת לאור במלאות 850 שנה להולדתו. שם, תשמ"ב, עמ' 91].
"..הכל מסכימים עליה שהיא מזויפת. הזייפן היה מחסידיו של הראב"ע ושל המיסטיקאי שבו דווקא!".

111] תמר, דוד
על טעיות סופרים וחכמים. **ידיעות אחרונות**, י"ט אייר תשמ"ה, עמ' 21.
שהצוואה מזויפת.

112] Abrahams, Israel, 1859-1925.
The Gate of Instruction attributed to Maimonides. In *Hebrew Ethical Wills*, part I, Philadelphia: Jewish Publication Society of America, 1926 (reprinted: 1946 and 1976), pp. 101-102. Compares the old version which includes a sharp criticism of the French rabbis, and the version published by M. Steinschneider (1952). The authenticity of this version is questionable and Abrahams omitted it from his collection. Although, in his opinion, Steinschneider's version "has no better claim to authenticity," he, nevertheless, included it in his collection "on its own merit." See also Hebrew translation of this introduction.

113] Bacher, Wilhelm, 1850-1913.
Die Bibelexegese Moses Maimuni's. Budapest, 1986 (reprint: Gregg International, 1987), p. 18.

114] Baron, Salo W., 1895-1989.
The Historical Outlook of Maimonides. PAAJR VI (1934-1935), p. 87; reprinted in his *History and Jewish Historians*. Philadelphia: Jewish Publication Society of America, 1964, p. 148, note 169. "The very uncomplimentary remarks concerning the French scholars are evidently spurious, as is the entire ethical will."

BIBLIOGRAPHY

115] Ginzberg, Louis, 1873-1953.
Allegorical Interpretation. *Jewish Encyclopedia* I (1901), p. 408 (bottom). States that the *Ethical Will* was "falsely ascribed to Maimonides." He was also cited to this effect by Solomon Goldman, *The Jew and The Universe.* New York: Harper & Brothers, 1936, p. 218, note 4.

116] Goslar, Naftali Hirsch, 18th century.
Letter to his son, Amsterdam, 11 Iyar 5520 (1760). In: B.H. Auerbach, *Geschichte der israelitischen Gemeinde Halberstadt.* Halberstadt: H. Meyer, 1866, p. 202 (top). Doubts the authenticity of the will attributed to Maimonides.

117] Graetz, Heinrich, 1817-1891.
Geschichte der Juden. 3. Auflage, 6. Band. Leipzig: Oskar Leiner, 1894, p. 389. Denies its authenticity.

118] Guedemann, Moritz, 1835-1918.
Geschichte des Erziehungswesens und der Cultur der Abendlaendischen Juden (vol. I). Wien: Alfred Holder, 1880, p. 73. Falsely ascribed to Maimonides. See also Hebrew translation.

119] Kaufmann, David, 1852-1899.
Geschichte der Attributenlehre in der juedischen Religionsphilosophie des Mittelalters von Saadja bis Maimuni. Gotha: F.A. Perthes, 1877, p. 490, note 175.

120] Minkin, Jacob S., 1885-1962.
The World of Moses Maimonides with Selections from his Writings. New York: Yoseloff, 1957 (reprint: Northvale, NJ: Jason Aronson, 1987), p. 421. Although scholars are divided on the authenticity of Maimonides' testamentary letter to his son, Minkin feels that the spirit of Maimonides as philosopher, theologian, and moral and ethical teacher is represented in almost every line and paragraph.

121] Oppenheim, David, 1816-1876.
R. Salomon Luria ueber Maimuni und dessen Epistel an seinen Sohn. *Jeschurun* (ed. J. Kabak), 3. Jahrgang (5619/1859), pp. 35-38 (German section). Affirms the authenticity of the *Ethical Will* ascribed to Maimonides in which he praises R. Abraham Ibn Ezra and criticizes the French rabbis as quoted by R. Solomon Luria. Written in opposition to Solomon Rapoport (ibid., 1857, pp. 46-55) who doubts its authenticity.

122] Poznanski, Samuel, 1864-1921.
Mose b. Samuel Hakkohen Ibn Chiquitilla. Leipzig: J.C. Hinrich, 1895, p. 59, note 4. Refutes the authenticity of the will ascribed to Maimonides.

123] Roth, Norman, 1938-
Maimonides as Spaniard: national consciousness of a medieval Jew. In his *Maimonides, Essays and Texts 850th Anniversary.* Madison: Hispanic

Seminary of Medieval Studies, Ltd., 1985, pp. 139-153. Pp. 145-146: Letter to his son *(Will of Maimonides)*; affirms its authenticity in which he criticizes French scholars.

124] Steinschneider, Moritz, 1816-1907.
Vorbericht des Herausgebers. In his *Ermahnungsschreiben des Jehuda Ibn Tibbon... des Moses Maimonides.* Berlin: A. Asher, 1852, pp. III-XIV. At that time, Steinschneider was inclined to accept the authenticity of this work, which was supposed to be an introduction to the older version, first printed in 1544. See, however, his review of: *Lekach Tob,* Catechismus des Abraham Jagel. [Koenigsberg, 1858]. *Hebr. Bibliographie,* II (1859), pp. 7-8. Steinschneider withdrew his earlier view when it came to his attention that the text had already been published anonymously under the title *Sefer ha-Mussar* in Cracow in 1586.

125] Steinschneider, Moritz, 1816-1907.
Review of: *He-Chaluz,* V (1860). *Hebr. Bibl.* IV (1861), 107. "Die Unaechtheit des Maimonidischen Briefes an seiner Sohn (s. 45)." Refers to J. Schor's article on this letter. See Hebrew section.

126] Stitskin, Leon D., 1910-1978.
Letters of Maimonides. New York: Yeshiva Univ. Press, 1977, pp. 137-142. The *Testament* in the light of Maimonides' other writings.

127] Waxman, Meyer, 1887-1969.
History of Jewish Literature, vol. I, New York: Bloch, 1930, pp. 373-374. Its authenticity has been somewhat doubted, but the teachings imparted there bear the stamp of his thought.

128] Zimmels, Hirsch Jacob, 1900-
Ashkenazim and Sephardim; their relations, differences and problems as reflected in the rabbinical responsa. London: Oxford Univ. Press, 1958, p. 15. On the alleged criticism of French scholars in the *Testament* attributed to Maimonides.

129] Zunz, Leopold, 1794-1886.
Zur Geschichte und Literatur. I. Band. Berlin: Veit and Co., 1845, pp. 199-200. On Maimonides' alleged negative attitude to the scholars of France according to the *Ethical Will* attributed to him. See S. D. Luzzatto, Hebrew section.

ד. ציונים ביבליוגראפיים (רובם לכתבי יד)

130] Adler, Elkan Nathan, 1861-1946.
Catalogue of Hebrew Manuscripts in the collection of Elkan Nathan Adler. Cambridge Univ. Press, 1921, p. 38, no. 1402. Now in the Jewish Theological Seminary of America, New York. no. 2435.

131] Assemani, Stephanus Evodius, 1707-1782.
Bibliothecae Apostolicae Vaticanae Codicum Manuscriptorum Catalogus. vol. 1: (Codices Ebraices). Romae, 1856 (photographic ed. Paris, 1926), no. CCCIII (13).

132] Freimann, Aron, 1871-1948.
Union catalog of Hebrew Manuscripts and their location. Vol. 2. New York: American Academy for Jewish Research, 1964, nos. 5163, 9009.

133] Kraft, Albrecht, and Deutsch, Simon, 1822-1877.
Die handschriftlichen hebraischen Werke der k.k. Hofbibliothek zu Wien. Wien, 1847, no. LXXX.

134] Luzzatto, S.D., 1800-1865.
Bibliotheque de feu Joseph Almanzi. *Hebr. Bibl.* V (1862), 104 (no. 195, II).

135] Margoliouth, G., 1853-1952.
Catalogue of the Hebrew and Samaritan Manuscripts in the British Museum, Part III, London, 1915 (reprint: 1965), no. 1076 (I).

136] Marx, Alexander, 1878-1953.
A New Collection of Manuscripts; a recent acquisition of the Library of the Jewish Theological Seminary. PAAJR, IV (1939), p. 152; reprinted in his *Bibliographical Studies and Notes on Rare Books and Manuscripts in the Library of the Jewish Theological Seminary of America*. New York: Jewish Theological Seminary of America and Ktav, 1977, p. 428.

137] Neubauer, Adolf, 1832-1907 and Cowley, Arthur Ernst, 1861-1931.
Catalogue of the Hebrew Manuscripts in the Bodleian Library and in the college Libraries of Oxford, 1886-1906, nos. 1318 (8); 2218 (2 r); 2386 (13); 2455 (2; fragment).

138] Rossi, Giovanni Bernardo de, 1742-1831.
Manuscripti codices Hebraici Biblioth. J.B. de Rossi. Accedit appendix qua continentur mss. codices reliqui al. linguarum. Parmae, 1803. Cod. 272 (3); 533 (4). Collection passed into possession of R. Biblioteca Palatina, Parma (cf. S. Shunami, *Bibliography of Jewish Bibliographies*, 1965, no. 3078).

139] Sacerdote, Gustavo, 1867-1948.
Catalogo dei Codici Ebraici della Biblioteca Casantense. Firenze, 1897, no. 216 (XIV).

140] Sassoon, David Solomon, 1880-1942.
Ohel Dawid; Descriptive Catalogue of the Hebrew and Samaritan Manuscripts in the Sassoon Library, London, with 73 facsimiles. London, 1932, nos. 46 (p. 516); 595 (p. 397a).

141] Steinschneider, Moritz, 1816-1907.
Catalogus Librorum Hebraeorum in Bibliotheca Bodleiana, Berlin, 1852-1860. Faksimile Auflage, Berlin, 1931; Hildesheim, 1964, col. 1934, nos. 157-158.

142] Steinschneider, Moritz, 1816-1907.
Karaitische Handschriften. *Hebraeische Bibliographie* XI (1871), 12.

143] Steinschneider, Moritz, 1816-1907.
Efraim ben Gerson. *Hebraeische Bibliographie* XIX (1879), 32. R. Efraim (mid-15th cent.) cites Maimonides' Testament in his sermons.

144] Steinschneider, Moritz, 1816-1907.
Die hebraeischen Uebersetzungen des Mittelalters und die Juden als Dolmetscher. Berlin, 1893 (facs. ed. Graz, 1956), p. 931.

145] Zotenberg, Hirsch
Catalogues des Manuscrits Hebreux et Samaritains de la Bibliotheque Imperials. Paris, 1866, no. 707 (7); 767 (10).

146] אלוני, נחמיה, 1906־1983 וד"ש לוינגר, 1904־1980.
רשימת תצלומי כתבי־היד העבריים במכון, חלק ג: כתבי־היד שבספריית הוואטיקן. ירושלים: מדינת ישראל; משרד החינוך והתרבות המכון לכתבי־היד העבריים. הוצאת ראובן מס, ירושלים, תשכ"ח, מספר 303 (כז).

147] זנה, ישעיהו, 1887־1960.
אגרת הרמב"ם לשמואל בן תבון עפ"י טופס בלתי ידוע בארכיון הקהלה בוירונה. **תרביץ** 10, ספר ב' (תרצ"ט), 148.
על נוסח שלישי של **צוואת הרמב"ם** בכתבי יד של הקהילה בוירונה.

148] שטיינשניידר, משה, 1816־1907.
דברים עתיקים ג: מגילת העופר. **הכרמל** (שבועון) 6 (תרכ"ו), 320. כתב יד באוקספורד נסמן, Pock. 28013 בשם **מוסר הרמב"ם**.

Part V

MEGILLAT SETARIM

THE SCROLL OF THE UNREVEALED

INTRODUCTION

It is difficult to translate into English the title of the work known as *Megillat Setarim* and falsely attributed to Moses Maimonides. The *Encyclopaedia Judaica* (Keter, Jerusalem, 1971, Volume 11, p. 1229), in describing a totally unrelated work with the same name discussed by Rav in two places in the Babylonian Talmud (*Shabbat* 6b and *Baba Metzia* 92a), calls it the *Concealed Scroll*. This work contains laws cited in the name of Isi ben Judah. *Rashi* (*ad loc*) explains that this scroll was concealed because it was forbidden in general to commit the Oral Law to writing, but since these laws were not generally taught, they were written down to save them from oblivion. Hence, the title *Concealed Scroll*.

The *Megillat Setarim* attributed to Maimonides, however, is a totally different work. It is essentially a letter with kabbalistic views that are foreign to all known authentic writings of Maimonides. Although the true author is unknown, it was clearly not written by Maimonides. Since the contents deal primarily with the secrets of the Torah and mystical and kabbalistic statements, it is better translated *Scroll of the Unrevealed*.

Maimonides was falsely accused of having adopted and

accepted kabbalistic ideations late in his life. Another kabbalistic work entitled *Nine Chapters on the Unity (of God)* was also falsely attributed to him. These pseudo-Maimonidean works are little known to the general public and heretofore only available in Hebrew. Hence, for the sake of historical interest and completeness, these small treatises and letters attributed to Maimonides are presented here in English translation with introduction, bibliography, and annotations.

Megillat Setarim was first published in 1778 in Karetz in the kabbalistic work entitled *Shoshan Sodot (Rose of Secrets)*. This book, whose author is not named, is said to have originated with the disciples of Moses Nachmanides and was printed by John Anton Krieger. Within this book is a statement by the author on page 31a that he found a letter called *Megaleh Amukot (Revealer of Profundities)* that was sent by Moses Maimonides to his distinguished disciple and scholar Rabbi Joseph.

The author of *Shoshan Sodot* calls this letter "the voice of Maimonides in his beautiful language" but then asserts that the contents of the letter concern matters that seem to be the words of kabbalists and astrologers. He therefore suggests that the letter may be by one of Maimonides' disciples who wrote it in his teacher's name. The author of *Shoshan Sodot* then adds that if what was written about Maimonides is true, and if at the end of his life Maimonides did lean toward kabbalistic views, then the letter may well have been written by him. However whether or not Maimonides wrote the letter, concludes the author of *Shoshan Sodot*, it is an important work whose words are "correct to those who understand, and straightforward to those with knowledge" and, therefore, he thought it worthy of publication. The book *Shoshan Sodot* containing this pseudo-Maimonidean letter on pages 31a to 32b was reprinted in Tel Aviv in 1970.

In 1856, Zvi Hirsch Edelman published a book in Koenigsberg entitled *Chemdah Genuzah (Concealed Delight)* containing a variety of "dear and esteemed treatises" that, heretofore, had been unavailable, which he edited and annotated from various manuscripts and other sources. Within this book, on pages 42 to 45 is a "Letter attributed to Moses Maimonides, and known by

INTRODUCTION

the name *Megillat Setarim*" (*Scroll of the Unrevealed*). The subtitle reads: "The pleasant and distinguished disciple, Rabbi Joseph, son of Judah, may his soul delight (in paradise)."

In a lengthy introductory footnote, Edelman states that the *Megillat Setarim* came from Rabbi Moses Alshakar in his commentary and criticism of a work known as *Sefer Ha-Emunot* (*Book of Beliefs*) authored by Rabbi Shem Tob. The latter's words there are: "I came to write the words of Rabbi Moses Maimonides who wrote in his *Megillat Setarim* to his distinguished pupil about profound matters." He then quotes extensively from the letter, beginning with the statement "the strong love that existed between me and you and your holy ancestors . . ."

Edelman points out that it was next copied by Rabbi Joseph Solomon Rophé (acronym *Yashar*) Delmedigo from Candiya in his book *Novlet Chochmah* (*Fruits of Wisdom*). Edelman motivates the readers to consult that work to see for themselves the numerous omissions of words and phrases in the printing of *Megillat Setarim*. He further states that Rabbi Chayim Joseph David Azulai, in his work *Shem HaGedolim* (*Names of Great Scholars*), cites the *Megillat Setarim* as follows:

> According to the words of Rabbi Chaim Vital it seems that during the last days of his life the reason he made use of the various divine names was related to the *Megillat Setarim* which has been attributed to Moses Maimonides and cited by Rabbi Moses Alshakar, section 117. However, I saw in the book *Shoshan Sodot* a copy of this work [*Megillat Setarim*] about which [the author of *Shoshan Sodot* expresses] doubt as to whether or not it is from Maimonides. [p.42]

"It appears to me," continues Edelman, "that these two scholars never saw *Megillat Setarim* and only had secondhand knowledge of this letter from its mention by Rabbi Moses Alshakar." Edelman decries the practice of scholars who quote writers and citations without consulting the original works themselves. Edelman quotes a critic who wrote in the periodical *Bikkurei Ha'itim* in 1831, adding his complaints about the authorship of *Megillat Setarim*. This unnamed critic argued against the attribution of authorship to Moses Maimonides. Edelman dismisses his arguments, saying that he, too, never saw a copy of *Megillat Setarim.*

By the grace of God, continues Edelman, among the various manuscripts that came to his attention were several that allowed him to edit and publish *Megillat Setarim* in its entirety "from beginning to end." He clearly states that his intent is not to support or negate the attribution of authorship to Maimonides and leaves it "up to the judges to judge." He allows himself the liberty, in his footnotes, of pointing out similarities in the contents of *Megillat Setarim* and certain writings of Maimonides and some of his predecessors, especially Rabbi Abraham ibn Ezra.

Edelman concludes his introductory remarks by saying that he himself considered it just and proper to disseminate the words of the letter by publishing it and asks for his reward from the Righteous Judge, Master of All That Is Hidden.

The letter *Megillat Setarim* was reprinted unchanged from Edelman's edition in part two of a collection of responsa and letters of Moses Maimonides called *Kovetz Teshuvot HaRambam Ve-Iggrotov* (*Collection of Responsa of Maimonides and His Letters*) published in Leipzig in 1859, on pages 35a to 36a. The *Kovetz* was reprinted in Jerusalem in 1967. Most of the Edelman version of *Megillat Setarim* was also reprinted by David Margolith in his book *Derech Yisrael Birefuah* (*The Way of Israel in Medicine*), published by the Jerusalem Academy of Medicine in 1950 (pp. 204–208).

In 1970, M. Bar-Joseph published a book containing letters of Maimonides and biographical material on his life. The book was published in Tel Aviv by the Mordechai Institute for Publishing Judaica and is entitled *Rabbenu Moshe ben Maimon: Iggrotov Ve-Toldot Chayav* (*Maimonides: His Letters and Biography of His Life*). Pages 110 to 118 are devoted to a brief analysis and new Hebrew version of *Megillat Setarim.* This version differs considerably from the first 1778 version and the 1856 Edelman version and is a rather free and loose rendition into modern and simple Hebrew since Bar Joseph's book, according to the title page, is intended for high school students. Difficult pas-

INTRODUCTION

sages from the original and Edelman versions are simply omitted by Bar Joseph. Regarding its authorship, Bar Joseph simply states in a brief footnote that "this letter (*Megillat Setarim*) is attributed to Maimonides but there are different views as to whether or not that supposition is correct."

In 1988, Yitzchak Shilat published a collection of Maimonides' letters in a two volume work called *Iggarot HaRambam (Letters of Maimonides)*. This book was published in Jerusalem by Ma'aliyot, associated with the Yeshiva *Birchat Moshe* of Maale Adumim, a suburb of Jerusalem. Shilat briefly cites six spurious works attributed to Maimonides. On pages 595 and 596 at the end of volume 2, Shilat discusses *Megillat Setarim* whose main contents comprise "praises of Kabbalah and its preference over philosophy, instructions in practical Kabbalah and the use of holy [that is divine] names."

Shilat cites the various published editions of *Megillat Setarim* including the first version in 1778 in *Shoshan Sodot*. He states that according to Azulai (also known as *Chidah*) in his work *Shem HaGedolim*, the author of *Shoshan Sodot* is Rabbi Moshe ben Jacob of Kiev who lived about 350 years after Maimonides. Shilat also expresses doubt whether Rabbi Moses Alshakar, who mentions *Megillat Setarim* in his Responsa 117, seriously attributed this letter to Maimonides or whether he used it only to protest against those who were disrespectful of Maimonides.

According to Shilat, "there is not even a shadow of a doubt" that *Megillat Setarim* is a forgery for the following reasons:

1. The author of the letter writes: "and by the strong bonds of love between me and you and your holy ancestors." However, in the introductory letter to the *Guide* there is first depicted the acquaintanceship between Maimonides and Rabbi Joseph, and there is no mention of the love between him and the ancestors of Rabbi Joseph. By contrast, see the introduction to *The Letter to Yemen* and the introduction of the letter to Rabbi Samuel ibn Tibbon.
2. The author also writes: "that which you studied before me about the science of astronomy and some of the wonderful remarks I made about the topic of Kabbalah, which is an

awesome and marvelous wisdom." The term "wisdom of Kabbalah" (*Chochmat HaKabbalah*) is used several times thereafter. However, nowhere does Maimonides use the term *Kabbalah* to depict the wisdom of the Secrets of the Torah, and more to the point, it seems to me that even the kabbalists of his era did not yet use the expression "wisdom of Kabbalah." It was not until a much later period that this term was used.

3. If Maimonides studied the science of astronomy as well as "practical Kabbalah" together with his disciple, he would have done so before he composed the *Guide*. How then does the author of the letter *Megillat Setarim* sustain the basic and strong opposition of Maimonides to the use of "[divine] names" in the *Guide of the Perplexed*, Part 1, Chapter 61? (See also *Mishneh Torah, Hilchot Mezuzah* 5:4.) The fact that the author mentions in *Megillat Setarim* the "book that I composed for you and which I called *Guide of the Perplexed*" should not, understandably, evoke surprise: this is the outstanding ingredient to the creation of the impression of authenticity and the "forger examined the barrel but not its contents."

In a general way, concludes Shilat, one can say that legends like "at the end of his day, Maimonides reverted," do not add honor either to Maimonides or to Kabbalah. The proper way to compare the philosophical teaching of Maimonides with the wisdom of Kabbalah is not by artificial coercion of one over the other, but to descend into the depths of the divine perceptions of both and to openly examine and compare them as was done by many sages and kabbalists throughout the generations.

The present English translation is based primarily on the 1856 Edelman edition of *Megillat Setarim* which was reprinted unchanged in Leipzig in 1859 in *Kovetz Teshuvot HaRambam Ve-Iggrotov* (vide supra). The earlier 1778 version of *Megillat Setarim* in *Shoshan Sodot* is incomplete and full of errors. It appears as if it was not even proofread nor corrected prior to its publication. Differences between these two versions are pointed out in the footnotes. Words in brackets are my own additions to help clarify the meaning of the text.

THE SCROLL
OF THE UNREVEALED[1]

The pleasant and distinguished disciple, Rabbi Joseph, son of Judah, may his soul delight [in Paradise].[2]

May the Lord grant you repose in the tabernacle of life and of wisdom, and keep you straight on the path of uprightness and integrity,[3] and give you understanding to comprehend[4] the prophetic allegories[5] and the spiritual assurances[6] that were created based on the fundamental principle of the knowledge of God[7] and the divine names that are alluded to in some of the verses of the prophecy.[8] With the knowledge of these general principles, you will inherit the eternal and everlasting inheritance and not fall under the boundary of want. You will rise to

---

[1] The 1778 earliest version of *Megillat Setarim* (see bibliography) entitles it *Megaleh Amukot (Revealer of Profundities)*.

[2] The 1778 version prefaces this subtitle with the phrase "these are the words of the letter."

[3] Literally: wonder or marvel.

[4] Literally: a heart to know.

[5] The 1778 version renders: allegories of the prophets.

[6] The 1778 version renders: assurances of the souls.

[7] The 1778 version renders: based on the knowledge of the secrets of God.

[8] The 1778 version renders: prophecies (plural).

the level of marvelous wisdom, and your soul will resemble the holy angels on high. Your paths will be exalted and you will be elevated above the paths of the general populace who are dull-hearted.[9] Your knowledge will be separate from the knowledge of fools whose ears are closed to listening.

Since I know that you love the wisdom of Kabbalah[10] about which you say, "she is my sister, and she, even she herself said, 'he is my brother,'"[11] I have combined what you studied before me[12] about the science of astronomy with certain wonderful remarks that I called to your attention about the topic of Kabbalah, which is an awesome and marvelous wisdom.

I also saw fit to cause you to inherit another enlightened inheritance[13] and to perfect you in one fundamental principle upon which depend all its branches and roots.[14] In the depiction of this fundamental principle that describes the proper path for you to follow, you will be among those who understand divine knowledge.[15] Your lust will be tranquilized, the power of your intellect will be strengthened, the divine desire will be awakened in you, and you will be among the group of the perfect. You will also attain all your wishes provided the requests are honorable and lead to perfection of your pure soul. Do not let your thoughts wander to vanishing materialistic images,[16] which suppress and cause the divine and free will to sink into the abyss.[17] Also conduct yourself virtuously[18] in relation to regulations of the land, your friends, and members of your household, and in your spiritual and physical activities.

---

[9] Hebrew: *areley lev*, literally: uncircumcised, that is, obtuse, stupid, or dull-hearted. The 1778 version renders *abirey lev*, literally hardhearted, or stubborn.

[10] The 1778 version renders: since this knowledge of yours includes a love of the wisdom of Kabbalah.

[11] Allusion to Genesis 20:5.

[12] The 1778 version renders: that which I saw before me.

[13] The 1778 version renders: enlightened wisdom.

[14] Literally: root.

[15] Literally: higher knowledge.

[16] The 1778 version renders: perdition of the Creator; obviously an error.

[17] Literally: the depths of the ocean.

[18] Literally: conduct your soul with virtues.

THE SCROLL OF THE UNREVEALED

Your free will should remain in your influence and prevail over everything that is contrary to your intellect except for those honorable and precious activities that are desired for the love of your spiritual glory.

I swear by the life of the strong love[19] between me and you and your holy ancestors that most of the time I was perplexed by inquiries into existences according to the view of the truth of their content, as much as is feasible by human perception. I toiled and found some of the truth. However, on faith I did not find the total truth from the standpoint of philosophical inquiry and the ways of their signs, not that I say that they are not correct in what they perceived.[20] However, it may be correct because what they have proven[21] through their wisdom has not been disproven.[22] Rather, they did not find individual ways in their inquiry into the general nature of existences other than intellectual toil;[23] but in respectable ways they distress[24] the intellect and confuse it. However, in regard to the wisdom of Kabbalah,[25] the truth of their ways is cleared of boulders[26] that act as stumbling blocks. It becomes very easily understood;[27] everything falls within the human perception.[28]

The prophets walked on this path[29] and perceived all that they perceived of the knowledge of the future, and performed strange activities that are outside the habit of nature. I too adopted some of their ways in the understanding of the nature of existences and there became known to me the enormous doubts that I had. There became opened before me all the

---

[19]The 1778 version renders: chosen love.
[20]The 1778 version renders: taught.
[21]Literally: does not contradict the sign.
[22]The 1778 version renders: to us.
[23]The 1778 version omits this entire phrase.
[24]The 1778 version renders: destroy.
[25]The 1778 version renders: scholars of Kabbalah.
[26]Literally: destoned.
[27]That is, Kabbalah.
[28]The 1778 version renders: the boundary of human perception.
[29]The 1778 version renders: a strange path.

doors[30] of perplexity and there was placed in my hands the key of wisdom and the clarification of all that was concealed from me. Herewith I adjure you not to reveal these secrets in public[31] and the marvelous comments except to one with a fine nature,[32] pure in deeds, pure in thoughts,[33] and who walks in the paths of learning and of knowledge.

Know, my brother, that it is explained in the books of the wisdom of Kabbalah that the holy, divine names are too numerous to count and all show the existence[34] of angels who have levels one above the other and degrees one above the other. There is one Prime Cause[35] that is straight[36] over them and which is not a physical body, nor a force in a body, nor essence in a body.[37] The prophet alludes to these three negatives in the general portrayal of the Prime Cause in the three-part description of the secret of holiness.[38] His connection with the other causes that are related to Him is like the connection between the king and the judges. Below the judges are the judicial enforcers, and below the judicial enforcers are the officials, and below the officials are the messengers who all went forth in haste by the king's commandment.[39]

The [divine] names are powers that emanate from angels who are fulfilling the wishes of their Creator.[40] These powers

---

[30] The 1778 version omits the word "all."

[31] The 1778 version omits the term "in public."

[32] The 1778 version renders: fine intellect.

[33] The 1778 version renders: dejected in his eyes, or humble in spirit.

[34] Hebrew: *mahut* meaning essence, nature, quality, existence, being.

[35] That is, Almighty God, the Most High.

[36] That is, singular or simple, not a combination of different substances.

[37] God is an incorporeal, not a corporeal, force; nor has he corporeal substance, but He rules over the angels. Bar Joseph distorts the meaning by rendering: the commonality [of angels] is that they are incorporeal, have no force and no essence in a [physical] body.

[38] Probable allusion to "Holy, Holy, Holy is the Lord of Hosts" (Isaiah 6:3).

[39] Probable allusion to Esther 3:15.

[40] Here Edelman has a lengthy footnote in which he speaks of a work called *Sefer Ha'atzamin* containing an essay by Rabbi Abraham ibn Ezra that cites the following in the name of Aristotle. They have already said that Aristotle has asserted that: the divine names are the powers that emanate from the power

rest in the lower world by the decree of their Creator as is requested of them[41] for good and for blessing, no matter how it turns out when it is mentioned by the requestor[42] in the name of the One who demonstrates the truth of His request.

If one perceives this matter of the holy names and mentions them with holiness and purity and includes his request [to God] with those names, they become an entity in his hand as a single request, and he will achieve[43] from Him whatever height he wishes. And it will be with him like whispered speech[44] with a soft voice so that he can hear it without sounds. And he will understand illusions from Him in those matters that he asks of Him. The clarification of the requested matters and advice will come to him from afar to remove him from his confusions. He will stir them up with deep thoughts[45] and the truth will be explained to him without any doubt.

And if it should happen because of preoccupations with confusion that perturb his mind so that he becomes confused in perplexity[46] or [he is perplexed] because of lack of holiness and purity, then all his doubts[47] will only melt with great difficulty. The Master of the Prophets[48] proved [this point] at the waters of Meribah.[49]

Therefore, my brother, I will elaborate and teach you wisdom because the matter of understanding the remainder of

---

of their names which are the heavenly intellects and powers arranged level below level like a king and a judge, and below that are judicial enforcers and below the judicial enforcers . . . etc. until the completion of all the things mentioned here about this matter. Edelman also cites a work, *Margoliyot Tovah*, which quotes biblical verses to comment on and "correct" Ibn Ezra's statements. Also cited are numerous places in Maimonides' *Guide of the Perplexed* for many of the topics discussed in the present work, *Megillat Setarim*.

[41] The term "of them" appears twice in the 1778 version.
[42] The 1778 version omits "the requestor."
[43] The 1778 version renders: will be helped.
[44] The 1778 version renders: with spiritual speech.
[45] Literally: deep matters.
[46] This entire phrase is missing in the 1778 version.
[47] The 1778 version renders: all the doubts.
[48] Moses.
[49] Numbers 20:13. Literally: waters of strife. See also Exodus 17:1–7.

wisdom, which is concealed, requires that you devote yourself[50] to holiness and purity as much as possible. You should beware of lascivious talk and be extremely careful and far removed from the sense of touch. Devote your soul to divine knowledge and become wise from the things that emanate therefrom because you are a delightful person.

After these matters[51] it is up to you to know that in the scriptural verse, "And there I will meet with thee, and I will speak with thee from above the ark cover, from between the two cherubim that are upon the ark of the testimony, of all things that I will give thee in commandment unto the children of Israel,"[52] you will find twenty-two words[53] to which the author of the *Book of Creation* alludes when he asserts that twenty-two letters are carved out for the Engraver.[54] He exchanges them and combines them and creates with them every creation and every soul that is to be created in the future and they are twenty-two simple letters. The intent therewith is that whatever is created of the spiritual angels in human beings[55] is carved out with these twenty-two words. Thereby, a person can attain knowledge in the world[56] and will remember that which he forgot of matters that are possible [to know].[57]

Know that Moses our Teacher, may he rest in peace, included in his perceptions these divine cognomens arranged from among the general names of the angels with whom he was in constant communication. This is alluded to when it is written: "He is faithful in all Mine house."[58] From this scriptural verse

---

[50] The 1778 version renders: prepare yourself.
[51] The 1778 version renders: all these matters.
[52] Exodus 25:22.
[53] In Hebrew, this scriptural verse has twenty-two words.
[54] Almighty God.
[55] Literally: external or human souls.
[56] The 1778 version renders: can attain knowledge of that which is concealed.
[57] Bar Joseph suggests that the author may here be alluding to the rabbinic adage that a fetus is taught the entire Torah but as soon as it is born, an angel comes and makes the fetus forget all it was taught.
[58] Numbers 12:7.

there emanate seven names from seven angels of the seven[59] heavens which comprise [the Hebrew acronym] *Shatzam Chanakal*[60] (Saturn, Jupiter, Mars, Sun, Venus, Mercury, Moon).[61] Parallel[62] to these are the seven sacrificial bullocks[63] and also the festival sacrifices—all follow the path of the sevens. Similarly the seven sevens of the years of the Jubilee[64], the seven years of the Sabbatical year,[65] the seven months until Rosh Hashanah,[66] the seven weeks until the receiving of the Torah,[67] the seven days of the Sabbath.[68] Also parallel to these are the seven altars that Balak built[69] and the sprinkling [of the blood] on the seventh day [to purify] the ritually unclean.[70]

You already know from having studied the science of astronomy with me that the moon returns to the planet opposite it on the seventh day of its cycle.[71] Its influence on the lower world does not change. All this is an allusion to and comment about the influence here of the forces that contact these seven planets.

Behold, [I here provide] for you the order of the seven names of the aforementioned scriptural verse.[72] The first line

---

[59] The 1778 version omits the word "seven."

[60] The first letter of each of the seven planets in Hebrew: *S*habatai (Saturn), *Tz*edek (Jupiter), *Ma*'adim (Mars), *Ch*amah (Sun), *N*ogah (Venus), *K*ochov (Mercury), *L*evanah (Moon).

[61] Edelman adds the names of the planets parenthetically in order to explain the Hebrew acronym. The parentheses do not appear in the 1778 version.

[62] Literally: opposite.

[63] Numbers 29:32.

[64] Leviticus 25:8.

[65] Leviticus 25:4.

[66] Rosh Hashanah occurs on the first day of the seventh month, the month of Tishri. Numbers 29:1.

[67] The holiday of Pentecost, which commemorates the receiving of the Torah at Mount Sinai, occurs seven weeks after Passover. Leviticus 23:15 and Deuteronomy 16:9.

[68] The seven days of the week of which the seventh is the Sabbath. Genesis 2:2.

[69] Numbers 23:1.

[70] Leviticus 4:6, 4:17, 8:11, 14:7, 14:16, 14:27, etc.

[71] Literally: event.

[72] Exodus 25:22.

represents the first letters[73] of the words and the second line represents the last letters of the words, and their punctuation should be as written forwards and backwards.[74] The following are the names: V-L-Sh[75] V-I-M[76] H-M-Sh[77] H-A-A[78] A-H-E[79] K-A-A[80] O-E-B-Y[81] I-Ch-M[82] I-Ch-L[83] T-N-E[84] M-R-L[85] N-T-T[86] L-R-H[87] K-L-E-L[88]

The[89] way to use [these names] in this matter[90] is as follows: one should fast on a Wednesday, which is the day of Mercury, and part of it is wisdom and knowledge of concealed things.[91] And one should conduct oneself with extreme purity and more timidity than all human beings.[92] When he goes to sleep during the first hour of the night, he should wash his head and all his flesh with water and clothe himself in a pure and clean shirt[93] and trousers and lie alone in bed and recite the aforementioned sentence with strong devotion and with a pure heart and with humble spirit. After that he should recite the aforementioned

---

[73] Literally: heads of words.

[74] In a footnote, Bar Joseph states that his intention was to omit "the section dealing with the names of angels." However, in response to a plea by Rabbi Yehuda Tzvi Brandwine, author of *Ma'alot Hasulam*, Bar Joseph retained this section for the sake of the completeness of the *Megillat Setarim*.

[75] *Veno'adti Lecha Sham* (and there I will meet with thee).

[76] *Vedibarti Itcha Meyal* (and I will speak with thee from above).

[77] *Hakaporet Meebayn Shne* (the ark cover, from between the two).

[78] *Hakerubim Asher Al* (cherubim that are upon).

[79] *Aron Ha'eydut Et* (the ark of the testimony).

[80] *Kol Asher Atzaveh* (of all things that I will give thee in commandment).

[81] *Otcha El Bnei Yisrael* (unto the children of Israel).

[82] *Veno'adti Lecha Sham*.

[83] *Vedibarti Itcha Meyal*.

[84] *Hakaporet Meebayn Shne*.

[85] *Hakerubim Asher Al*.

[86] *Aron Ha'eydut Et*.

[87] *Kol Asher Atzaveh*.

[88] *Otcha El Bne Yisrael*.

[89] Here the 1778 version adds the names of the seven planets: Saturn, Jupiter, Mars, Sun, Venus, Mercury, Moon.

[90] The 1778 version omits the phrase: in this matter.

[91] The 1778 version renders: the concealed knowledge.

[92] Literally: creations.

[93] Hebrew: *chaluk*, also refers to a robe, jacket, or gown.

holy names. His heart should be constantly directed toward heaven. He should do this seven times, that is to say, he should read the aforementioned sentence [seven times] and then the seven names of the angels and become fluent in them.[94] After complete introspection, he should direct his thoughts toward the doubt that he had about this or any other matter.

Afterwards he should sleep on his left side. You will find that in the middle of your sleep the spirit of the Holy God[95] will affect you and the hair on your flesh will bristle as you fall into a sleep of confusion and fear of your thoughts. During the nocturnal dream you will see the appearance of a man who will awaken you from your sleep. He will come to judge with you and will relate to you the mysteries of wisdom and [give you] twice as much insight or[96] he will appear as if he is arguing with you.[97] He will clarify for you[98] the things[99] about which you are in doubt. As your solitude becomes intense, conduct yourself according to the rule of this powerful art and the doubt will become clarified for you like true and righteous light.[100] The expanse[101] of your intellect will be purified from the great doubts with complete purification and there will not remain any point of doubt in the matters[102] of your request.

Behold, my brother, my dear one,[103] that mostly the true clarification will come to you through parables and riddles. From this point of view, the words of influence of the interpreting angel and his riddles will make the power of your intellect strong to understand the parables and riddles. This is not astounding because even in regard to the true prophecies that the prophets, other than Moses our Teacher, may he rest

---

[94] Literally: arrange them in the mouth.
[95] The 1778 version renders: a holy spirit.
[96] The 1778 version substitutes "their" for "or."
[97] The 1778 version omits this phrase.
[98] Literally: teach you.
[99] Literally: the place.
[100] The 1778 version renders: a true and righteous explanation.
[101] The 1778 version omits this phrase.
[102] The 1778 version renders: matter, in the singular.
[103] The 1778 version omits: my dear one; Bar Joseph renders: my son.

in peace, prophesied, all they related and the mysteries of their prophecies were in the form of parables as stated by the Holy One, blessed be He: "if there is a prophet among you, I the Lord will make Myself known unto him in a vision" [I will speak with him in a dream].[104] I have explained this matter similarly in the book I composed for you and that I called *Guide of the Perplexed* and its explanation is in the second section.

Distinguished disciple, consider well the seven names and how each, except for the seventh, is made up of three[105] letters.[106] This means that the first six, that is to say the angels who are related to them, have in them parts of three natures, the nature of the upper world because they are separate intellects, the nature of the middle world because for each figure,[107] one of them[108] is responsible for that planet and its orbit,[109] and the nature of the lower world according to its designated arrangement in the lower world. However, the name of the angel appointed over the planet moon has [four][110] letters and the completeness of this planet controls all the planets. The four simple fundamental elements[111] emanate from its concavity and below from the center [of the moon].

Open your eyes, my dear son,[112] [and observe] how the enigmas and secrets of divine wisdom will become known to you. All that about which you were in doubt concerning the clarifications[113] of the Torah and its explanations[114] will be-

---

[104] Numbers 12:6.

[105] Edelman omits the word "three" which is found in the 1778 version and helps to clarify the text.

[106] See notes 75 to 88.

[107] Planet.

[108] Angels.

[109] The entire phrase about the middle world is not in the 1778 version.

[110] The 1778 version adds "four" which helps in understanding the meaning of the sentence; that is, the other planets are represented by an acronym of three letters but the moon's acronym has four letters. (See footnotes 81 and 88.)

[111] Fire, wind, water, and dust.

[112] Allusion to Jeremiah 31:19.

[113] The 1778 version renders "clarification" in the singular.

[114] The 1778 version renders "explanation" in the singular.

come clear to you in the way that I have revealed to you its reason and its greatness and its mighty hand[115] through Kabbalah from the letters.[116] My probings into most doubts were clarified. Because of my love for you it[117] will be for you only and not for any laymen[118] with you except for those whom God[119] granted understanding. Concerning you and those who are comparable to you the prophet said: "the secret of the Lord is with them that fear Him, and His covenant, to make them know it."[120]

Another secret [I will reveal to you will] enable you to be close to the king[121] and to find favor in his eyes over all the sages of the time, to have divine power attached to you, to stand in his palace, and to have his attendants ask your [advice] and request your presence. I saw fit to help you in a matter that is accepted and useful and dear[122] in its existence. Thereby you will rise to an even greater level, kings will exalt you, all the judges of the land will honor you, and they will turn to bear the significance of all that you ask of them. You will be among the group of their advisors, and their leaders will seek out your advice and reject the advice of others. They will encourage you[123] like an advocating angel and ask things from your mouth just like from the mouth of a prophet who asks [advice] from the *Urim and Thummin*.[124]

---

[115] Perhaps an allusion to *The Mighty Hand* which is one of the names of Maimonides' *Mishneh Torah*.

[116] The 1778 version renders: through the authentic Kabbalah.

[117] The knowledge and understanding of the secrets, riddles, and parables of the Torah.

[118] Literally: strangers, aliens, foreigners.

[119] The 1778 version renders: the Creator.

[120] Psalm 25:14.

[121] Literally: kingdom or royal family, that is, the government in power.

[122] The 1778 version renders: draw close to.

[123] Literally: strengthen you.

[124] The last phrase here is translated from the 1778 version. Edelman renders: and they ask (advice) from the *Urim and Thummin*. The *Urim and Thummin* is a priestly device for obtaining oracles. On the high priest's *ephod* (an apron-like garment) lay a breastplate known as *choshen*—a plate inlaid with twelve precious stones engraved with the names of the twelve tribes of

In the book of Exodus[125] you will find a sentence in which the Lord, may He be blessed, said the following to the most distinguished man of the human race[126] when He promised the Israelites that they would find favor in the eyes of the Egyptians: "And I will give this people favor in the sight of the Egyptians; and it shall come to pass that when you go, you shall not go empty."[127] I will instruct you, my son, that in this sentence there are divine secrets which are not conjectured because of their great virtues, for a great portion of divine influence rests on the compounding of all the constellations. In it[128] are thirteen [Hebrew] words corresponding to the thirteen [divine] attributes of the Creator, may He be blessed, alluded to in the scriptural verse: "And the Lord passed by before him."[129]

You already know the allusion that I alluded to you in person[130] concerning the wisdom of the thirteen attributes. I revealed to you their explanations and their mystique in that they are incorporated into this number and not another number. It is not necessary for me to repeat my dissertation because I know that I am speaking to a listening ear. You will also find that the letters of this scriptural verse[131] are forty-six in number and that the sum total of this number is alluded to in the first letter of this verse and in the last.[132] Behold, there are no two letters in the Hebrew alphabet[133] that are duplicated

---

Israel—that held the *Urim and Thummin* (Exodus 28:15–30 and Leviticus 8:8). By means of the *Urim*, the priest inquired of God on behalf of the king or high court (Numbers 27:21 and *Yoma* 7:5). For more details consult the *Encyclopedia Judaica*, Jerusalem: Keter, 1971, Vol. 16, pp. 8–9.

[125]Literally: in the portion (of the Torah that begins with the words): "Now these are the names" that is, the Book of Exodus.

[126]Moses our Teacher.

[127]Exodus 3:21.

[128]In this sentence.

[129]Exodus 34:6–7. There are thirteen distinct divine attributes in these two verses, though there are differences among the rabbis as to their precise enumeration.

[130]Literally: face to face.

[131]Exodus 3:21: "And I will give this people favor."

[132]The 1778 version renders: the last letter.

[133]Literally: in the *aleph-bet*.

THE SCROLL OF THE UNREVEALED   213

in their pronunciation other than the *mem* and the *vav*.[134] This demonstrates the simplicity of their composition. They are close and resemble the simple [letters] which are further distanced from the three names.[135]

You will also find therein[136] that the [letter] *vav* as it is written has the numerical value of twelve[137] which is an allusion to the twelve constellations that allude to the twelve precious stones [on the breastplate of the high priest][138] upon which all matters of the world are dependent. Behold, the [Hebrew letter] *mem* as it is written has the numerical value of eighty[139] which is double the number forty. The four letters of the Tetragrammaton [multiplied] by ten[140] and doubled [also

---

[134] Exodus 3:21 begins with the letter *vav* and ends with the letter *mem*.

[135] The 1778 version renders: greatly distanced from the corporeal (Hebrew: *gashmiyot*), whereas Edelman renders the Hebrew: *gimmel shemot* (three names) rather than fusing the two words into *gashmiyot*, which has a totally different meaning. In a lengthy footnote, Edelman suggests that the author is referring to other letters duplicated from the three letters. Thus, in his words, we find an explanation of the words of the *Book of Creation*: "twenty-four letters are engraved, etc.," that is to say, everything that is created is carved out with these twenty-two words. Perhaps also the fact that each letter, in its pronunciation, is comprised of three letters (such as the Hebrew letter *aleph* which in its pronunciation is comprised of three letters (*aleph, lamed,* and *pheh*), led the author to call them words rather than letters. Therefore, each letter, which can be divided into three letters, is itself in its pronunciation comprised of three letters. Thus he portrays them as names comprised of three letters. "This is correct in my opinion," concludes Edelman, "but I cannot coerce anyone to accept my opinion."

[136] In Exodus 3:21.

[137] Double its usual value of six because, when written, the word *vav* has the letter *vav* twice in it.

[138] Hebrew: *avnei chen*. The 1778 version has *avner choshen*, literally: stones of the breastplate. See footnote 124.

[139] Double its usual value of forty because, when written, the word *mem* has the letter *mem* twice in it.

[140] In a footnote Edelman suggests that the author refers to the development of the ten heavenly intellects together with the lower world which receives its influence through them. All of them are influenced by the Tetragrammaton, and this is the reason for the doubling of each of its four letters; double ten gives twenty for each letter, times four equals eighty.

produces eighty] and this is an allusion to the tenth planet, which is holy, giving praise to the Lord.[141]

Now listen, my son, I will give you counsel and may God be with you.[142] I will teach you to follow this path, [the path of] this marvelous Kabbalah. The following is what you should do:[143] Take a pen made of refined silver on Thursday, which is the day of Jupiter, and watch it. Make ink from the juice of roses and saffron[144] on Wednesday, which is the day of the planet that is appointed over wisdom and grace. Prepare parchment that is extremely well cultivated on Sunday, which is the day of the sun that is appointed[145] over the sultanate. When everything is prepared before you, begin writing on Monday during the first hour of the day. Also on that day, fast and conduct yourself with holiness and purity. Similarly, delineate[146] on the parchment and write one word thereon on one day[147] during the first hour. So too shall you do for each word until the completion of the entire scriptural verse of thirteen consecutive words.[148]

After you have completed it, carry it on you[149] constantly.[150] However, be careful, my son, that as long as it is fastened upon you, beware of any [bad] action or thought because then the influencing power of the celestial bodies on it will weaken and become nullified. You too will bear the responsibility for[151] your sin and you will be punished. In a place where your perception [of these hidden matters] could benefit you, you will, heaven forbid, achieve just the opposite. Therefore, ob-

---

[141] Allusion to Leviticus 19:24.
[142] Allusion to Exodus 18:19.
[143] Literally: this is its practice.
[144] The 1778 version omits roses and saffron and substitutes another plant.
[145] The 1778 version omits this entire sentence as well as the words "wisdom and grace" in the previous sentence.
[146] Alternate translations: draw, sketch, portray, stripe, make lines.
[147] The 1778 version renders: Monday.
[148] Exodus 3:21.
[149] The 1778 version renders: with you.
[150] Perhaps the author refers to an amulet upon which is written the scriptural verse from Exodus 3:21 and which is to be worn at all times.
[151] Literally: will have to carry.

serve and listen. Because if one gives to a wise man, he will become yet wiser,[152] I point out to you[153] that the righteous Joseph found favor in the eyes of his master because of one of these reasons about which it is not necessary to speak at length because you are a wise man. So too Queen Esther before the king as it is written: "and she obtained grace and favor in his sight."[154] In this [understanding of kabbalistic ideas], I too achieved what I achieved in the eyes of the Arabian kings in Egypt and Alexandria, and all were of this type.

Behold, I have alluded to you hidden and concealed secrets. Protect them on the tablet of your heart. Tie them to your windpipe and accept them[155] with the proper judgment and God will be with you. I know that you pursue and practice love of compassion.[156] And walk humbly with your God[157] who loves peace and pursues peace.[158] And if you will conduct yourself[159] with holiness and purity and reverence for your Creator and investigate the nature of existing things and the order of existing things that are influenced by the upper world[160] according to Kabbalah, I have given you a way in which to succeed.[161] I saw fit to show you the way about these two straight and honorable approaches which encompass much of the beginning of the prophetic, rabbinic, and practical aspects of Kabbalah.

May these bring you to an understanding[162] of things that are concealed from you and things about which you have doubts and bring you to a love for all creations and specifically before kings and princes; that is to say, through the second

---

[152] Allusion to Proverbs 9:9.
[153] Literally: I arrange or prepare or set before you.
[154] Esther 2:17.
[155] The 1778 version renders: tie them.
[156] The performance of personal acts of loving kindness.
[157] Allusion to Micah 6:8.
[158] Perhaps a reference to Aaron the high priest. See *Pirké Abot* 1:12.
[159] Literally: place your ways.
[160] The 1778 version omits the word "world."
[161] The latter phrase is not in the 1778 version.
[162] Literally: approaching, touching, reaching.

teaching that I taught you and through the first teaching in regard to the revealing of what is concealed and about that concerning where there are doubts. Together with these two perceptions you will achieve eternal spiritual life and you will delight in the resplendence of the divine influence, which cleaves to those who cleave to Him as it is written: "but you that cleave to the Lord your God," and so on.[163]

You will also achieve thereby[164] life in this world with love and peace together with your overall political conduct[165] and thoughts. You will be preserved in all your ways, which are ways of pleasantness, and all your paths are peace.[166] May the Lord refine you in the crucible of wisdom[167] and lead you in the proper path and make you dwell in a perfect tent[168] and [grant you] peace like a soul praying for your peace.

Amen—Eternity—Selah[169]

---

[163] Deuteronomy 4:4.

[164] The 1778 version omits the word "thereby."

[165] The latter phrase is not in the 1778 version.

[166] Allusion to Proverbs 3:17.

[167] The crucible of wisdom is apparently a phrase used in kabbalistic works. It is found repeatedly in another kabbalistic essay falsely attributed to Maimonides, entitled *Nine Chapters on the Unity (of God)*, in my *The Existence and Unity of God: Three Treatises Attributed to Moses Maimonide* (1990), Northvale, NJ: Jason Aronson.

[168] Literally: complete tent. The 1778 version renders: a tent of peace.

[169] The Hebrew abbreviation A-N-S representing the Hebrew letters *Aleph*, *Nun* and *Samech* is found at the end of *Megillat Setarim* and is an acronym for *Amen, Netzach, Selah*. Bar Joseph erroneously has the last letter as a *mem* rather than a *samech*.

BIBLIOGRAPHY

by Jacob I. Dienstag

תקמ"ד 1784

1] מגלה עמוקות. בתוך: ספר **שושן סודות** לר' משה מקיוב. והוא חיבור... סודות עליונות... מתלמידי הרמב"ן... קארעץ: דרוקרייא פון יאהן אנטאן קריגר, [תקמ"ד], דף לא, א-לב, ב.

"אמר המחבר מצאתי אגרת אחת שלוחה מהרמב"ם... לתלמידיו ...רבי יוסף... וקראן מגלה עמוקות... ואולי אחד מתלמידיו כתבם בשמו...". הערכה על ספר זה ומחברו, ראה: חיים ליברמן, "דפוסי קארעץ", **סיני**, כרך 68 (תשל"א), קפב-קפט =[**אהל רחל**, כרך א'. ניו-יורק, תש"ם, עמ' 93-104].

תרט"ז 1856

2] מגילת סתרים. בתוך: **חמדה גנוזה**, מחברת ראשונה. הועתקו... ממני... צבי הירש עדעלמאן. קאניגסבערג, [תרט"ז] 1856, דף מב-מה.

תרי"ט 1859

3] מגילת סתרים. בתוך: **קובץ תשובות הרמב"ם ואגרותיו**... לפסיא: דפוס ה.ל. שנויס, תרי"ט 1859, חלק ב', דף לה-לו.
צלומים מדפוס זה, עיין להלן בשנים 1967, 1969.

תשכ"ב 1962

4] מכתב המיוחס למרן הרמב"ם ונודע בשם מגילת סתרים. **בפירושי רבינו שלמה בן אדרת** [**תרשב"א**]... **ורבינו דוד ב"ר יוסף קמחי** [**הרד"ק**]... על חמשה חומשי תורה... [יצא לאור ע"י] חיים יוסף איסר גד. לונדון: חי"ל האניג, תשכ"ב, עמ' קכד-קכו.

"יש להעיר שנדפסה עפ"י כ"י בס' **האח נפשנו** לר' אברהם חמוי, אזמיר תר"ל, דף לד-לה (בסי' ג' יש שנויים בינו לבין מהד' אדלמן ולפיהם א"צ להערת אדלמן)" (פרופ' יעקב שפיגל בהשלמות והוספות **לשרי האלף**, כרך ב', ירושלים, תשמ"ד, עמ' תרע).

תשכ"ג 1963

5] מגלה עמוקות. בריש ס' **טעמי המצוות** לר' מנחם ריקנטי, י"ל על ידי שמחה בונם ליבערמאן. לונדון: מכון אוצר החכמה, תשכ"ג, עמ' כה.
קטע עם שינויים והערות מאת המהדיר.

תשכ"ו 1966

6] מגילת סתרים. בתוך: **אגרות אקטואליות** של רבינו משה בן מימון הספרדי. תורגם ועובד ע"י מ. בר-יוסף. חלק ב. בני-ברק: מכון למדעי יהדות [מכון מרדכי להוצאת ספרי יהדות], תשכ"ו. ספירת עמודים שניה. 10 עמ'. °4. משוכפל.
פאראפרזה "מיועד לקוראי ימינו". וראה גם להלן מספר 7.

תשכ"ז 1967

7] מגילת סתרים. בתוך **אגרות קנאות, אגרות הרמב"ם**. ירושלים, תשכ"ז, ספירת עמודים שניה, דף לה-לו.
ד"צ מתוך **קובץ תשובות הרמב"ם ואגרותיו**, חלק ב', לפסיא תרי"ט, (לעיל מס' 3).

תשכ"ט 1969

8] מגילת סתרים. בתוך: **קבץ תשובות הרמב"ם ואגרותיו**, חלק ב'. 1969, דף לה-לו.
ד"צ של הוצאת לפסיא תרי"ט (לעיל מס' 3).

תש"ל 1970

9] מגילת סתרים. בתוך: **רבינו משה בן מימון-אגרותיו ותולדות חייו**. [בעריכת מרדכי בר-יוסף]. תל-אביב: מכון מרדכי להוצאת ספרי יהדות, תש"ל 1970, עמ' 110-118.
"בעברית המדוברת בימינו," בלווית "תוכן העניינים בראשי פרקים" והערות. (מהדורה משוכפלת, ראה לעיל מס' 6).

תשמ"ט 1989

10] מגילת סתרים. בתוך: **רבינו משה בן מימון — אגרותיו ותולדות חייו** [בעריכת מרדכי בר-יוסף]. בני-ברק: הוצאת מכון מרדכי, תשמ"ט 1989, עמ' 110-118.
זהה להוצאת תש"ל.

תש"ן 1990

11] Megillat Setarim (Scroll of the Unrevealed). In: *Five Spurious Treatises Attributed to Moses Maimonides.* Translated and Annotated from the Hebrew by Fred Rosner. Northvale, NJ: Jason Aronson, 1990.

מגילת סתרים בספרות ימי הביניים

12] אירגאס, ר' יוסף, 1685-1730.
שומר אמונים, אמשטרדם, תצ"ו, דף ה'.
הוא שמע אודות האגדה שהרמב"ם חזר בסוף ימיו ונעשה למקובל, אבל הוא אינו מאמין באגדה זו, כי נפלט מקולמוסו משפט שכזה: "וסוף דבר יהיה איך שיהיה אין אנו צריכין לעדות הרמב"ם על אמיתות הקבלה" (דף ה', ע"א).

[13] אבן יחיא, ר' גדליה, 1515-1587 בערך.
שלשלת הקבלה, ויניציא, שמ"ז, אמשטרדם, תנ"ז.
נכנס ב**ספרות ההיסטוריה הישראלית**, מאת אברהם כהנא, כרך ב'. ורשה, תרפ"ג
(דפוס צלום: ירושלים: מקור, תשכ"ט), עמ' 136.
מעתיק דברי גינזנו (ראה להלן).

[14] אברבנאל, דן יצחק, 1437-1508.
נחלת אבות על פרקי אבות, סוף פרק ג'.
"וגם אני שהרב הגדול המימוני כתב באגרת שלו אלה הדברים: בסוף ימי בא
אלי אדם אחד ואמר לי דברים של טעם ואלולי שהייתי בסוף ימי ונתפשטו חבורי
בעולם הייתי חוזר מדברים רבים שכתבתי בהם. ואין ספק שדברי קבלה היו אשר
שמע באחרית ימיו".

[15] אלשקר, ר' משה, 1466-1542.
תשובות, סימן קי"ז [= השגות שהשיג החכם ר' משה אלשקר על מה שכתב רבי
שם טוב בספר האמונות שלו נגד הרמב"ם... פירארא, שי"ז, נלוה גם כן לס' האמונת,
שם שי"ז].

[16] גינזנו, ר' אליהו חיים, המאה הט"ז.
אגרת חמודות על הקבלה ותורת ח"ן. לונדון, תרע"ב, עמ' 3-4
"והנני מעיד על הרב הגדול הרמב"ם ז"ל כי בסוף ימיו נתחרט ממה שכתב
בטעמי המצות בספר המורה ואלה דבריו באגרת אחת שלוחה במצרים ובכל ארץ
התימן: אחרי בואי בארץ הצבי מצאתי זקן אחד שהאיר עיני בדרכי הקבלה ואילו
ידעתי אז מה שהשגתי עתה, דברים רבים כתבתי שלא כתבתים [=שלא הייתי
כותב]".

[17] יוסף משושן, המאה הי"ד.
פירושי רבינו יוסף בן שושן על מסכת אבות. יוצא לאור בפעם הראשונה ע"י
משה שלמה כשר ויעקב יהושע בלכרוביץ. ירושלים: מכון תורה שלמה, תשכ"ח, עמ'
פ.

[18] מט, ר' משה בן אברהם, 1551-1606 בערך.
מטה משה, שער ב'... קראקא, שנ"א: פרנקפורט א.מ. ת"פ: מהדורה חדשה
בתוספת הערות וציונים בשם באר מרדכי מאת הרב מרדכי חנוך קנאבלאווייטש,
לונדון, תשי"ח (דפוס צלום: ירושלים).
"...גם כתב במגילת סתרים שישלח לתלמידיו החשוב וז"ל: ובחיי האהבה
הנמרצה אשר נהיתה בינך וביני... עד הנני משביעך שלא תגלה הסודות הדקות
וההערות הנפלאות אלא למי שהוא דק בשכלו ובטבעו ונקי במעשיו ונזדככו רעיוניו
והלך בדרכי הלמוד והידיעה..." (עמ' יט).

[19] ר' משה בן יהושע הנרבוני, נפטר 1362 בערך.
באור לספר מורה נבוכים, חלק א, פרק כא.
"...ובאגרת הסודות אשר שלח הרב לתלמידו בהשבעה שלא יגלהו לזולתו
הערים התלמיד החשוב להשפיע בלי עבור על שבועת הרב..."

[20] ר' משה בן יעקב הגולה מקיב, 1449-1520.
שושן סודות. והוא חיבור... סודות עליונות... קארעץ, תקמ"ד.
מכיל (בדף לא, א-לב, ב) את מגילת סתרים — ראה למעלה, סימן 1.

"אמר המחבר מצאתי אגרת אחת שלוחה מהרמב"ם... לתלמידו... רבי יוסף...
וקראן מגלה עמוקות... ואולי אחד מתלמידיו כתבם בשמו...".

[21] סמברי, יוסף בן יצחק, 1640־1703.
לקוטים מדברי יוסף. **בסדר החכמים וקורות הימים** חלק א', בעריכת א. נויבאור,
אוקספורד, תרמ"ח, עמ' 122.
Reprinted in A. Berliner, *Quellenschriften*. I. Frankfurt a.M.: J. Kaufmann, 1896, p. 13.

[22] שלום, ר' אברהם בן יצחק, נפטר 1492.
נוה שלום...קושטאנטינה, רצ"ח־רצ"ט (ללא מספור עמודים). מאמר יא, פרק ה.

[23] שלום, ר' אברהם בן יצחק, נפטר 1492.
נוה שלום...ויניציאה, של"ה (דפוס צילום: ירושלים, תשכ"ז). מאמר יא, פרק ה
(דף בשם "אגרת הסודות".

מאמרים ומחקרים

[24] אזולאי, ר' חיים יוסף דוד, 1724־1806.
שם הגדולים, חלק א, הוצאת יצחק אייזיק בן־יעקב, ווילנא: יוסף ראם,
תרי"ג/1852, אות מ', סימן 150, עמ' 156.
מסתפק אם הוא מהרמב"ם.

[25] דינסטאג, ישראל יעקב
מגילת סתרים (או: מגלה עמוקות) המיוחס לרמב"ם. ביבליוגרפיה. ב־
Six Treatises Attributed to Maimonides. Translated and annotated from the Hebrew Editions by Fred Rosner. Northvale, NJ: Jason Aronson, 1991.

[26] זלטקין, מנחם מנדל, 1875־
אוצר הספרים, חלק ב'. ירושלים: "קרית ספר", תשכ"ה/1965, עמ' 147, סימן 418.
הספר הוא זיוף.

[27] חורין, אהרון, 1766־1844.
מכתב לי"ש ריגיו. **כרם חמד** א' (1833), 47.
סותר דעות אלו שהרמב"ם בסוף ימיו חזר בו מהפילוסופיה; שהמגילה לא יצאה
מפי הרמב"ם. "ומה שנראה אצלי הוא שהמגילה הזאת כתבה איש אחר שהיה בימיו
ושמו ושם אביו כשמו כר' משה בן מיימון מקרטבא שהביא הכסף משנה בה'
תפילין". על חורין, ראה הרב א. בנדיקט, **מוריה**, שנה ח', גליון י"ב (סיון, תשל"ט),
עמ' פט־צה.

[28] מיזס, יהודה ליב, 1798־1831.
מכתב. **בכורי העתים**, 11 (תקצ"א), 131־142: נדפס שוב בספרו **קנאת האמת**,
לבוב, תרל"ט, עמ' 257־269.
בדבר הידיעה המזויפת שהרמב"ם נסתלק בסוף ימיו מהשקפותיו הפילוסופיות
ודבק בקבלה; שמגילת **סתרים** לא נתחבר ע"י הרמב"ם.

29] מיכל, חיים יוסף, 1792-1846.
אור החיים, פרנקפורט א.מ.: י. קויפמן, תרנ"א (ד"צ: ירושלים: מוסד הרב קוק, תשכ"ה; ניו יורק: חרמון), עמ' 551-552.
מראי מקומות למגילה בספרות ימי הביניים. הערך על הרמב"ם מאת מיכל, הופיע ג"כ בספר **בי ביצחק** מאת יצחק בדאהב, ירושלים, תרפ"ח, עמ' ד-כב.

30] שילת, יצחק
איגרות הרמב"ם. מהדורה מדויקת של האיגרות העבריות והערביות ירושלים: הוצאת מעליות ליד ישיבת "ברכת משה" ומעלה אדומים, תשמ"ח, עמ' תרצה-תרצו.
"לעניות דעתי אין אפילו צל של ספק שלפנינו זיוף מגמתי".

31] שלום, גרשם, 1897-1982.
מחוקר למקובל (אגדת המקובלים על הרמב"ם). **תרביץ**, שנה ו', ספר ג' (ניסן תרצ"ה), 338-339 [= ספר הרמב"ם של התרביץ, ירושלים: האוניברסיטה העברית, תרצ"ה, עמ' 94-95; **מיקראה בחקר הרמב"ם**, יוצאת לאור במלאות 850 שנה להולדתו. ירושלים: האוניברסיטה העברית, תשמ"ה, עמ' 94-95].

32] Beer, Bernhard, 1801-1861.
Anmerkungen des Uebersetzers. In S. Munk, *Philosophie und Philosphische Schriftsteller der Juden*. Leipzig: Heinrich Hunger, 1852, pp. 76-77.

33] Dukes, Leopold, 1810-1891.
Kurze Anzeigen. *Literaturblatt des Orients*, IX (1848), 325.

34] Scholem, Gerhardt, 1897-1982.
Maimonide dans l'oeuvre des Kabbalistes. *Cahiers Juifs*, no. 16/17 (July-Oct. 1935), pp. 107-108. Translation from his study in *Tarbiz*, 1935.

ציונים ביבליוגראפיים לכתבי-יד של מגילת סתרים

35] הלברשטם, שז"ח, 1832-1900.
קהלת שלמה והיא רשימת הספרים כ"י הנמצאים ביד ש' ז' ח' ה' בביעליטץ. ויען, תר"ן, מספר 288.

36] זק"ש, שניאור, 1815-1892.
קטלוג ברון גינצבורג (בכתב יד). בספרית בית מדרש לרבנים, כרך א' מספר 222; כרך ב', מספר 374.

37] חלמיש, משה
אהל חיים. קטלוג כתבי-היד העבריים בספרית משפחת מנשה רפאל ושרה ליהמן. יוצא לאור על שם בנם ר' חיים מנחם ז"ל (תש"ו-תשמ"ב). כרך א: כתבי-יד בקבלה, ניו-יורק: הוצאת קרן מנשה רפאל ושרה ליהמן, תשמ"ח, סימן 130 (עמ' 283).

38] ליברמן, ר' חיים, 1892-
דפוסי קארעץ. **סיני**, כרך 68 (תשל"א), קפב-קפט [=**אהל רחל**, כרך א'. ניו יורק, תש"ם, עמ' 93-104].
מתיחס לספר **שושן סודות**, קארעץ, תקמ"ד, שבו הופיעה, בפעם הראשונה המגילת סתרים. ליברמן השוה את תכנו עם הכתב-יד של הספר בספרית ייווא, בניו-

יורק. בדקתי את הכתב-יד, שהוא מאוסף אנסקי, והמגילה נמצאת בדף 67, ב-69, א.
(Collection of Rabbinic Mss. RG 128, folder 404).

[39 עפשטיין, אברהם, 1841-1918.
ר' משה הגולה מקיוב בן יעקב בן משה. **האשכול** א' (תרנ"ח), 149 = **כתבי ר'
אברהם עפשטיין**, כרך א'. ירושלים: מוסד הרב קוק, תשכ"ה, עמ' שז.
על כתבי יד של הספר **שושן סודות**.

[40 שווגר, ל' ודוד פרנקיל, מוכרי ספרים
אוצר כלי חמדה; רשימת כתבי-יד (רשימת מס' 11)
חוסיאטין, 1906, מספר 161.

41] Fuerst, D.
Aus einem Schreiben des Herrn D. Fuerst in Leipzig von 5. Februar 1837. *Wissenschaftliche Zeitung f. juedische Theologie* 3 (1837), 283, no. 1.

42] Freimann, Aaron, 1871-1948.
Union Catalog of Hebrew Manuscripts and their location, vol. 2. New York: American Academy for Jewish Research, 1964, p. 189, no. 4940.

43] Hirschfeld, Hartwig, 1854-1934.
Descriptive Catalogue of Hebrew Manuscripts of the Montefiore Library. London, 1904 (reprint from JQR, 14-15 (1902-03), no. 481, 4 Halberstam collection, no. 288.

44] Kraft, Albrecht, and Deutsch, Simon, 1822-1877.
Die handschriftlichen hebraeischen Werke des k.k. Hofbibliothek zu Wien. Wien, 1847, no. LXXXI (pp. 97-98).

45] Margoliouth, G., 1853-1952.
Catalogue of the Hebrew and Samaritan Manuscripts in the British Museum, part 3. London, 1909 (reprint: 1965), 749, I (Add. 19, 788).

46] Neubauer, Adolf, 1832-1907 and Arthur Ernst Cowley, 1861-1931.
Catalogue of the Hebrew Manuscripts in the Bodleian Library and in the College Libraries of Oxford, 1886-1906, no. 2246, 6 (fol. 75).

Part VI

LETTER TO THE JEWS OF FEZ ABOUT THE MESSIAH IN ISFAHAN

INTRODUCTION

In 1881, Adolf Neubauer published a pseudobiography in Hebrew of the renowned rabbi, philosopher, and physician Moses Maimonides, based on manuscript no. 1767 of the *Beth HaMidrash* in London.[1] The following year Neubauer published, in Hebrew and in French translation, an analogous apocryphal document that he considered:

> of much greater interest because of the pseudomessianic movement of David Alroy, which is described therein with numerous details. Besides, it contains an account about the Jews in Yemen, the history of which is not yet complete, and certain names and dates that might be of help for historians of the Jewish people in the Middle Ages.[2] [p. 173]

The document in question is found in the Oxford Bodleian Library, marked Oppenheim, add. 80–36. In the Neubauer catalogue, it is part of manuscript no. 2425, written in Spanish

---

[1] A. Neubauer, Pseudo-Biographie von Maimonides. *Israelitische Letterbode* (Amsterdam), 1881–1882, 7:14–17.

[2] A. Neubauer, Une pseudo-biographie de Moïse Maïmonide. *Revue des Études Juives* (Paris) 1882, 4:173–188.

rabbinic characters, and begins on folio 63b.[3] It consists of a pseudo-biographical account of the life of Maimonides and includes a letter supposedly written by Maimonides to the Jewish community in Fez, about the Messiah who appeared in Isfahan. The letter states that the reason the Messiah is delaying the redemption of the Jewish people is that the time for the messianic redemption has not arrived, but is near. Maimonides describes how he investigated the authenticity of the Messiah by eighteen talmudic questions on Jewish law that he sent him.

Neubauer's 1882 Hebrew edition of this pseudo-Maimonidean letter faithfully reproduces the text according to the unique manuscript. Neubauer added words and letters in brackets for those obliterated in the manuscript, and put words in parentheses that he thought were redundant. In a brief introductory paragraph in French, he states that it is not necessary to prove that the document is apocryphal, certainly not as it concerns Maimonides. One need only compare it with the famous letter that Maimonides addressed to the Jews in Yemen (*Epistle to Yemen*) about the messianic movement in that land.[4] Therein, concludes Neubauer, one finds, without difficulty, the divergences from this document.

In 1888, Neubauer wrote about the false Messiah in Yemen and about the letter that Rabbi Jacob ben Nathaniel sent to Maimonides asking for direction.[5] Maimonides, in his *Epistle to Yemen,* answered that the man in Yemen claiming to be the Messiah was an impostor and that the true Messiah will be recognizable by appropriate signs. Neubauer also writes about the false Messiah, David Alroy, who studied in Bagdad under prominent rabbinic scholars. He was also knowledgeable in secular subjects, Arabic works, and books of sorcery, witchcraft,

---

[3] A. Neubauer, *Catalogue of the Hebrew Manuscripts in the Bodleian Library.* Oxford, 3 vols, 1886–1906.

[4] A. S. Halkin, *Moses Maimonides' Epistle to Yemen.* The Arabic original and the three Hebrew versions, with an English translation by Boaz Cohen. New York: American Academy for Jewish Research, 1952.

[5] A. Neubauer, *Seder Hachachamim Vekorot Hayamim.* Oxford: Clarendon Press, 1888, pp. 122–123. Reprinted in Jerusalem in 1957.

and wizardry. He decided to challenge the king of Persia, to gather the Jews to wage war against the Gentiles, and to conquer Jerusalem. A lengthy biography of David Alroy is provided by Neubauer.

In 1892, David Kaufmann wrote about the falsification of part or all of the letter that Maimonides sent to the Jews of Yemen.[6] Kaufmann points out that the false letter, edited and published by Neubauer in 1882, exemplifies one of many historical or literary movements that tried to find support for their position in the writings of Maimonides and, therefore, falsified letters and whole books that they attributed to him. Similarly, false passages were interpolated into authentic Maimonidean writings in order to support an opinion or accredit an impostor. Thus, Kabbalah tried to make Maimonides one of its partisans.[7] Bacher considers the passage on the Messiah in Maimonides' *Epistle to Yemen* to be authentic.[8]

The pseudo-biographical letter of Maimonides to the Jews in Fez concerning the Messiah of Isfahan is discussed in some detail by Fritz Baer in his study on messianic movements in 1186.[9] Baer summarizes the contents of the letter and distinguishes between the pseudo-biographical material and the letter itself. He contends that the writer of the obviously false biographical material did not write the letter but found it in Fez with Maimonides' name on it, since his biographical dates are at variance with those in the letter. For example, Maimonides' brother David, supposedly the carrier of the letter, died in the year 1179 or even before, but the biographer considers him to have been alive in 1189. Furthermore, Saladin sojourned in Syria in 1187, but the biographer writes that Saladin reigned in

---

[6] D. Kaufmann, Une falsification dans la lettre envoyée par Maïmonide aux Juifs du Yemen. *Revue des Études Juives* (Paris), 1894, 24:112–117.

[7] F. Rosner, Nine Chapters on Kabbalah in *Existence and Unity of God: Three Treatises Attributed to Moses Maimonides*. Northvale, N.J.: Jason Aronson, 1990.

[8] W. Bacher, Le passage relatif au Messie dans la lettre de Maïmonide aux Juifs du Yemen. *Revue des Études Juives* (Paris), 1894, 34:101–105.

[9] E. F. Baer, Eine juedische Messiaprophezie aus des Jahr 1186 und der dritte Kreuzzug. *Monatsschrift fuer Geschichte und Wissenschaft des Judentums* (Breslau), 1926, 70:155–165.

Egypt in 1189. Other legendary accounts, such as the residence of Maimonides in a cave, are blatantly false. Baer proves the falseness of the pseudo-biography of Maimonides concerning the Messiah of Isfahan with historical detail.

In an appendix to his Arabic and Hebrew edition of Maimonides' *Epistle to Yemen*,[10] Abraham Halkin comments on and cites the text of the letter on the Messiah of Isfahan. He states that at first, he paid no attention to the letter since its 1882 editor, Adolf Neubauer, himself concluded that it is a forgery and should not be attributed to Maimonides. Halkin also distinguishes between the pseudo-biography and the letter contained therein. The former is a collection of legends. The first paragraph concerning the exodus from Spain to Fez and the flight from there to Eastern lands, according to Halkin, is reminiscent of the story told in the historical work of Saadiah ibn Danan. The description of the average workday of Maimonides is reminiscent of the letter he sent to his friend, disciple, and translator, Rabbi Samuel ibn Tibbon of France, in 1199.[11] These portrayals and other biographical statements about Maimonides are obviously false and often internally inconsistent.

The letter contained within the pseudo-biography is different in that it, too, was not written by Maimonides but is *referred* to by him in *his* letter on astrology[12] to the sages of Montpellier. He wrote:

> Concerning the message about the Messiah that you mentioned had reached you in my name—the matter was not as you had heard, and it was not in the East [in Isfahan]. Rather, in Yemen a man arose—and said that he was the messenger of the Messiah to pave the path for his coming. He told them that the Messiah will reveal himself in Yemen. Many people, both Jews and

---

[10] Halkin, *op. cit*, pp. 108–111.

[11] F. Rosner, *Medicine in the Mishneh Torah of Maimonides*. New York: Ktav Publishing, 1984, pp. 2–3.

[12] A. Marx, The correspondence between the rabbis of southern France and Maimonides about astrology. *Hebrew Union College Annual*, 1926, 3:311–358; 1927, 4:493–494.

> Arabs, flocked to him and surrounded him on the mountains. He misled them and constantly told them: "Come with me, let us go to meet the Messiah for he sent me to you to prepare the way for him," . . . I understood that . . . that poor man was lacking in understanding but was a pious man . . . without any knowledge . . . after a year all those who had flocked to him fled from him. . . .If you heard that my letter reached Fez, it is possible that the message I sent to Yemen [*The Epistle to Yemen*] was copied and reached Fez. [pp. 356–357]

There is obviously a similarity between the spurious letter to the Jews of Fez concerning the Messiah of Isfahan and the authentic Maimonidean work *Epistle to Yemen* in that both deal, at least in part, with the Messiah. It is also understandable why the Jews of Provence were not aware of the *Epistle to Yemen*. In the year 1194, asserts Halkin, there was no Hebrew translation of the *Epistle to Yemen*, and the Arabic original had not yet reached them. Furthermore, Arabic was a totally foreign language, not spoken or even understood in Provence (see Ibn Tibbon's foreword to his translation of Maimonides' *Commentary on the Mishnah*). Halkin concludes that it is obvious that the Messiah of Isfahan is Menachem ben David Aldagi, better known as David Alroy. Although Maimonides clearly states that he never addressed the matter of the Messiah of Isfahan but spoke only about the Messiah in Yemen, the author of *Shevet Yehudah* cites another version of the letter to the Jews of Fez about the Persian Messiah in the name of Maimonides.[13] This author considers the Yemenite Messiah to be David Alroy. This opinion is also held by David Gans in his book *Tzemach David*.[14]

In his book entitled *Letters of Maimonides*,[15] Isaac Shailat briefly describes the spurious letter (and biography) attributed

---

[13]Ibn Verga S., *Sefer Shevet Yehudah*. Jerusalem: Mossad Bialik, 1947, pp. 74–77.

[14]D. Gans, *Sefer Tzemach David*. Jerusalem: Hebrew University, 1983, p. 120.

[15]I. Shailat, *Iggrot HaRambam* (Letters and Essays of Moses Maimonides). Maaleh Alumim, Israel; Maaliyot Press of Yeshivat Birkat Moshe, 1988 (5748), Vol. 2, p. 693.

to Maimonides on the Messiah of Isfahan. Shailat states that this work is full of imaginary legends and stories. He confirms that the letter was written in Maimonides' lifetime since the latter refers to it in his letter on astrology to the Jews in Montpellier. Shailat concludes that the forger was not concerned that his goal was the exact opposite of Maimonides' in his *Epistle to Yemen*. Furthermore, the story of the appearance of the Messiah of Isfahan is portrayed in the *Epistle to Yemen* as an example of the ancient trap of the false Messiahs who date from the beginning of Islam. Maimonides warned against this type of false Messiah. Shailat wonders whether the forger made use of the story in a cynical manner or was totally unaware that Maimonides mentioned it in his *Epistle to Yemen*! Future scholars may shed light on this matter.

There are many biographical errors in the letter to the Jews of Fez about the Messiah of Isfahan. The following prove beyond a doubt that the letter is a hoax. The biography states that Maimonides and his father and brother sailed from Fez to Alexandria, whereas they actually sailed to Acco, Palestine. The biography states that Maimonides lived hidden in a cave for several years. There is no mention in any other source to support this fantasy. The entire story of Maimonides' servant and the interpretation of the king's dream is not found in any biography of Maimonides and is no doubt a fabrication. The biography states that the king gave Maimonides a wife from among the women of Fez and that he had a son named David, but there is no evidence to support this claim. Maimonides, as far as is known, had only one son, Abraham. The biography states that David, the brother of Maimonides, died of a serious illness, whereas in actuality he died in a shipwreck.

The average day in the life of Maimonides, as described in the pseudo-biography, is totally at variance with the authentic description by Maimonides himself of his busy schedule, found in his famous letter to Samuel ibn Tibbon. Finally, the biography erroneously states that Maimonides died in the year 1202 instead of the known 1204 and that he was buried in Egypt instead of Tiberias, where his gravesite can be visited by all.

Since false Messiahs first made their appearance, they—or

INTRODUCTION

Since false Messiahs first made their appearance, they—or their followers—frequently forged letters from the great sages of their generation endorsing their Messiahs. Examples are Shabbetai Tzvi, Frank, and others. Even the literary forgers of supposed classics always engaged in producing spurious letters testifying to the authenticity of their forgeries, as is clearly shown in the *Parshat Hayerushalmi al Seder Kodoshim* by the master forger Friedlander-Azoulai.

In spite of the obvious forgery of the biographical material surrounding the letter attributed to Maimonides on the Messiah of Isfahan, it is included in this book for its historical interest as another example of a medieval hoax.

My translation is based entirely on the 1882 Hebrew edition by Neubauer. Neubauer's French translation is very free with major omissions of words and phrases and was, therefore, not used at all.

LETTER TO THE JEWS OF FEZ ABOUT THE MESSIAH IN ISFAHAN

There was a man in Spain named Maimon. This man was very pious and walked in the paths of his Father in Heaven and occupied himself with the Torah, day and night. This man had two sons, one was named Moses and the other David. This man heard that in the city of Fez, in the West,[1] there lived a great and righteous individual who occupied himself with the study of the Torah of God, and who was a great scholar in all sciences and an authority on metaphysics and speculative philosophy. This man and his entire household went to find the great *Gaon* Rabbi Judah the-Kohen, of blessed memory.[2]

Rabbi Moses, son of Maimon, studied under the *Gaon* throughout his life and learned Torah from him because he taught Torah publicly. At that time the tyrant Machmud[3] arose and killed the *Gaon,* who martyred himself to sanctify the unity of God, after great torture. The cruel tyrant tried to force the

---

[1] The West refers to Morocco or Mughrab.

[2] In a footnote, Neubauer states that this *Gaon* is probably Rabbi Judah Kohen ibn Soussan who is mentioned by Saadyah ibn Däman as having been a martyr. See Graetz's *History of the Jews*, Vol. 6, p. 172.

[3] According to Neubauer, it probably refers to Mohammed Almoumen. Perhaps one should read *Toumart,* suggests Neubauer.

Gaon to renounce his faith and adopt Islam, but he refused and was therefore killed by a violent death. Let him repose in honor. May the Lord preserve us and preserve all the Jewish people!

When Rabbi Maimon observed this [martyrdom], he took his two sons, Rabbi Moses and Rabbi David, and fled during the night. They traveled at night and hid during the day until they arrived at the town of Sabata. The three boarded a ship and sailed to Alexandria, and from there they traveled to Jerusalem where Rabbi Maimon died. His sons buried him [there]. Rabbi Moses returned to Egypt and grew in wisdom more than all his contemporaries because he was a great scholar.

His fame came to the attention of the king of Egypt whose name was Salah Ad-din [Saladin]. Rabbi Moses was introduced to the king and was elevated in rank above all the princes that were there. He taught Torah publicly and his books and his letters arrived constantly in the West, and he looked after the well-being of the Jews.

I, the copyist of this letter, am a resident of Toledo, and was born in Spain. I, too, fled that tyrant to Toledo. I left Toledo in the year 4946[4] on the fourteenth day[5] of the month of Tammuz, and I remained on business in Spain for a period of fourteen months. Then I traveled to the city of Fez to engage in mundane commerce. I lived in an inn among Jews for four months. On the Sabbath, some of the notables of the community told me: "We have here an old man who is a great sage. He is ill. Let us visit him." I went with them.

That sick Jew was a sage and very pious. We sat before him discussing the extortions of the various governments and our servitude among the nations. This sick sage, whom we had come to visit and whose name was Rabbi Isaac, son of Nathan, told us, "My brothers, be aware that I have received a letter from Egypt from the *Gaon,* our revered teacher, Rabbi Moses Maimonides." He took out the letter and placed it before us.

The following is the text [of the letter] that came from Egypt

---

[4]Equivalent to the year 1186 of the Common Era.
[5]The Neubauer French translation erroneously has *twelfth.*

from the *Gaon* Rabbi Moses. The letter was written in Arabic[6] but here is the text of the letter [in Hebrew]:

In honor of our brothers and dear ones of the holy [Jewish] communities, holy people, the children of Abraham, descendants of the Perfect Man,[7] Congregation of The West and My brothers and friends of the community of Fez.[8] I, your humble[9] brother Moses, son of Maimon, write to inform you of good tidings from before God.[10] Let us rejoice in the coming of the Messiah[11] who will console us with the consolation of Zion. I hereby notify you, my masters and my brothers, that I heard these good tidings from the merchants who came from Babylon[12] to Egypt and to Jerusalem. They said that the Jewish king, who was long hoped for, finally arrived and was observed in Isfahan. Every merchant brought the same news. Even those who came from Acco and Damascus and other cities said the same thing.

I, Moses, heard but paid no attention to these things because I thought that these [non-Jewish] merchants were deriding us and laughing at us and scorning us. I was aggrieved about this matter regarding their scorn and mockery. But when everyone who came said the same and the reports came one after another, doubt entered my heart and I said: "Perhaps it is true!"

I was contemplating these matters in my heart when two rich and prominent merchants from the community of Damascus passed before me. These merchants traveled to Mecca where the tomb of the Moslem prophet is located and from there they came to Egypt. When they saw me, they turned to me and

---

[6] Literally: the language of the Ishmaelites.
[7] Alternate translation: the straightforward man, that is, Jacob. cf. Genesis 25:27.
[8] This flowery introduction is rendered simply in French by Neubauer, "To my brothers and friends, to the holy people of the holy community of Fez."
[9] Literally: younger.
[10] Literally: He who dwells in the heavens.
[11] Hebrew: *Yinnon*, symbolic name of the Messiah.
[12] The French version has *Bagdad*.

greeted me[13] and I returned their greeting. I entreated them to sit with me as I wished to engage them in conversation. They sat at my side. I inquired about their welfare, the safety of the roads, and the welfare of our brethren of the Babylonian communities and other distant places.

Then I said to them: "You, my very dear, close,[14] and beloved friends, I will ask you a question but please answer it truthfully and do not deceive me." They said: "We will not deceive you, but will tell you the truth. What are you asking about?" I said to them: "What is this tiding that I heard from you? Is it true or not?" Those Ishmaelite merchants replied: "What you heard is certainly true. We were in Babylon at the inn frequented by merchants. We were sitting at the entrance of the inn talking about things when a Jew passed before us and was seized by two mockers, frivolous and empty men.[15] They scorned and mocked that Jew. We, too, were laughing because of the mockers and the Jew, when two merchants from Sheba and Seba[16] arrived and said to those mockers: 'Oh, vain and stupid people, are you not afraid of the Lord, and are you not ashamed [to act in this manner] before people? Know that the cornerstone of the Jew you are scorning and mocking was lifted up[17] and his fortune[18] has been raised by God. The Messiah[19] for whom they had been waiting has arrived and he is in Isfahan. All the nations came to him as did the two great [Arabic] families of Kedar and Nebaiot,[20] which flocked to him and believed in him.'" Those Ishmaelite [merchants] also told me: "If you do not believe what we are saying, two wealthy

---

[13]Literally: they gave me peace.
[14]Literally: with heart and soul.
[15]Allusion to Judges 9:4.
[16]Allusion to Psalm 72:10. Sheba is the southeastern part of Arabia, a country of great wealth. Seba (Genesis 10:7) is identified by Josephus as the capital of Merse in Ethiopia. Neubauer renders Sheba and Seba as Yemen in his French translation.
[17]Perhaps an allusion to 1 Chronicles 25:5.
[18]Hebrew: *mazel*, meaning luck, fortune, fate, or destiny.
[19]Literally: anointed one.
[20]Sons of Ishmael. See Genesis 25:13.

Jewish [merchants] from Babylon are coming. They will tell it to you and you will believe it."

I waited for those Jews for four days and [finally] they arrived. I sat with them and questioned them. I said to them: "What is this tiding that I heard from the Ishmaelites? Are they speaking the truth or are they mocking us?" Those Jews replied: "The Lord saw our affliction[21] and delivered us, just as He delivered our forefathers." They [further] said that they were in Babylon[22] and saw Jewish merchants who said: "Verily, a Jew arose in Isfahan whose name is Abi Said ben Daudi[23] who claimed that he was the general of the Messiah's army. Seven years have already passed and there have flocked to him a large community of Israel, as numerous as the sand [on the seashore], and also from [the other] nations. They are innumerable and include Nabateans and Kedarites."[24] When he saw that all those [Jewish and Ishmaelite] families gathered around him, he said to them: "The time of redemption is not yet here," and he hid himself for seven years. These Jews further told me that during the present year more people flocked to him than did the previous time. And these Jews also told me that Jews related to them that other Jews claimed to have seen a thick pillar of cloud[25] over his head that reached to the heavens whenever he stood to ask for something or when he prayed.

After that, there came to him Jews and elders of the Nabateans and Kedarites and said to him: "Our Master, our king, Messiah of God, we live here in tranquility, a large

---

[21] Allusion to Deuteronomy 26:7.

[22] The Neubauer French version always substitutes Bagdad for Babylon.

[23] This is the Arabic name of David Alroy, leader of a twelfth-century messianic movement in Kurdistan. According to the *Encyclopaedia Judaica* (Vol. 2, p. 750), the movement gathered momentum from the ferment that accompanied the struggle waged between Christendom and Islam in the wake of the First Crusade, and during the wars preceding the second. The tribulations of the period and massacres, in which they were the victims, appeared to many Jews as the pangs heralding the advent of the Messiah. The principal leader of the movement was initially Solomon, Alroy's father, who claimed to be the prophet Elijah.

[24] Ishmaelites or Arabs of the Moslem faith.

[25] Exodus 13:22; 14:19; 33:9–10, etc.

community, prosperous and flourishing.[26] But our Jewish brethren live in captivity. How long shall this be for us?[27] Command us and we will go forward [to liberate] our brethren that are among the nations and oppressed by the kingdoms." He said to them: "No, my brothers! The time for the redemption has not yet arrived. I was only sent because the outcry of the daughters of my people[28] from distant lands was heard [by God], and their outcry reached the throne of the One who dwells in the heavens.[29] I went out and was sent to reassure the melancholic hearts of the children of Israel so that they bear the burden of the remaining years [ordained by God] for them among the nations. I was also commanded not to reveal [the end of the] exile, but it is close."

When I, your brother Moses, heard this from the mouths of these Jews, my soul became calmed and I rejoiced. At the end of the night, I was unable to sleep.[30] I arose and delved into the Talmud and found eighteen legal ordinances[31] where the sages of the world said: "Until the [Messiah] will come and correctly clarify them."[32] I arose and prepared a letter, according to my humble opinion, with verses and matters appropriate to be presented to that man.[33] I called my brother David[34] and spoke

---

[26]Literally: we have no number, we are innumerable.

[27]Allusion to Exodus 10:7.

[28]Allusion to Jeremiah 4:11; 6:26; 8:11; 19, 21, and so forth, and Lamentations 2:11; 3:48; 4:3, 6, 10.

[29]Hebrew: *Shochen Shechakim,* taken from the High Holy Day liturgy.

[30]Literally: sleep escaped from my eyes. Allusion to Esther 6:1.

[31]Hebrew: *halachot,* plural of *halachah.*

[32]In a footnote, Neubauer states that this tradition is unknown in the Talmud and in the Midrash. Halkin suggests that these are questions to which the Talmud says *teku,* which is an acrostic that states that only Elijah the Prophet will answer the legal questions and, thereby, solve the problems.

[33]To test whether he was truly the Messiah, in which case he would satisfactorily answer all the questions posed to him.

[34]In a footnote, Halkin points out that this statement is an obvious error since Maimonides' brother David died in 1166 or 1167. If this letter attributed to Maimonides was written in 1186, one must conclude that its writer was unaware that David had died.

heartily to him and assured him that I would aggrandize him[35] and do him honor. I gave David 200 Egyptian *denars* together with the letter containing the questions and dispatched him to Isfahan. I also gave him a letter to the princes and governors[36] stating that they should honor him[37] when he passes before them.

David traveled to Isfahan and remained there for ten days. He returned to me after a year and a half. Were it not that it would take me lengthy discourses, I would write to you all that my brother related to me. My brother David saw him and they swore by his name[38] saying: "By the life of our King, Messiah of the Lord." My brother David brought me four[39] letters. In one of the letters he explained fifteen of the questions; concerning the other three, he said: "They were not told to me."

Also, I, your brother Moses, had previously delved into those legal questions and explained some of them;[40] others I was unable to clarify, but when they were addressed to that man,[41] he explained them well, properly, and appropriately. I said to myself: "Had he explained to me the remaining three questions, I would have said that he is not truthful because our Sages[42] left them concealed and unrevealed until the teacher of righteousness[43] will come [and explain them]." Since he did not explain them, I reasoned that he must be truthful. Similarly, he said: "They were not told to me, and it is not up to me to explain them until the Messiah will come."[44] When the community of Isfahan said to me, in the letter that they sent me in

---

[35] The "Messiah in Isfahan."
[36] Perhaps an allusion to Esther 3:12.
[37] The "Messiah in Isfahan."
[38] It was the custom to swear "by the life of" the reigning monarch to establish the truth of what was being testified to.
[39] The Neubauer French version has "two" instead of four.
[40] In a footnote, Halkin points out that in order to aggrandize the honor of Maimonides, the author of the letter impresses the reader with the miraculous power of Maimonides.
[41] Literally: when they came into the hand of that man.
[42] Literally: my teachers.
[43] That is, the Messiah.
[44] Literally: until he comes and teaches righteousness.

return through my brother, that many families joined them, including the Nabateans and the Kedarites, I rejoiced and said [to myself]: "This is what the prophet predicted:[45] 'and the flocks of Kedar shall be gathered together unto thee; the rams of the Nabateans shall minister unto thee.'"[46] In his[47] letter that he sent with my brother David, he wrote: "For three more years I cannot leave my cave because the time for me to leave has not yet arrived; the end of the time period will be on the fourteenth day of [the month of] Marcheshvan. Then my fortune will be good."

I will also relate to you an event that transpired there concerning a king in the south of Egypt, descended from the families of Togarma [Turkey?] and Yaphet, who believed in the faith of the prophet Mohammed. His [capital] city is Aden and 12,000 Israelites live under his dominion. They have one judge[48] named Rabbi Menachem who is a great man in Israel, scholarly and pious.[49] The king summoned them saying: "The Jews[50] must convert [to Islam] or perish." Rabbi Menachem replied and said to the king: "My master, give us seven days' time." After they left, Rabbi Menachem and the elders of the community who were wailing before the princes and the governors, made a compromise with the king and gave him fourteen bars[51] of silver and he let them retain their Jewish faith.

The following year, he told them: "Give me an additional fourteen bars of silver, or the Jews must convert [to Islam] or perish." They gave it to him. They sold everything they had [to pay the ransom] and they had nothing left as it is written "and they will be consumed [by evil]."[52] During the third year he sent

---

[45] Literally: said.
[46] Isaiah 60:7.
[47] The man who claimed to be the Messiah in Isfahan.
[48] Hebrew: *dayan*.
[49] Literally: heaven-fearing.
[50] In Hebrew the euphemistic term "enemies of the Jews" is here used.
[51] Hebrew: *kikare*, usually translated "talents," here refers to bars or "loaves."
[52] Deuteronomy 21:17.

for them and killed some of them. Many of them fled.[53] Those who remained were the poorest in the land and they renounced the Jewish faith. Synagogues and houses of study were destroyed.

Rabbi Menachem fled and escaped, wearing a sackcloth on his loins, to the top of a mountain in the realm of another king. After some fifteen or eighteen months, the [wicked] king heard the tidings [of the Messiah of Isfahan] and was stricken with trembling, his countenance withered, and his mind became confused, and he had no strength to stand. He sent letters to Rabbi Menachem until he found him and promised him complete peace, and entreated him, saying to him: "I, myself, know that I sinned in that act. Send for and gather all your brethren and rebuild the synagogues and houses of study." The king returned to them twenty-five bars of gold, and gave them silver and gold to rebuild the synagogues as they previously were. And so they did.

He mustered about 4,000 men. Those who had remained also heard this tiding. The elders of the community came to Rabbi Menachem and said: "How long shall this man be a snare for us?[54] Let us got to Isfahan." Rabbi Menachem replied to them: "No, my brethren. It is not yet the time for redemption." Since they distanced him with words,[55] he said to them: "Do not uproot yourselves. Give me some community funds and I will go [to Isfahan and investigate]. If the matter is true, I will send for you." So Rabbi Menachem and fifteen of the great men of the community went. After fifteen months, twelve of them reached Isfahan: twelve of them and Rabbi Menachem, three having died of thirst as it was a long journey and they passed through deserts. When they entered the city they came before the man [purported to be the Messiah]. Rabbi Menachem went

---

[53]In a footnote, Halkin points out that Margolies suggests the farfetched notion that this letter about the "Messiah in Isfahan" provides evidence that the captives, for whose redemption Maimonides solicited funds in North Africa, were the remnants of the persecutions in Yemen.

[54]Exodus 10:7.

[55]That is, he could not convince them.

out and wrote to the remainder of the community telling them: "The matter and the tidings [about the Messiah] are true. He appears to me like Moses our teacher, of blessed memory." Those in the community who were able to leave, left in secrecy.[56]

I, Moses, sat for some time after receiving this tiding. The secretary of the king[57] came to me. The king instructed me to supervise the [royal] treasury, to take the gold and to send it to him, because the king was involved in a war. The king was Salah Ad-din.[58] The secretary of the king who brought me the king's letter also told me that the king stood up and announced in a loud voice: "Know ye that these Christians[59] came from distant lands, kings of the East and the West, to wage war with me over Jerusalem and the Holy Temple." Thus speaks Salah Ad-din: "The Lord placed into them a spirit of foolishness[60] so that they died at the hands of my sword and from famine and from pestilence. Also, I cannot reign over the kingdom of the Lord because I know that the King of the Jews will now come and take these lands from me and from them. However, it was my good fortune that the King of the Jews will take it from my hand in tranquility and not in war. Perhaps, I will find favor in his eyes."

I, the writer of this letter, saw all these things in the letter of the *Gaon* Moses, which he sent to the West and to the community of Fez, except that I translated it[61] from Arabic into Hebrew. When I came to Rome, I related it to Rabbi Leon, may

---

[56] In a footnote, Neubauer states that according to our document, the letter of Maimonides addressed to the Jews of Yemen concerns the messianic movement in Isfahan and not that of another Messiah who appeared in Yemen, as is the opinion of Graetz (*History of the Jews*, Vol. 6).

[57] Literally: scribe of the king.

[58] Neubauer states it was Saladin who recaptured Jerusalem from the Christians and allowed the Jews to establish themselves in the holy city.

[59] Literally: uncircumcised.

[60] Isaiah 19:14.

[61] Literally: these things.

the Lord watch over him and preserve him,[62] and he rejoiced and asked me to write all these things down for him.

As soon as I heard about the letter of my master, Rabbi Moses, and that he is living in Egypt,[63] I rejoiced greatly and swore in the name of the Almighty that I will not sit quietly nor rest[64] until I see my master. I set out and traveled for nine months until I arrived in Egypt. I asked secretly about his whereabouts and did not locate him for a full fifteen days. I went to see him and searched for him in a cave until I found him. As soon as he saw me, he recognized me and rejoiced greatly with me. I said to him: "Behold, my master, I came to see you and to serve you until God will have mercy upon you."

I stayed with him for a year until one day he had a dream in which he saw a tall tree with tall branches and he was standing over it. He awoke from his sleep and called to his servant and described his dream to him and said: "Perhaps I can interpret it but I am not sure of myself. Rather, rise and go to the city and seek out a wise man who knows how to interpret dreams. Tell him that the dream was yours and let no man know anything[65] about me." The servant arose and sought out a wise man capable of interpreting dreams, and told him his dream. The dream-interpreter said: "Give me time until tomorrow and I will go tonight and look into the stars and then tell you [the significance of the dream]." The next day, the servant went to him at the end of the day and asked him for the interpretation of the dream. He said to him: "This was not your dream but that of Moses, who is concealed in a cave. Know that the dream is very good because the tall tree represents a great place that he will have in the house of the king. The branches over which he is standing represent all the people of the king's house who speak evil of him [Moses] and who wish to harm him and who will speak good of him and serve him with all their might. For

---

[62]In a footnote, Halkin refers the reader to the work of Fogelstein and Rieger, *The Jews in Rome*, Vol. 1, pp. 227 and 372.
[63]Neubauer's French version substitutes Cairo for Egypt.
[64]Literally: remain tranquil.
[65]Allusion to 1 Samuel 21:3.

this matter emanates from God and cannot be questioned because He has mercy on all His creatures who place their hope in His name,[66] and Moses will reign over them."

The servant went and told him all these things and his master was full of anger[67] because he said to himself: "Perhaps the matter will be revealed and the king will kill me." He left the cave and fled and escaped to the mountain. He studied there for a full fifteen months until his supplication and prayer came[68] before the King of Kings, the Holy One, blessed be He.

The king, while reclining on his divan, had a dream that troubled his spirit.[69] He arose and sent for all the wizards and wise men of Egypt[70] to interpret his dream. All the people in the city who were knowledgeable in witchcraft came before him but they were not able to relate to him the interpretation of his dream. He sent throughout the land and there was no person who knew anything about that [type of] dream until the Lord, may He be praised, revealed Himself to him and he saw in a dream that He said to him: "Behold, Moses, whom you drove away sinless—he will explain your dream."

The king arose from his sleep and sent for the runners and sent them throughout the land to find Moses. The runners departed and publicized that the king will give such and such [a recompense] to any man who shows him the whereabouts of Moses. The news reached the ears[71] of Rabbi Moses but he paid no attention thereto for he said: "Perhaps the king wishes to kill me." The runners continued to search daily, according to the word of the king[72] until Rabbi Moses saw in a dream that he was told: "The time has come for you to leave the cave because the Lord has heard your voice." He awoke from his sleep, joyful and with a good heart.[73] He related [this dream] to his servant

---

[66] Perhaps an allusion to Psalms 31:25.
[67] Allusion to Esther 3:5.
[68] Literally: reached.
[69] Allusion to Exodus 41:8.
[70] Allusion to Exodus 41:8.
[71] Literally: reached up to.
[72] Perhaps an allusion to Esther 5:8.
[73] Allusion to Esther 5:9.

and told him: "Go to the palace[74] and stay there until we know that the matter is true, for now the three years that our master, the messenger of the Messiah, has referred to are complete."[75]

The servant went and, after he heard what he heard, returned to the cave to Rabbi Moses and told him all that he had learned from the ministers who sat first in the kingdom.[76] Rabbi Moses told him: "Go to the king and say to him, 'My master, I will deliver Rabbi Moses to you if you give me 5,000 Egyptian *denars*.' If he agrees, tell him, 'Give me time until tomorrow and I will go for him; I will bring him to you tomorrow.'" The servant did so and he came to the palace and did exactly as his master had instructed him. The king gave him the *denars* and clothes[77] and a horse to bring Rabbi Moses to him.

The servant departed and came to the cave. He clothed Rabbi Moses in the [royal] clothes and placed him on the horse. Rabbi Moses took seven books with him, which he had composed in the cave, and he came to the inner gate of the palace.[78] He approached the king, kissed his hands and feet, and bowed down with his forehead to the ground. The king arose before him and took him by his hand and placed him next to himself and rejoiced greatly with him and told him his dream.

He said to the king: "Give me until tomorrow and I will explain your dream, with God's help." The king instructed that he be given a house nearby and he instructed all his servants to honor him. After a day, he came before the king and told him the interpretation of his dream, and stated to the king: "Eight days from today you will see that the interpretation of your dream is correct,"[79] and thus it was.

When the king saw that what my master told him was true, he

---

[74]Literally: house of the king.
[75]Literally: reached.
[76]Allusion to Esther 1:14.
[77]The implication is that special "kingly" or royal clothing befits a ministerial visitor to the monarch. This special clothing is replete throughout ancient and medieval writing, for example, Genesis 41:14, Exodus 28:2, Esther 6:8.
[78]Allusion to Esther 5:1.
[79]Literally: well-explained. Allusion to Deuteronomy 27:8.

rejoiced greatly and instructed that he be given great wealth and that his servants honor him. He appointed him over his office and over his treasury[80] and placed him second [to the king] because of his great wisdom and understanding. At his word, people went out and at his word they came in.[81] He [the king] swore to him [Rabbi Moses] by the prophet [Mohammed] that all the days of his life he will not believe the things that slanderers say about him.

Moses, the servant of God, became established as a wise and discerning man, good in the eyes of God and good in the eyes of people, and his reputation spread throughout the land. He was a greater physician than all his contemporaries. The king loved Moses greatly and gave him a wife from among the women of Fez and gave him riches and honor. Moses loved his wife and she gave birth to a son, and his name was Abraham because he said: "The God of Abraham was my help."

I, [the servant] cannot even partially describe[82] all the goodness and riches and honor that were bestowed upon my master by the king and by the ministers who stood before the king, and some of the gifts came from distant lands. My master gave a wife to his brother, Rabbi David, from the women of Egypt, and he gave him great wealth. He also appointed him over his treasury because he [Moses] was unable to carry out all the responsibilities placed upon him.

I will now tell you what he [Moses] did all his days. He would rise in the morning and go to his synagogue to pray with two hundred of his disciples who lived in his house, excluding the others who came from distant lands to see him, to learn from him, and to ask him questions. Then he would go to see all the sick people in the city, both Jews and Ishmaelites, until three hours into the day. Then he would go to see the king and be with him for an additional three hours. Then he would return to his house and eat and sleep until the evening. Then he would perform computations of the [king's] expenses and taxes and

---

[80] He was restored to his previous position as treasurer to the king.
[81] Allusion to Numbers 27:21.
[82] Literally: explain a little.

money brought to him by the royal clerks, until nightfall. Then he would write all the books that he composed, which number twenty-five. He wrote [books] at night and during the day he gave them to the scribes to copy them in other books.

This is the way he conducted himself all his days until an old well-respected man came before him from the land of Damiette to see my master, because he had heard of his wisdom and his understanding. He left his home to come before him. My master received him with cordiality and instructed that he be honored and served. The old man, named Rabbi Nehemiah, saw the situation of my master and his toil but said to him: "My master, there is one question that I wish to pose to you." My master said to that old man: "Ask whatever you wish." The old man said: "I come from a distant land to see you and to study before you and from the day I arrived in Egypt I was unable to speak with you privately because of the marked pressure and toil under which I observed you were [straining]." My master, Rabbi Moses, said to him: "Verily, this is my lot every day, but wait until I complete the computations of the taxes and the clerks have left, and then the Lord will fulfill our wishes." He did just as my master had instructed him. He remained there and studied before him for three years until that old man died.[83] My master, Rabbi Moses, treated him with great honor and they buried him in Egypt.

Later, a son was born to Rabbi Moses and he named him David, after his [Moses'] brother David. The child grew up[84] and increased in wisdom and understanding greater than his brother [Abraham]. Rabbi Moses loved his son David because he was the son of his old age,[85] but his wife loved Rabbi Abraham because he was beloved by all the ministers in the palace. My master took two women [as wives] for his sons, daughters of Rabbi Joseph the Prince from the family of [—].[86] Their father gave them property and riches and honor.

---

[83] Literally: took leave of his world.
[84] Allusion to 1 Samuel 2:26.
[85] Allusion to Genesis 37:3.
[86] The family name is not in the manuscript.

In the year 4939,[87] Rabbi David, brother of my master, developed a very serious illness and died on the eleventh of [the Hebrew month of] Ab. They buried him in Egypt. My master delivered a major eulogy as did all the disciples who studied Torah from the mouth of our teacher Moses. They eulogized him more than had been done for any man in the previous five years. My master then took his two daughters and gave them to the two sons of his brother David [as wives], because of his great love for him. He also gave them property and great wealth.

He then took the books that he composed and sent them to Spain, and to France, and to Alexandria, and to Allemagne, and to Fez, and to Isfahan, and to all the lands where he heard there are scholarly and intelligent men.[88] His books were disseminated throughout the lands but they were looked at with malevolence[89] since they did not know his ways and did not understand his actions because of the impatience of their spirit,[90] and they slandered him inappropriately.[91] This matter reached the ears of Rabbi Moses and he composed for them a book which he called "Light for the Blind"[92] in which he explained all these matters very well,[93] including all the doubts they had. He said: "This [book] is for you, for people who have eyes but do not see,[94] and who have ears but do not hear."[95] Then he wrote a letter that he sent to all lands.

I cannot [adequately] explain even part of the good deeds and the great love that the Ishmaelites and the Jews had for him. All the days that Rabbi Moses lived on the earth, not one

---

[87] Corresponding to the year 1179 of the Common Era.
[88] That is, rabbinic scholars.
[89] Literally: a bad eye.
[90] Allusion to Exodus 6:9.
[91] In a footnote, Neubauer refers the reader to Graetz's classic *History of the Jews*, Vol. 6, and the *Histoire Litéraire de la France*, Vol. 27, p. 650 for more information about this opposition to Maimonides and his writings.
[92] Neubauer says this book is the *Guide of the Perplexed*.
[93] Literally: a good explanation, that is, plainly. See Deuteronomy 27:8.
[94] Allusion to Psalm 115:5.
[95] Allusion to Psalm 115:6.

ABOUT THE MESSIAH IN ISFAHAN

of the children of Israel that resided in Egypt[96] and surrounding villages was persecuted.[97] He was a man of great scholarship and understanding, a righteous and God-fearing man. He established five synagogues and houses of study in Egypt. There lived in Egypt more Jews who came from all countries to Rabbi Moses than Jews who lived there before [his arrival] which numbered two thousand, two hundred and thirty. He taught Torah to all passing travelers and established a large inn for all who came there and who wished to study Torah, so that they could be provided for from the inn where they would receive daily bread to eat and clothes to wear.[98] Most people left their occupations and came there to eat and be clothed and study [Torah]. The sum of money that the inn received every year was ten thousand Egyptian *denars*. Every week he distributed two hundred small *denars* of the currency of Fez in the city and outside [the city], to Jews and to Ishmaelites. This is how he conducted himself all his life. Many books cannot [adequately reflect] his great wisdom, his understanding, his riches, and his righteousness.

In the year 4962[99] Rabbi Moses developed a serious illness and died and was gathered to his people, an old man, and full of years.[100] He was buried in Egypt and was accorded great honor by all the Jews and all the Ishmaelites who were there. I cannot properly relate the numerous eulogies and honors that were bestowed upon him, nor the great honor that the king accorded him all the days of mourning for him. May the Lord have mercy upon us and upon all of Israel, Amen. Peace and tranquility.

---

[96]Hebrew: *mitzrayim*, literally Egypt. Neubauer translates: Cairo.
[97]Literally: exiled.
[98]Allusion to Genesis 28:20.
[99]Corresponding to the year 1202 of the Common Era. Neubauer correctly points out that Maimonides died in the year 1204.
[100]Allusion to Genesis 25:8.

BIBLIOGRAPHY

by Jacob I. Dienstag

I. Editions

1] Neubauer, Adolf
Une pseudo-biographie de Moise Maimonide. *Revue des Etudes Juives* 4 (1882), 173-188.
Hebrew text and French translation.

2] נספח. **באגרת תימן** לרבנו משה בן מימון...ערוך בידי אברהם שלמה הלקין. ניו־יורק: האקדימיה האמריקנית למדעי היהדות. תשי״ב, עמ' 108־111.

3] איגרת מזויפת על שם הרמב״ם על משיח באיצפאהאן. בהתנועות המשיחיות **בישראל** מאת אהרן זאב אשכולי. ירושלים: מוסד ביאליק, תשט״ו/1956, עמ' 183־187.
עם הערכה והערות.

4] **בישראל בגולה**, מאת בן־ציון דינור, כרך ב, ספר 3, תל־אביב: דביר, ירושלים: מוסד ביאליק, תשכ״ח/1968, עמ' 433־435. קטעים.

5] In *Six Treatises Attributed to Maimonides*. Edited and annotated by Fred Rosner. Northvale, NJ: Jason Aronson, 1991.

II. Studies

6] Ashtor Strauss, E., 1914-
Saladin and the Jews. *Hebrew Union College Annual* 27 (1956), 320-321.
That "the falsified letter must have been written under the impression of the great victory of Saladin and the capture of Jerusalem."

7] Baron, Salo Wittmayer, 1895-1989.
A Social and Religious History of the Jews. 2nd edition. Volume V.

Philadelphia: The Jewish Publication Society of America, 1957, pp. 204-205; 386-387 (notes).

8] Dienstag, Jacob I.
Personages associated with the eschatological teachings of Maimonides and the scholarship thereon. An alphabetical survey. In: Jacob I. Dienstag, ed. *Eschatology in Maimonidean Thought*. New York: Ktav, 1983, pp. XXV-XXVII, XL-XLI.

9] Rosner, Fred, 1935-
Preface to his translation of *Letter to Moses Maimonides* on "The Messiah of Isfahan." In *Six Treatises Attributed to Maimonides*. Northvale, NJ: Jason Aronson, 1991.

10] אשכולי, אהרן זאב, 1901‎־1948.
התנועות המשיחיות בישראל. ירושלים: מוסד ביאליק, תשט"ז/1956, עמ' 186‎־187.

11] הלקין, אברהם שלמה, 1903‎־1990.
נספח. **באגרת תימן**. ניו־יורק: האקדמיה האמריקנית למדעי היהדות. תשי"ב/1952, עמ' 108‎־109.

12] מלאכי, אליעזר רפאל, 1895‎־1980.
הביוגרפיות הראשונות של הרמב"ם. **הדואר** 34, גליון 22 (ט' ניסן תשט"ו), 422‎־424.

13] שילת, יצחק
איגרות הרמב"ם. מהדורה מדויקת... כרך ב. ירושלים: ליד "ברכת משה", תשמ"ח, עמ' תרצג.

14] שלום, גרשם, 1897‎־1982.
מחוקר למקובל. **תרביץ** 6, ספר ג' (ניסן, תרצ"ה), 334‎־335. [—**ספר הרמב"ם של התרביץ**. ירושלים: האוניברסיטה העברית, תרצ"ה, עמ' 90‎־91; **מיקראה בחקר הרמב"ם**. ירושלים: האוניברסיטה העברית, תשמ"ה, עמ' 90‎־91].

III. References to Manuscripts

15] Freimann, Aron, 1871-1948.
Union Catalog of Hebrew Manuscripts and their Location. New York: American Academy for Jewish Research, 1964, no. 10, 993.

16] Neubauer, Adolf, 1832-1907, and Cowley, Arthur Ernst, 1861-1931.
Catalogue of the Hebrew Manuscripts in the Bodleian Library and in the College Libraries of Oxford. Oxford, 1886-1906, no. 2425 (11).

INDEX

Abraham ben David, Rabbi (Raibad), xi
Abraham ibn Ezra, Rabbi, xv, 198
Abrahams, Israel, 150–151, 152, 155
Allgemeine Zeitung des Judenthums (newspaper), 104
Alroy, David, 226–227, 229
Alshakar, Rabbi Moses, 197
American Israelite, The (newspaper), 107
Arimon, 69
Aristotle, xviii, 12
Asaph, 119
Ashkenazi, Shmuel, 69
Asthma (Maimonides), xviii
Azulai, Rabbi Chayim Joseph David, 197

Baal Shem Tov, Rabbi Israel, xiii, 197
Bacher, W., 5–7, 10, 13, 14–15
Baer, Fritz, 3, 4, 227–228

Baneth, D. H., 3, 8, 12
Bar-Joseph, M., 198, 199
Bennigson, W., 110, 112, 114
Berner, H., 114
Bogen, Emil, 110, 112, 115, 117
Boie, Christian, 103
Book of Commandments (Maimonides), xviii
Book of Creation, The, xi
Book of Poisons (Maimonides), xviii
Book of Remedies, The, (attributed to Maimonides), xviii, 67–100
　bibliography to, 99–100
　editor's foreword to, 71–75
　introduction to, 67–75
　text of, 77–97
Book of Logic (Maimonides), xviii
Bresslau, M. M., 149

Commentary on the Mishnah (Maimonides), xiv, xvii

Davidowitz, H. S., 3, 4, 8, 8–10, 11–12, 15

Delmedigo, Rabbi Joseph Solomon Rophé, 197
Deutsch, Gotthard, 106, 107–109, 110, 115, 117
Dienstag, Jacob I., 57–64, 99–100, 127–146, 152, 155, 173–192
Dinor, B. Z., 13
Distel, Theodor, 105, 109, 110, 113
Dohm, Christian Wilhelm, 103
Don Beneviste ben Labi, 4
Dukes, L., 151

Edelman, Zvi Hirsch, 149, 151, 196–200
Eichel, Itzig, 104
Epistle to Yemen (Maimonides), xviii
Euchel, Isaac, 104, 118
Existence and Unity of God, The (Maimonides), xv

Forgery, 231
Franklin, Benjamin, x
Friedenwald, H., 109, 113
Friedlander-Azoulai, 231

Gans, David, 229
Gates of Moral Instruction, The (attributed to Maimonides), xviii, 149–192
  bibliography to, 173–192
  introduction to, 149–155
  text of, 157–172
Gershenfeld, L., 111
Gershon Henoch of Radzin, Rabbi, xi
Golden, William W., 105, 107
Graetz, H., 7, 12, 152
Greenes, Rabbi Moshe, ix–xv
Grossberg, Menashe, 67, 69, 71–75, 77n

Guide of the Perplexed (Maimonides), xi–xii, xiv, xviii, 5, 8, 9, 11, 155

Haeser, H., 109
Halevi, Rabbi Zerachyah, 3, 4
Halevy, Judah, 119
Halkin, Abraham, 228, 229
Ha-Massef (periodical), 104, 105
Hasidism, xiv
Hemorrhoids (Maimonides), xviii
Hertz, Joseph H., 111–112, 115, 117
Herz, Marcus, x, 104, 105, 106, 107, 108–109, 111, 112, 114, 115, 116, 117–118, 119
Hippocratic Oath, 110–111

Illevitz, A. B., 111, 115, 117
Ingra, Rabbi Meshulam, xiii

Jacob ben Nathaniel, Rabbi, 226
Jakobovits, Immanuel Lord (Rabbi), 119
Jews and Medicine, The (Friedenwald), 113
Jose Ben Halafta, Rabbi, 108
Joseph, Rabbi, 196, 197
Joseph ben Eleazar, 4
Journal of the American Medical Association, 106, 110, 114
Judah ibn Tibbon, Rabbi, 149, 150
Justice to the Jew (Peters), 105

Kabbalah. *See* Maimonides
Kabbalism, 196
Kagan, S. R., 110, 112, 114, 115, 116, 117
Kaufmann, David, 227
Keller, H., 110
Kottek, Samuel, 70

INDEX

Kreditor, L. S., 13
Krieger, John Anton, 196
Kroner, H., 71, 110, 115, 116

Landau, Rabbi Ezekiel, xiii
Lanzkron, J., 114
Last Will and Testament, The (attributed to Maimonides). See *Gates of Moral Instruction, The* (attributed to Maimonides)
Lehrman, Simon Maurice, 151
Leibowitz, J. O., 114, 117–118
Letter to the Jews of Fez about the Messiah in Isfahan (attributed to Maimonides), xviii, 225–249
  bibliography to, 251–252
  introduction to, 225–231
  text of, 233–249
Levinson, A., 113
Levy, Heinrich, 113
Lull, Raymon, 67, 68, 69, 70
Luria, Rabbi Isaac, xiii
Luzzatto, Rabbi Moshe Chaim, xiv–xv

Maimon, Yehudah Leib, 151–152
Maimonides, Moses
  importance of, xvii
  Kabbalah and, x–xv
  works attributed to, xviii–xix
  works of, xvii–xviii
Margalith, David, 154–155
Medical Aphorisms (Maimonides), xviii
Menachem ben Abraham of Perpignan, 5
Menachem ben David Aldagi. See Alroy
Mendelssohn, Moses, 108
Mesilat Yesharim (Luzzatto), xiv–xv

Messianic movements, 227
Metzik, Yitzchok Zev, 67
Meyerhof, M., 111, 115, 117
Minkin, Jacob, 152, 153
Mishneh Torah (Maimonides), xvii
Münz, I., 112
Moshe ben Jacob, Rabbi, 199
Muntner, Süssman, 71, 110, 113–114, 117, 118

Nachmanides, Rabbi Moses (Rambam), xi–xii, 72, 77n, 196
Neo-Platonism, 12
Neubauer, Adolf, 225–226, 227, 228, 231
New Era (journal), 149
Nine Chapters on the Unity (of God) (attributed to Maimonides), 196

Osler, Sir William, 111

Pagel, Julius, 105, 110, 116
Peters, Madison C., 105, 107
Philippson, Ludwig, 104, 107, 109
Physician's Prayer, The (attributed to Maimonides)
  bibliography to, 127–146
  introduction to, 103–122
  text of, 123–125
Pines, J., 115
Pinto, Rabbi Isaiah, 153
Premsela, M. J., 110

Raibad. See Abraham ben David, Rabbi
Raminos. See Lull
Regimen on Health (Maimonides), xviii
Richler, Benjamin, 67–68, 70

Saladin (vizier of Egypt), 227–228
Salomo del Megido, Joseph, 5
Samuel ibn Tibbon, Rabbi, 228, 229
Sarne, Rabbi Yechezkel, xiv, xv
Schmiedl, A., 7
Schreiber, Rabbi Moshe, xiii
Schwab, Moïse, 105, 106, 108, 115, 117
Scroll of the Unrevealed (attributed to Maimonides), xviii, 195–222
  bibliography to, 217–222
  introduction to, 195–200
  text of, 201–216
Seeligmann, S., 109–110, 115, 117
Sefer Hashoroshim (Yonah ibn Ganach), 11
Serach ben Nathan, 5
Sexual Intercourse (Maimonides), xviii
Shailat, Isaac, 229–230
Shalom, G., 13
Shilat, Yitzchak, 199–200
Simon, I., 115
Singer, E., 111
Soveiv, Galgal, 113
Steinschneider, Moritz, 3–4, 5, 6, 7, 8, 68, 71, 113, 151, 152, 155
Stitskin, Leon D., 13, 154

Tama, Mordechai, 5
Thirteen Middos of Reb Yisrael Salanter, x
Torah, Maimonides and, xii
Treatise on Eternal Bliss (attributed to Maimonides), xviii, 3–64
  bibliography on, 57–64
  introduction to, 3–15
  text of, 17–56
  text of, *Allegorical Interpretation of Psalm 45*, 28–36
  text of, *Allegory of the Sanctuary* . . . , 18–24
  text of, *Biblical Evidence for the Continuation of the Soul after Death*, 43–47
  text of, *Ceremonial Commandments* . . . , 24–26
  text of, *Chupah* . . . , 37–43
  text of, *Miscellaneous Remarks on Eternal Salvation*, 48–56
  text of, *Repentance. Isaiah 6*, 26–28
Treatise on Resurrection (Maimonides), xviii
Treub, Hektor, 110
Tzvifel, Eliezer Tzvi, 150

Vajda, G., 5, 12
Vidor, N., 13
Vital, Rabbi Chaim, 197
Voice of Jacob, The (newspaper), 104

Wertheimer, Shlomo Aharon, 152
Wolff, Rabbi Jules, 105–106, 107, 115, 116

Yabetz, Rabbi Joseph, 5
Yagal, Abraham, 149, 155
Yonah ibn Ganach, Rabbi, 11

Zacutus, Abraham, 119
Zahalon, Jacob, 113, 119
Zaks, S., 12
Zerachyah ben Yitzchok ben Shealtiel Chen, Rabbi, 4

About the Author

Dr. Fred Rosner has written, translated, and edited many books on Maimonides, including *Maimonides' Introduction to the Mishnah, The Existence and Unity of God: Three Treatises Attributed to Moses Maimonides*, and *Medicine and Jewish Law*. A nationally known authority on medical ethics and a popular lecturer, Dr. Rosner is director of the Department of Medicine at the Queens Hospital Center Affiliation of the Long Island Jewish Medical Center. He is also assistant dean and professor of medicine at the Albert Einstein College of Medicine of Yeshiva University in New York City.